Ius Gentium: Comparative Perspectives on Law and Justice

Volume 83

More information about this series at http://www.springer.com/series/7888

Pablo Bravo-Hurtado • Cornelis Hendrik van Rhee
Editors

Supreme Courts Under Pressure

Controlling Caseload in the Administration of Civil Justice

Springer

Editors
Pablo Bravo-Hurtado
Catholic University of Valparaíso
Valparaíso, Chile

Cornelis Hendrik van Rhee
Maastricht University
Maastricht, The Netherlands

ISSN 1534-6781 ISSN 2214-9902 (electronic)
Ius Gentium: Comparative Perspectives on Law and Justice
ISBN 978-3-030-63730-9 ISBN 978-3-030-63731-6 (eBook)
https://doi.org/10.1007/978-3-030-63731-6

This Springer imprint is published by the registered company Springer Nature Switzerland AG.
The registered company address is: Gewerbestrasse 11, 6330 Cham, Switzerland

Contents

Abbreviations

BGB	German Civil Code (*Bürgerliches Gesetzbuch*)
CPC	Civil Procedure Code
CPQ	Constitutional Priority Question
DDR	German Democratic Republic (*Deutsche Demokratische Republik*)
ECJ	European Court of Justice
ECtHR	European Court of Human Rights
GDP	Gross Domestic Product
GDR	German Democratic Republic
GG	Basic Law (*Grundgesetz*)
GVG	Judicature Act (*Gerichtsverfassungsgesetz*)
HGB	Commercial Code (*Handelsgesetzbuch*)
JN	Statute on Jurisdiction (*Jurisdiktionsnorm*)
JCPC	Judicial Committee of the Privy Council
QPC	Constitutional Priority Question (*Question Prioritaire de Constitutionnalité*)
UK	United Kingdom
UKSC	United Kingdom Supreme Court
US	United States (of America)
ZPO	Code of Civil Procedure (*Zivilprozessordnung*)

Part I
Introduction

Introduction

Pablo Bravo-Hurtado and Cornelis Hendrik van Rhee

Abstract The book discusses civil litigation at the Supreme Courts of nine jurisdictions: Argentina, Austria, Croatia, England & Wales, France, Germany, Italy, Spain and the United States of America. It focuses on the problem of excessive caseload and measures to keep caseload within acceptable boundaries. This introductory chapter analyses, from a comparative perspective, the different dimensions of the problem. The first and most evident dimension of an excessive caseload is undue delay. The problem, however, also exhibits a second dimension in which a heavy caseload affects the performance of Supreme Courts, especially where it concerns the balancing of the private and public purposes of adjudication at these courts. Solutions to an excessive caseload need to take into account both dimensions. Solutions may go in the direction of increasing the capacity of the court to resolve more cases or reducing the number of cases. A variety of factors—ranging from different understandings of the caseload problem, local conceptions about the purpose of the Supreme Court, strong entitlement to a right to appeal, budgetary restrictions and rigidity of legal rules—may explain why some jurisdictions prefer certain solutions over others. A comparative analysis shows that the implementation of similar solutions, such as access filters, in different jurisdictions may not have similar effects, but effects even opposite to those sought. Since the problem of overburdened courts is multifactorial and context-dependent, reforms need to be multifactorial and context-dependent too.

P. Bravo-Hurtado
Catholic University of Valparaíso, Valparaíso, Chile
e-mail: pablo.bravo@pucv.cl

C. H. van Rhee (✉)
Maastricht University, Maastricht, Netherlands
e-mail: remco.vanrhee@maastrichtuniversity.nl

P. Bravo-Hurtado, C. H. van Rhee (eds.), *Supreme Courts Under Pressure*, Ius Gentium: Comparative Perspectives on Law and Justice 83,
https://doi.org/10.1007/978-3-030-63731-6_1

1 'Under Pressure'

Supreme courts—i.e. courts situated at the apex of the judicial hierarchy issuing final decisions at the domestic level[1]—serve various purposes. Since the Rule of Law commands the application of the law in an equal manner to everyone,[2] Supreme Courts should ideally serve as shining beacons that guide us in the (sometimes obscure) interpretation of the law. Rulings of Supreme Courts should shed light on ambiguities and loopholes in the law, while updating the legal criteria to current circumstances.[3] Supreme Courts should be the key players for increasing legal certainty, maintaining a well-working justice system and contributing to predictable 'rules of the game.'

Having the final word means that Supreme Courts are the last stop in the appeals route.[4] Supreme Courts are often the only chance that remains (at least at the domestic level) to reverse an unfavourable judgment. In principle, appeals at the Supreme Court are meant to concentrate on erroneous decisions issued by lower courts.[5] Litigants, however, tend to consider unfavourable judgments as mistakes that should be amended on appeal. As a result, Supreme Courts may receive large numbers of complaints filed by thousands of litigants eager to roll the dice one last time.

Consequently, Supreme Courts may face an increase in their caseload if no adequate access filters are in place. In some jurisdictions the increase may be steady—e.g. at the Austrian *Oberster Gerichtshof* discussed in the chapter "Access to the Austrian *Oberster Gerichtshof*: Attempts to Strike a Balance Between Adequate Workload and Adequate Review"—while in others the caseload may 'explode'—e.g. at the Italian *Corte Suprema di Cassazione* discussed in the chapter "Finding a Cure or Simply Relieving Symptoms? The Case of the Italian Supreme Court." Certain Supreme Courts may have reduced their caseload several decades ago—e.g. the US and UK Supreme Courts discussed in the chapters "The Supreme Court of the United Kingdom and the Court of Appeal in England and Wales: Sharing the Appellate Load" and "A Happy-Go-Lucky Story: The American Supreme Court and Overload Problems," respectively—while for many other jurisdictions this is still a pressing problem—e.g. the Croatian *Vrhovni sud Republike Hrvatske* discussed in the chapter "Croatia: Supreme Court Between Individual Justice and System Management." In either situation, a heavy caseload compromises

[1]Other definitions of 'Supreme Court' in Van Rhee and Fu (2017), pp. 1–5; Yessiou-Faltsi (1998). Similar denominations such as 'top courts' in Le Sueur and Cornes (2000); Taruffo (1998), p. 102; 'highest courts' in Huls et al. (2009), Muller and Loth (2009) and Muller and Richards (2010), or 'court of last resort' in Silvestri (1986) and Mitidiero (2015).

[2]On the Rule of Law, Dicey ([1979] 2013).

[3]Chiarloni (2014), p. 82; Bravo-Hurtado (2014), pp. 322–325.

[4]In jurisdictions with separate constitutional courts, however, the 'last-resort' at a domestic level could be disputed between the Supreme Court and the Constitutional Court, see Garlicki (2007).

[5]Uzelac and Van Rhee (2014), p. 3; Shapiro (1980), p. 629.

the Supreme Court's performance, resulting in lower quality standards or undue delay (or both). Sooner or later, changes are needed in order improve the situation.

1.1 Two Dimensions of Case Overload

This book finds its inspiration in the 'bewildering variety'—using Professor Jolowicz's words[6]—among jurisdictions when dealing with the problems just mentioned. The most fundamental difference is due to the standard according to which local actors evaluate what counts as an 'overloaded' Supreme Court. Let us imagine a Supreme Court that is burdened with deciding around 4000 cases per year. For the US Supreme Court, which hears 100–150 cases annually,[7] this would count as an unprecedented crisis. For the French *Cour de cassation*, however, accustomed to resolve around 22,000 cases a year in civil matters only,[8] (just) 4000 cases per year may sound, quite the contrary, as though the court is 'underused.' And for the German *Bundesgerichtshof*, close to 4000 cases would be considered normal according to current practices.[9]

Jurisdictions also diverge as regards the reasons for heavy caseloads and, perhaps more interestingly, as regards the reasons that need to be addressed urgently in order to solve this problem. Undue delay is the most palpable result of an overloaded court. When the number of cases brought to the Supreme Court exceeds the number that can be resolved within an acceptable period of time, waiting lists start to grow longer. The delay can be measured from the number of cases that remain unresolved every year.[10] Undue delay, thus, can be a symptom that the court is receiving too many cases in proportion to its working capability.

The disadvantages of undue delay are also palpable. The aphorism 'justice delayed is justice denied' means that the court becomes irrelevant when it cannot address relevant cases in a timely manner.[11] A result may be that fewer people are willing to bring appeals before the Supreme Court or will desist continuing appeals that have already been lodged. Gravelle—among many other economists—holds that 'paying' for access to justice through waiting time has a regressive effect.[12] Undue delay excludes litigants whose cases are so urgent that they cannot pay the price in waiting time, and it excludes litigants without enough financial means to endure a long and expensive procedure.

---

[6]Jolowicz (1998), p. 35.

[7] US Supreme Court – Caseload (2020).

[8]Ferrand (2017), p. 196.

[9]See in this book Stürner (Chapter "Sharing Responsibility: The German Federal Court of Justice and the Civil Appellate System").

[10]Pastor Prieto (1993), pp. 235–237.

[11]From a comparative perspective, Van Rhee (2004).

[12]Gravelle (1990), pp. 255–270. See also, Barzel (1974), pp. 73–95.

To consider undue delay to be the only symptom of case overload, however, would lead to serious misunderstandings. From this perspective, a court would be overloaded only in the case of undue delay. Vice versa, the court's caseload would not be problematic if delays were reduced, usually to less than a year. The consequence of this approach would be that reforms will mainly aim at reducing delay.[13] However, Jolowicz rightly pointed out that case overload has more dimensions than only delay. In his words:

> A court is overloaded not only if it has a growing backlog of pending cases, but also if it cannot adequately fulfil the purpose or purposes for which it exists.[14]

The problem of case overload, thus, has other dimensions. Superior Courts obviously serve public and private purposes. On the one hand, the private purpose responds to the natural desire of the losing party to have the case reconsidered by a court higher in the court hierarchy. The public purpose, on the other hand, is supervision of the lower courts and to contribute to the unification of case law and the development and clarification of the law.[15]

The latter dimension is important since it affects the role played by Supreme Courts in modern society. The development of the Rule of Law requires guarantees that similar cases are judged according to equal legal criteria and that these legal criteria should be known in advance.[16]

Appeals of last resort are meant to serve both purposes, at least to some extent.[17] When resolving a dispute, the Supreme Court aims to correct the misapplication of the law by the inferior court, but at the same time to provide the public at large with information on the legal criterion that should be applied in future similar cases.

This dimension of case overload needs to be taken into account seriously because an overburdened Supreme Court cannot fulfil its tasks in a meaningful manner and various aspects of the Rule of Law may be infringed. With too many cases to resolve, the court will need to reduce the time spent on individual cases, and the quality of judgments will suffer. The Supreme Court may end up concentrating on formal mistakes in order to close cases as quickly as possible. For the appellant that scenario is risky. An overburdened Supreme Court makes it likely that cases will be resolved on the basis of erratic criteria. The court will not be able to provide justice in individual cases, nor will it be able to give guidance to the uniform interpretation and development of the law. An overburdened court may not be able to provide for internal consistency[18] since it does not have enough time to analyse previous,

[13] See, e.g., Pekkanen et al. (2012), pp. 94–103.

[14] Jolowicz (2000), p. 55.

[15] Ibid., pp. 31–32.

[16] Cotterrell (1992), p. 158.

[17] For instance, Woolf (1996), p. 153; Jolowicz (1998); Taruffo (1998); Galič (2014); Norkus (2015); Ferraris (2015), pp. 6–7.

[18] Bravo-Hurtado (2014), p. 328.

pertinent case law. If internal consistency is lost, the externalities of Supreme Court judgments will be negative, increasing uncertainty.

The various dimensions of case overload are not necessarily correlated. In one extreme, a small number of cases may be brought before the court, allowing it to spend sufficient time on each case, but even so undue delay may occur in resolving cases. It may also happen that delay is minimal, but at the cost of spending insufficient amounts of time on individual cases. Therefore, it is not a good idea to focus solely on reducing backlogs at the cost of reducing the court time available for individual cases. Case overload is a problem that needs a balanced approach in order to be solved in a satisfactory manner.

1.2 Various Solutions

The jurisdictions discussed in this book exhibit not only a variety of understandings of the problem of case overload, but also a variety of proposed solutions. In general, the solutions can be clustered in two groups: (1) increasing the capacity of the Supreme Court and (2) reducing the number of cases.[19]

The various measures that can be implemented may have counter-productive effects. GRAVELLE, for instance, argues that:

> With a given supply of trials, the aims of reducing the delay and cost of the legal process are contradictory since any reduction in litigant's costs stimulates demand and increases delay.[20]

In other words, it should be kept in mind that measures increasing the capacity of the Supreme Court may have the side effect of a further increase in the number of cases. Obviously, in the long run this may aggravate the problem of case overload.

Increasing Capacity Increasing the number of judges is one of the most common approaches that is being chosen to increase the capacity of Supreme Courts. However, there are other measures that may have the same effect. For example, judges could be given more support staff to whom specific tasks may be delegated. One may also think of dividing the court into smaller chambers or sections. Additionally, procedural reforms may be introduced to accelerate litigation. For example, eliminating oral hearings or creating different tracks for different types of cases may result in more efficiency.

Reducing the Number of Cases Where it concerns a reduction of the number of cases that are brought before Supreme Courts, access filters have received considerable attention in comparative legal studies.[21] Important aspects of such filters are

---

[19]See also Del Rio (2015) on Chile.

[20]Gravelle (1995), p. 289.

[21]For instance, Taruffo (2001), Silvestri (2001), Amrani-Mekki (2014), Drago et al. (2015), Ferraris (2015), and Norkus (2015), among many others.

the selection criteria, the procedure of filtering cases and whether the screening is done by the lower court that issued the judgment, the Supreme Court itself, or both courts. Other solutions that deserve attention are increasing court fees[22] and determining a select group of Supreme Court lawyers. Provisional enforcement of the judgments of the lower courts may also reduce Supreme Court cases since litigants will not be able to postpone enforcement simply by filing an appeal.

Different Approaches The contributions to the present volume provide information on various approaches to counter case overload at the Supreme Court:

(a) Some jurisdictions focus on measures reducing delay. When delay is under control, no further measures are introduced even though the quality of the Supreme Court judgments may be under threat.
(b) Some jurisdictions focus on the private purpose of Supreme Court litigation. Increasing the capacity of the court instead of reducing the number of cases is then preferred. However, where the predominant conception is the public purpose of the Supreme Court, reducing the quantity of cases is a more acceptable approach.
(c) Some jurisdictions are under the threat of sanctions due to problems related to case overload. Jurisdictions that face sanctions, for example due to infringement of the right to a judgment within a reasonable time, may opt for measures solving the problem of delay without concentrating on the quality of judgments.[23]
(d) In some jurisdictions, obvious solutions to case overload may not be feasible. A strong entitlement to a right to appeal—for example enshrined in the Constitution—will be problematic where access filters are under discussion.
(e) Some jurisdictions have stricter rules than others where it concerns changing the court's organisation and procedure. If every change affecting the court requires legislative intervention, such change can only be introduced at a slow pace, if at all. On the contrary, in jurisdictions in which the Supreme Court may itself provide for its rules, changes are easier and faster.
(f) Budgetary restrictions may hinder Supreme Court reform as well, for example where it concerns appointing more judges, clerks and other staff, and where it concerns improving the infrastructure of the court.
(g) Finally, lobbying by interest groups should not be underestimated. Lawyers litigating at the Supreme Court may oppose the introduction of access filters. Frequent litigants may oppose an increase of court fees or the introduction of additional fees. And Supreme Court judges may lobby in favour of (or against) certain solutions, for example against an increase in the number of judges at the Supreme Court when they feel that such an increase will affect the power-balance within the court.

[22] On the effect of costs and fees on litigation, see Vogenauer et al. (2010), pp. 110–115.

[23] See Van Rhee (2010) for a historical perspective.

Obviously, this list is not exhaustive. Further historical, political, cultural or economic circumstances may need to be analysed. However, the goal of this comparative introduction is not to exhaust the topic of case overload, but to provide a theoretical framework to facilitate further debate on the matter.

1.3 Content

This book covers nine jurisdictions: Argentina, Austria, Croatia, England & Wales, France, Germany, Italy, Spain and the United States of America. Therefore, the experiences of jurisdictions on both sides of the Atlantic, and belonging to both the civil law and the common law worlds, are discussed. The authors of the contributions to this volume have been asked to address at least four questions:

- To what extent is case overload a problem at the Supreme Court in your jurisdiction?
- Which solutions to this problem have been discussed and/or introduced?
- Have these solutions proven to be effective?
- Has use been made of legal transplants to solve the problem of case overload?

For reasons of convenience, this book consists of an introductory part (I) and three additional parts (II-IV) devoted to three legal traditions (or families).[24] Part II is devoted to the Romanic legal tradition (France, Italy and Spain). Part III discusses systems belonging to the Germanic legal tradition (Germany, Austria and Croatia), while Part IV addresses the Anglo-American legal tradition (England & Wales, the United States of America, and, perhaps surprisingly, Argentina).

2 Romanic Legal Tradition

2.1 France

From an outsider's perspective, the French *Cour de cassation* is clearly overburdened. The court has to cope with around 30,000 cases on a yearly basis. However, in his contribution Emmanuel Jeuland explains that caseload is not viewed as the main problem of the court. The approximately 200 judges are able to keep the average duration of cassation cases close to a year. The main problem the French Court of Cassation faces is, according to Jeuland, the increasing relevance of other courts—both at the national level (*Conseil d'état* and *Conseil constitutionnel*) and at the international level (ECJ and ECtHR). These other courts seem to eclipse

[24]On legal families, see Zweigert and Kötz (1998); David and Brierley (1978); Glenn (2006); Örücü (2007), pp. 169–187.

the *Cour de cassation* as the ultimate instance in the French court hierarchy. In order to increase the relevance of the Court of Cassation, reforms such as extending the grounds of the court's judgments in important cases and focusing on the most relevant cases only are considered.

2.2 Italy

The Italian *Corte Suprema di Cassazione* is, as is commonly known, an overburdened court with around 87,000 cases per year. Combined with other factors, this overload has increased the duration of cases far beyond the reasonable-time standard of Article 6 ECHR and Article 47 of the EU Charter of Fundamental Rights. In his contribution, FEDERICO FERRARIS analyses the latest reforms that have been introduced in Italy to counter this situation. The creation of a specialised chamber entrusted with the task of filtering cases and new admissibility rules will not, in FERRARIS's opinion, cure the disease but merely provide some temporary relief. A strong entitlement to a third instance in the Italian legal culture, together with a right of access to cassation enshrined in the Constitution, tend to frustrate any efforts to reduce the incoming caseload of the Supreme Court. Italy, in this regard, is a good example of how reforms may face cultural and constitutional barriers which are difficult to overcome despite the fact that the case overload reaches critical levels.

2.3 Spain

MARCO DE BENITO provides a historical account of the Spanish Supreme Court (*Tribunal Supremo*) and its current interaction with the Constitutional Court. Since its early conception in 1812, Spanish cassation appeal has gone through several reforms with different effects as regards case overload. Reforms from the 1990s, for example, were mainly focused on increasing the capacity of the court by speeding up the cassation procedure, increasing the number of panels by reducing the number of judges per panel and limiting the scope of review. Following these reforms, the *Tribunal Supremo*'s caseload increased rather than decreased. This necessitated further reforms. In 2000 and 2011, filters based on 'cassational interest'—i.e. selecting cases based on infringements of fundamental rights, contradictory case law and a monetary threshold—were introduced and subsequently reinterpreted. This approach seems to have solved the case overload problem in Spain. Subsequent reform proposals aimed at restricting access to the *Tribunal Supremo* even further have been rejected.

3 Germanic Legal Tradition

3.1 Germany

Germany provides an example of successful attempts to solve the problem of case overload. Michael Stürner holds that this is not exclusively due to restricting access to the German Supreme Court (*Bundesgerichtshof*) in civil and criminal matters by way of access filters. Apart from the introduction of permission to appeal, the 2001 Reform introduced major changes to appeal proceedings at the lower courts. Moreover, a small and highly qualified cassation bar guarantees rigorous selection of cases since the professional prestige of the members of that bar depends on the quality of the services provided. Even though the German Supreme Court still conceives its role as serving both private and public purposes, in recent years the balance has clearly shifted towards the latter. As a result, the German Supreme Court now has a caseload that remains constant, whereas the caseload in civil matters of the lower courts is decreasing due to the popularity of ADR. The popularity of ADR results, according to Stürner, in a situation in which not every important case may reach the German Supreme Court, which is problematic in itself.

3.2 Austria

Florian Scholz-Berger analyses the Austrian Supreme Court (*Oberster Gerichtshof*). The Austrian legal system often draws inspiration from reforms in Germany and vice versa. Nonetheless, as regards appeal at last resort (*Revision*), at least three important differences may be observed between Austria and Germany. First, apart from qualitative filtering criteria ('significant question of law'), Austria has maintained a monetary threshold. Second, a lower court's positive decision as regards granting permission to appeal does not bind the Austrian Supreme Court. Third, in proportion to the Austrian population, the size of the Austrian Supreme Court is much larger than the German *Bundesgerichtshof* (60 full-time judges for 8.3 million inhabitants). These differences are very relevant when it comes to case overload, a problem that in Austria—according to Scholz-Berger—has been countered by way of frequent reforms of proceedings and court organisation without reaching a state of crisis.

3.3 Croatia

Croatia is the last jurisdiction discussed in the section on the Germanic legal family in this volume. In their contribution Alan Uzelac and Marko Bratković state that the evolution of the Croatian Supreme Court (*Vrhovni sud Republike Hrvatske*) was influenced by ideas from the Socialist era. Particularly interesting are the efforts at this court to combine the private and public purposes of adjudication at the highest level by way of two separate means of recourse: ordinary and extraordinary revision (*revizija*). However, the Croatian experience demonstrates that combining these two purposes may have counterproductive effects. In fact, since the introduction in 2003 of extraordinary revision, the caseload of the Croatian Supreme Court has increased dramatically. On top of that, a low level of trust in the judiciary combined with a constitutional court reluctant to introduce access filters hinder solutions for the caseload problems in Croatia.

4 Anglo-American Legal Tradition

4.1 England & Wales

John Sorabji analyses the UK Supreme Court and the English Court of Appeal. The civil justice system in England and Wales is hierarchical in terms of both its first instance jurisdiction and its appellate jurisdiction. Appeals lie from first instance decisions to either the next judicial tier within a court or to a superior court. The High Court has both a trial jurisdiction and is the appellate court for appeals from the County Court. The Court of Appeal, while it has no trial jurisdiction, hears appeals from first instance decisions from the High Court or, exceptionally the County Court. It also hears second appeals from the High Court. The House of Lords, which exercised judicial appellate jurisdiction from the middle ages, and its statutory successor the UK Supreme Court, only hear appeals from inferior territorial appellate courts within the United Kingdom. This hierarchical structure has, historically, ensured that neither the House of Lords nor the UK Supreme Court have suffered from a surfeit of appeals. Furthermore, the fact that appeals to the House of Lords and the UK Supreme Court (*a*) are limited to appeals on questions of law, and only those which raise issues of general public importance, and (*b*) are only permitted if permission to appeal is granted, has ensured that the number of appeals they hear has remained relatively static historically. By way of contrast, the appellate jurisdiction of the Court of Appeal in England and Wales has undergone periods of severe increases in its caseload; it is currently undergoing such an increase, and reforms have been introduced to reduce its burgeoning caseload. This increase comes despite appeals to the Court of Appeal being subject to a permission to appeal requirement, albeit one that is not as restrictive as that to the UK Supreme Court.

4.2 United States of America

The situation in the United States of America is to some extent similar to that in England & Wales, since the highest court, i.e. the US Supreme Court, has a 'shrinking docket' while the Courts of Appeal receive larger numbers of cases. This is, according to Richard Marcus, the result of a combination of historical, political and constitutional circumstances. Originally, the US Supreme Court had limited relevance. When its relevance increased it attracted a larger number of cases, but quickly many cases were diverted to the Federal Courts of Appeal that were created to absorb part of the burden. Consequently, the present Supreme Court may focus on the most important cases and has gained (almost) full control of its docket, especially due to reforms in the 1930s. As a result, case overload at the US Supreme Court is not a matter of concern. Matters of concern exist, but they are different in nature. For example, the fact that the Supreme Court is a highly politicised court is a matter that is becoming more and more problematic.

4.3 Argentina

Argentina obviously does not belong to the Anglo-American legal family but to the civil law legal tradition. From a comparative perspective, however, the current Supreme Court of Argentina (*Corte Suprema de la Nación Argentina*) is more comparable to the US Supreme Court than, for instance, the French *Cour de cassation*. Argentina is a federal state and its Supreme Court has strong powers where judicial review of legislation is concerned. It has adopted the US writ of certiorari, but as Leandro Giannini explains in this volume, case selection at the Argentinian Supreme Court is different from case selection at the US Supreme Court. The Argentinian version of the writ of certiorari provides for a discretional selection of cases based on the criterion of 'transcendence' or relevance beyond the individual case submitted to the court. The particularity of this Argentinian certiorari is that, instead of excluding cases, the Supreme Court has used its discretionary powers to grant permission to appeal in cases that do not meet the requirements of transcendence or relevance. According to Giannini, this may be due to an interpretation of the court's discretional selection powers in accordance with the public purposes of adjudication at the Argentinian Supreme Court.

References

Amrani-Mekki S (2014) L'accès aux cours suprêmes: Rapport français. In: Warsaw Conference, The functions of the Supreme Court—issues of process and administration of justice. Warsaw, pp 1–12. http://colloquium2014.uw.edu.pl/wp-content/uploads/sites/21/2014/06/AMRANI_MEKKI_L%E2%80%99ACCES-AUX-COURS-SUPREMES-final.pdf. Accessed 1 June 2020

Barzel Y (1974) A theory of rationing by waiting. J Law Econ 17(1):73–95

Bravo-Hurtado P (2014) Two ways to uniformity: recourse to the Supreme Court in the civil law and common law world. In: Uzelac A, Van Rhee CH (eds) Nobody's perfect. Comparative essays on appeals and other means of recourse against judicial decisions in civil matters. Intersentia, Cambridge, pp 319–335

Chiarloni S (2014) General judicial functions of the Supreme Courts in the European legal culture with some critical remarks about the Italian Corte di Cassazione. In: Adolphsen J et al (eds) Festschrift für Peter Gottwald zum 70. Geburtstag. CH Beck, München, pp 81–88
Cotterrell R (1992) The sociology of law. An introduction. Oxford University Press, New York
David R, Brierley J (1978) Major legal systems in the world today: an introduction to the comparative study of law, 2nd edn. The Free Press, New York
Del Rio C (2015) Casación Civil: El desafío de la correcta racionalización y iurisprudencia novit curia en una futura reforma legal. Revista Chilena de Derecho XLII(2):483–513
Dicey AV ([1979] 2013) The law of the constitution, 10th edn. Oxford University Press, London
Drago G, Fauvarque-Cosson B, Goré M (eds) (2015) L'accès au juge de cassation. Colloque du 15 juin 2015. Société de Législation Comparée, Paris
Ferrand F (2017) The French Court of Cassation: on the threshold of a quiet revolution? In: Van Rhee CH, Fu Y (eds) Supreme Courts in China and the West: adjudication at the service of public goals. Springer, Cham, pp 175–206
Ferraris F (2015) Rationing Justice. La selezione dei ricorsi nelle Corti Supreme di Stati Uniti e Italia. G Giappichelli Editore, Torino
Galič A (2014) A civil law perspective on the Supreme Court and its functions. In: Warsaw Conference (eds) The functions of the Supreme Court—issues of process and administration of justice. Warsaw, June 2014, pp 1–32. http://colloquium2014.uw.edu.pl/wp-content/uploads/sites/21/2014/01/Ales-Galic.pdf. Accessed 1 June 2020
Garlicki L (2007) Constitutional Courts versus Supreme Courts. Int J Constitutional Law 5 (1):44–68
Glenn P (2006) Comparative legal families and comparative legal traditions. In: Reimann M, Zimmermann R (eds) The Oxford handbook of comparative law. Oxford University Press, Oxford, pp 421–440
Gravelle H (1990) Rationing trials by waiting: welfare implications. Int Rev Law Econ 10 (3):255–270
Gravelle H (1995) Regulating the market of civil justice. In: Zuckerman AAS, Cranston R (eds) Reform of civil procedure: essays on 'Access to Justice'. Oxford University Press, New York, pp 279–303
Huls N, Adams M, Bomhoff J (eds) (2009) The legitimacy of the highest courts' rulings: judicial deliberations and beyond. TMC Asser Press, The Hague
Jolowicz JA (1998) General report. In: Yessiou-Faltsi P (ed) The role of the Supreme Courts at the national and international level. Sakkoulas Publications, Thessaloniki, pp 37–63
Jolowicz JA (2000) Managing overload in appellate courts: western countries. In: Jolowicz JA (ed) On civil procedure. Cambridge University Press, Oxford, pp 328–352
Le Sueur A, Cornes R (2000) What do the top courts do? Curr Leg Probl 53(1):53–97
Mitidiero D (2015) The ideal court of last resort: a court of interpretation and precedent. Int J Procedural Law 5(2):201–218
Muller S, Loth M (eds) (2009) Highest courts and the internationalization of law: challenges and changes. Hague Academic Press: The Hague
Muller S, Richards S (eds) (2010) Highest courts and globalization. Hague Academic Press, The Hague
Norkus R (2015) The filtering of appeals to the Supreme Courts. In: Network of the Presidents of the Supreme Judicial Courts of the European Union; Dublin Conference, pp 1–16. www.lat.lt/download/1369/introductory%20report%20-%20the%20filtering%20of%20appeals%20to%20supreme%20courts%20(president%20rimvydas%20norkus).pdf. Accessed 1 June 2020
Örücü E (2007) A general view of 'Legal Families' and of 'Mixing Jurisdictions'. In: Örücü E, Nelken D (eds) Comparative law: a handbook. Hart, Oxford, pp 169–187
Pastor Prieto S (1993) ¡Ah de la justicia!, política judicial y economía. Civitas, Madrid
Pekkanen P et al (2012) Designing and implementing delay reduction projects in courts. Int J Court Admin 9:94–103
Shapiro MM (1980) Appeals. Law Soc Rev 14(3):629–661

Silvestri E (1986) Access to the court of last resort: a comparative overview. Civil Just Q 5:304–320
Silvestri E (2001) Corti Supreme Europee: Accesso, Filtri e Selezione. In: Centro Studi Giuridici e Policitic e Centro Internazionale Magistrati (eds) Le Corti Supreme. Atti del Convengno. Giuffrè, Milano, pp 105–116
Taruffo M (1998) Civil law countries. In: Yessiou-Faltsi P (ed) The role of the Supreme Courts at the national and international level. Sakkoulas Publisher, Thessaloniki, pp 101–126
Taruffo M (2001) Le Corti Supreme Europee: Acceso, Filtri, Selezione. In: Centro Studi Giuridici e Policitic e Centro Internazionale Magistrati (eds) Le Corti Supreme. Atti del Convengno. Giuffrè, Milano, pp 95–104
US Supreme Court (2020) The Supreme Court at work. https://www.supremecourt.gov/about/courtatwork.aspx. Accessed 4 Dec 2020
Uzelac A, Van Rhee CH (2014) Appeals and other means of recourse against judgments in the context of the effective protection of civil rights and obligations. In: Uzelac A, Van Rhee CH (eds) Nobody's perfect. Comparative essays on appeals and other means of recourse against judicial decisions in civil matters. Intersentia, Cambridge, pp 3–13
Van Rhee CH (2004) The law's delay: essays on undue delay in civil litigation. Intersentia, Cambridge
Van Rhee CH (2010) Within a reasonable time: the history of due and undue delay in civil litigation. Duncker & Humblot, Berlin
Van Rhee CH, Fu Y (2017) Introduction. In: Van Rhee CH, Fu Y (eds) Supreme Courts in China and the West: adjudication at the service of public goals. Springer, Cham, pp 1–12
Vogenauer S, Tulibacka M, Hodges C (eds) (2010) The costs and funding of civil litigation: a comparative perspective. Hart, Oxford
Woolf H (1996) Access to justice. Final report. HMSO, London
Yessiou-Faltsi P (ed) (1998) The role of the Supreme Courts at the national and international level. Sakkoulas Publisher, Thessaloniki
Zweigert K, Kötz H (1998) Introduction to comparative law, 3rd edn (translation from German by Tony Weir). Clarendon Press, Oxford

Part II
Romanic Legal Tradition

Towards a Reform of the French Court of Cassation?

Emmanuel Jeuland

Abstract The French judicial system seems to be in a transitional phase. In France, the Court of Cassation, the Council of State and the Constitutional Council compete for the status of 'Supreme Court.' Nowadays, however, these three courts not only compete with each other but also with the European Court of Justice and the European Court of Human Rights. A new consensus is emerging in France about the need to reform the organisation or practices of these Supreme Courts in some way. The French Court of Cassation, particularly, has suffered detrimental consequences of the existing situation over the course of the last few decades. The main consequence is that the Court of Cassation seems to have lost part of its traditional influence. The court is no longer the undisputed highest authority in settling national legal debates. As a reaction, in recent years discussions on changes have been under way inside the court. Several working groups have been organised: one on access filters, one on grounds of cassation judgments, one on public prosecutors and one on the principle of proportionality. All of these topics are in some way connected and could lead to a major reform of the court. This contribution presents an overview of the French judicial system, it describes the place of the Court of Cassation within the system and it discusses the on-going reforms aimed at enabling the court to regain its traditional influence.

1 The French Court of Cassation in Its Context

Today, there are about 8000 professional judges in France. In relation to the total population, that means there are 9.1 judges per 100,000 people. The proportion of the public budget spent in the administration of justice represents 0.18% of the total French GDP. In civil and criminal matters, the court of last resort in France is the Court of Cassation (*Cour de cassation*), located within the premises of the Palace of

E. Jeuland (✉)
University Pantheon Sorbonne, Faculty of Law, Paris, France
e-mail: emmanuel.jeuland@univ-paris1.fr

P. Bravo-Hurtado, C. H. van Rhee (eds.), *Supreme Courts Under Pressure*, Ius Gentium: Comparative Perspectives on Law and Justice 83,
https://doi.org/10.1007/978-3-030-63731-6_2

Justice (*Palais de Justice*) in Paris. The same building—in which the *Parliament de Paris* sat during the sixteenth century, as we shall see—now houses the current Paris Court of Appeal, as well.

From a historical perspective, the origin of the Court of Cassation can be traced back to the period of the Ancien Régime.[1] During that time, the King of France exercised supreme authority, also as regards the administration of justice. Therefore, the King held the power to review every decision delivered by local judges or the regional (judicial) parliaments. In practice, the King delegated this task to various types of 'councils' (*Conseils*) whose composition and competences changed over time. For instance, the *Conseil d'État et des finances* was one of the King's councils devoted to resolving disputes concerning taxes and other conflicts with the royal administration—something that roughly resembles the current Council of State (*Conseil d'État*) as the court of last resort for administrative law. Another example, more relevant for the particular history of the Court of Cassation, was the 'Council of the Parties'—i.e. *Conseil des parties*, also known as *Conseil privé* or *Conseil d'État privé*. In fact, the Court of Cassation may be seen as the successor of this Council of the Parties, whose goal during the Ancien Régime was to act as the court of last resort, centralising the case law and controlling the regional parliaments, such as the *Parlement de Paris*.

After the French Revolution, the goal of the recently established *Tribunal de cassation*—later on renamed *Cour de cassation*—was similar to that of the previous Council of the Parties in the sense of acting as a court of last resort too. The new Court of Cassation aimed at controlling the former regional (judicial) parliaments which, in turn, were transformed into 'Courts of Appeal' (*Cours d'appel*) after the French Revolution.[2] The difference between the new Court of Cassation and the previous Council of the Parties was that instead of applying the King's law, the new Court of Cassation had to strictly apply the statutes voted by the National Assembly and the Senate. According to the notions of the Revolution, the Court of Cassation should only act as *bouche de la loi* (mouth of the law) and had no power to create laws.[3] This restriction implies that the Court of Cassation should not issue 'judgments providing general rules' (*jugements de réglement*)—i.e. judgments having a general scope similar to a regulation or a statute.[4]

One of the most salient aspects of the French Court of Cassation, particularly for a foreign observer, is the extreme conciseness of its judgments even though the reasons of its decisions are longer now.[5] The explanation for this relates to events that happened before and after the French Revolution. During the Ancien Régime, the Council of the Parties rendered judgments without providing grounds or reasons for the decision. The rationale behind this was related to the notion of the Council of

---

[1]Wijffels (2013a), pp. 62–73; Boulet-Sautel (1990), pp. 1–24.

[2]Wijffels (2013b), pp. 74–85.

[3]Montesquieu ([1747] 1998), Book XI, Chapter 6; Bell (2001), p. viii; Garapon and Papadopoulos (2003), pp. 50–51.

[4]See Wijffels (2013b), p. 80, and *Code civil*, Art. 5.

[5]Hortala (2020), p. 999.

the Parties as a representative body of the King. Supposedly, the Council could not know the precise reasons that the King himself had in mind when enacting a given statute. Acting on behalf of the King, therefore, the decision of the Council of the Parties should not mention any of the King's reasons since the Council itself could ignore them. After the Revolution, however, providing reasons became mandatory, but they had to remain rather concise.[6] It seems that there were two justifications for this. First, the rule establishing that the grounds for the decision had to remain short is a compromise with the workings of the old practice. Requiring (at least) concise grounds for the decision appears to be an improvement when compared to the total absence of grounds during the Ancien Régime. Second, the Court of Cassation could not create law but only apply statutes, especially the Civil Code (*Code civile*). Accordingly, the grounds for the decision should be presented as a brief judicial syllogism: the pertinent legal rule (major premise), a very short presentation of the facts of the case (minor premise) and the final part of the judgment containing the decision in respect of the dispute (conclusion). Following the tradition of the procedural rule that requires concise grounds, on the one hand, and the reasoning based on judicial syllogism, on the other, today the judgments issued by the French Court of Cassation usually consist of a *visa*, a *chapeau* and the 'operative' part. The *visa* is the equivalent of the major premise of the syllogism, in which the court states that it took into consideration Articles X and Y which apply to the current case. The *chapeau*—literally meaning 'hat' or top of the judgment—is the equivalent of the minor premise, in which the court mentions the rule contained in the cited articles and gives a brief presentation of the facts of the case. Lastly, the 'operative' part of the judgment is the equivalent of the conclusion of the syllogism, in which the court finally applies the cited rule to the current facts, resolving the dispute. As a result, a judgment of the Court of Cassation is extremely concise even for large and complex cases. The judgment fits onto one or two pages at most, rarely extending to a couple of additional pages.[7] This conciseness, and any criticism that comes with it, explains why a working group on legal reasoning has been established to reconsider the manner in which grounds should be provided by the Court of Cassation.

In addition to the Court of Cassation, at the top of the French judicial system there are two other 'courts of last resort'—i.e. a court that may issue final decisions from which no further appeal is allowed: the Constitutional Council and the Council of State. None of these three, however, can be properly called the 'Supreme' Court of France since none of them is clearly 'on top' of the other two.

The Constitutional Council is not composed of career judges but of (career) politicians coming from the executive and legislative branches. In that sense, the Council is not referred to as a proper 'judicial' tribunal but, more generally speaking, as the highest constitutional 'authority' in France. It has nine members: three of them appointed by the President of the Republic, three by the President of the National

[6]Troper et al. (1991), p. 197; Gillet (2012), pp. 173–174.

[7]Elliott et al. (2006), p. 197; Lasser (2004), pp. 31–32.

Assembly and three by the President of the Senate.[8] In addition, former French Presidents of the Republic are entitled to sit as members of the Constitutional Council too. But their level of involvement in the daily sessions of the Council varies from case to case. For example, former French presidents such as Valéry Giscard d'Estaing and Jacques Chirac have been active members indeed. Nicolas Sarkozy, quite the contrary, has not been very active when sitting in the Council. The current President of the Constitutional Council is Laurent Fabius, the former Minister of Foreign Affairs. As we may observe, the Council is a highly political body. Originally, membership of the Constitutional Council was viewed as an honour, particularly for former presidents during the beginning of the Fifth Republic (around 1958). Nowadays, however, their membership is seen as rather problematic. The active participation of former presidents raises the criticism of compromising the independence and impartiality of the Constitutional Council itself. A reform in this matter is under way.

The Constitutional Council deals with around 300 cases per year. It has jurisdiction over three areas: national elections, legislative policy and legislative review. More recently it has become possible to file an application for a priority preliminary ruling on an issue of constitutionality—known as a 'constitutional priority question' (CPQ), which in French is *QPC*.[9] Article 61(1) of the French Constitution, enacted by the constitutional reform of 23 July 2008, provides for such applications and has been invoked frequently—i.e. more than 100 decisions per year are rendered by the Constitutional Council by virtue of CPQ—since it came into force in 2010. The procedure for such applications is defined in a statute of 10 December 2009. At any hierarchical level of the judicial proceedings—i.e. first instance, appeal or cassation—a litigant may file one of these 'constitutional priority questions' at the Constitutional Council. The court in charge of the case must check whether the issue involves, on the one hand, a fundamental principle of the Constitution and, on the other hand, raises a new and serious issue.[10] Then the CPQ application is passed on to the Court of Cassation or to the Council of State, depending on whether the case comes from the ordinary courts for civil and criminal matters or the administrative courts, respectively. After review by the Court of Cassation or Council of State, the CPQ application reaches the Constitutional Council, which renders a decision within 3 months. A CPQ application is said to have 'priority' in order to anticipate that a complainant will bring his or her case before the European Court of Justice (ECJ). A litigant must go to the Constitutional Council first. After a CPQ application is resolved by the Constitutional Council, only then, if necessary, may the litigant apply for a preliminary ruling of the ECJ. In this last scenario, the ECJ's view will prevail.

The Court of Cassation has jurisdiction in private and criminal matters as the third instance and court of last resort. The court may review the case after a court of appeal

[8]On the Constitutional Council before the 2008 reform see Stone Sweet (1992), pp. 57–59.

[9]Heringa and Kiiver (2012), p. 160; Mathieu (2011), pp. 475–476.

[10]Roussillon and Espulgas (2015).

and court of first instance decision, but only on points of law.[11] It must be stressed that the Court of Cassation is the highest court in the 'judicial order'; the Council of State, in its turn, is the highest court in the 'administrative order.'[12] In France, there is a clear separation between public law and private law, which corresponds to the clear separation between administrative and criminal justice vis-à-vis civil justice. In the 'judicial order,' thus, it is necessary to distinguish between the cases resolved by lower criminal courts and civil courts.

There are five civil chambers, in a broad sense, within the Court of Cassation: a Commercial Chamber, a Labour Chamber and three Civil Chambers *stricto sensu.*[13] The first civil chamber deals with international litigation, arbitration and personal rights of private law and family matters; the second with procedural law and social security issues; and the third with real estate. The Court of Cassation heard 19,855 civil cases in 2010 and 20,049 in 2013; the average time spent on a case was 15.2 months.[14] The 36 Courts of Appeal heard 233,577 cases in 2010.[15] The average time spent on a case was 11.7 months.

At the lower levels of the French judicial system there are ordinary courts separate from the specialised tribunals for civil matters in a broad sense. The subject matter jurisdiction of ordinary courts depends on the amount of money at stake. The courts of first instance (*tribunaux d'instance*) have jurisdiction in cases in which the amount in dispute is less than €10,000. Above €10,000, cases are resolved by the Civil High Courts (*tribunaux de grande instance*) instead. But both, first instance courts and Civil High Courts, are composed of professional judges appointed by the President of the Republic based on the proposal of the High Council of the Judiciary (*Conseil supérior de la magistrature*). In 2013, the 161 Civil High Courts across France heard 923,313 cases in total; the average time spent on a case was 9.6 months (including summary judgments). The 307 first instance courts rendered 735,928 judgments in 2013. Here, the average duration of a case was 4.8 months. The French Parliament aims at reducing the duration of the proceedings in the ordinary courts, setting a goal of 6 months for Civil High Courts and 3 months for first instance courts. A statute of 23 March 2019 has merged (beginning in 2020) the first instance courts (*tribunaux de grande instance*) with the local courts (*tribunaux d'instance*) in a new court called *Tribunal judiciaire.*

Apart from the aforementioned ordinary courts, as noted, the French judicial system also contemplates specialised tribunals. Among them we can find the Business Courts (*tribunaux de commerce*), the Labour Courts (*conseils de prud'hommes*) and the Rural-Lease Courts (*tribunaux paritaire des baux ruraux*). These last do not sit on a permanent basis and hear around 2945 cases per year in all of France. Unlike the ordinary courts, all of whose members are professional career judges, some

[11] Ferrand (2017), p. 188; Boré and Boré (2015), pp. 239–240.

[12] See Gonod (2014).

[13] Boré and Boré (2015), pp. 58–60; Weber (2010), pp. 187–188.

[14] Ferrand (2017), pp. 202–203.

[15] Couchez (2004), p. 19.

members of the specialised tribunals could be lay judges appointed through local elections.

To avoid getting lost in translation, it should be noted here that in English the word 'court' refers to an ordinary and permanent court. The English word 'tribunal,' on the other hand, points at a special and transitory court, such as an arbitration tribunal. In French legal terminology, however, the word *tribunal* is used mainly for courts at the first instance of the judicial hierarchy, permanent or not, whereas the word *cour* is reserved for the Courts of Appeal and the Court of Cassation. Moreover, only a *tribunal* delivers a decision that, according to French terminology, is properly named a 'judgment' (*jugement*). The decisions issued by a *cour*, however, are not labelled as 'judgments' but as *arrêt*. *Arrêt* literally translates into English as 'interruption' or 'stop.' In the sense that all or part of the litigation stops or concludes with it, *arrêt* refers to a final judgment. The *arrêt* of the Courts of Appeal concludes the litigation on points of fact, while the *arrêt* of the Court of Cassation concludes the litigation on points of law.

In criminal matters, there are three kinds of courts whose jurisdiction depends on the seriousness of the offence. First, the Police Court (*tribunal de police*) has jurisdiction over traffic violations and other minor *contraventions*. Second, the Correctional Court (*tribunal correctionnel*) has jurisdiction mainly in regard to misdemeanours. Appeals against judgments delivered by a Correctional Court are lodged before the respective 'correctional chamber' of the local Court of Appeal, and, subsequently, the Criminal Court (named *cour d'assises*), which has both original and appellate jurisdiction for serious felonies or 'crimes,' properly speaking.

Lastly, similar to the Court of Cassation but in administrative matters, the Council of State is the third instance and court of last resort, restricted to points of law.[16] Historically, the ordinary judges for civil and criminal matters could not make decisions regarding public administration and civil servants (statute of 16–24 August 1790, Article 13). The Council of State, which succeeded the King's Council, acquired jurisdiction during the nineteenth century to decide on cases between the administration and French citizens. The Council of State pronounced 9235 judgments in 2013.

2 On-Going Reform

It has to be stressed here that, nowadays, the Court of Cassation does not seem to have a serious problem in handling its caseload. Some may say, in short, that the court works well. There is a sufficient number of judges, litigation is digitalised and the quality of the court's judgments is generally considered to be high. There are about 115 senior judges, or *conseillers*, in the court, 60 junior judges, or *conseillers*

[16]Gonod (2014).

référendaires,[17] 30 public prosecutors, one advocate general and 20 law clerks. Also, there is a specialised bar of lawyers for the court comprising about 60 law firms. Until 1947 there was a separate chamber inside the court (*Chambre des requêtes*) devoted to filtering cases by deciding on the admissibility of cassation complaints.[18] Since the elimination of this chamber, the court has not had an internal filtering mechanism anymore. By choosing which cases to bring to the court, the specialised bar of cassation lawyers performed a task comparable to an external filter. During the 1990s, however, the court became overburdened with cassation complaints. In reaction to that overload, a new access filter was put in place in the cassation procedure in 2001. The new Article L131-6 of the Code of Judicial Organisation (*Code de l'organisation judiciaire*) now requires that the cassation complaint should raise a 'serious point of law' since, otherwise, the complaint will be screened out.[19] Subsequently, the court was staffed with additional senior and junior judges. In 2005, the court's backlog reached 25,000 civil judgments annually, with 24,000 pending cases; in 2014, there were 21,295 judgments and 21,000 pending cases. As a matter of fact, there were enough judges to deal with 30,000 cases (civil and criminal) per year, and the proceedings were totally digitalised. The access filter resulted in the non-admission of around 25% of cassation complaints.

The Court of Cassation delivers, in total, around 30,000 civil and criminal judgments per year.[20] This figure seems enormous in comparison with the yearly caseload of the US Supreme Court, the UK Supreme Court or the equivalent to the Court of Cassation in Germany, the *Bundesgerichtshof*.[21] Nevertheless, the time-frame for deciding cases, which is now close to 15 months, appears reasonable from the French perspective.[22] One may therefore ask why reforms are needed. One reason may be that the Court of Cassation has become less influential over the last 20 years. The court's traditional influence came from having the power of the last word or final decision for all private and criminal matters in France. But the European Court of Justice, the European Court of Human Rights (ECtHR) and, most recently, the Constitutional Council too have become courts that provide the final decision in France. Moreover, they may even annul judgments issued by the Court of Cassation.[23] The Council of State has also managed to increase its influence above the Court of Cassation. The explanation for the different evolution of the level

---

[17]Weber (2010), pp. 31–33; Boré and Boré (2015), pp. 34–35.

[18]Ferrand (2017), pp. 190–191.

[19]Amrani-Mekki (2005), pp. 19–31.

[20]Ferrand (2017), p. 180.

[21]See, respectively, Marcus (Chapter "A Happy-Go-Lucky Story: The American Supreme Court and Overload Problems"), Sorabji (Chapter "The Supreme Court of the United Kingdom and the Court of Appeal in England and Wales: Sharing the Appellate Load") and Stürner (Chapter "Sharing Responsibility: The German Federal Court of Justice and the Civil Appellate System") in this volume.

[22]Ferrand (2017), pp. 181–183.

[23]In general, Garlicki (2007); Benvenisti and Downs (2009), pp. 59–72; Boré and Boré (2015), p. 3.

of influence of these two courts lies in the fact that, more than 10 years ago, the former introduced a fast-track procedure for cases of infringement of fundamental liberties, a fast-track procedure that does not have a clear equivalent in the latter. As a result, today some of the most high-profile media cases are adjudicated before the Council of State and not before the Court of Cassation—e.g. a case about euthanasia, another about a famous comic actor who made racist comments and, most recently, a case concerning the legality of some administrative decisions made during the state of emergency. In a metaphorical sense, it can be said that the Court of Cassation is now 'eclipsed' by other courts.

The particular division of labour between judges and public prosecutors within the Court of Cassation led to the finding in 1998 by the ECtHR as being contrary to the principle of equality of arms from the perspective of other litigants.[24] One of the problematic issues was that the cassation judge in charge of a case and the public prosecutor would convene before the main hearing in relevant cases.[25] This is now prohibited under the argument that the public prosecutor should not be privileged when compared to other participants in the lawsuit.[26] Currently, and as a result of the reform in France triggered by the ECtHR's sanction, the influence of the public prosecutor has decreased.

The daily practices of the Court of Cassation are not characterised by close teamwork. Unlike the common image of a court in which the panel of judges gathers on a daily basis to deliberate over each case, in reality the job of the cassation judges could be better described as individual or 'solitary' in nature. Normally, most of the work will be done by a single reporting judge who proposes one or two drafts of a judgment for a 'yes or no' approval by the other colleagues of the panel. Another indirect symptom of the lack of teamwork seems to be that about half of the cassation judges reside outside Paris. The reason they can do so is that the occasions on which the judges need to gather in person for hearings and deliberations are infrequent to the extent that the judges need to travel to the Palace of Justice usually no more than twice per month.

The question as to which should have priority over the other—i.e. the Constitutional Council or the Court of Cassation—has been disadvantageous for the Court of Cassation. As a counterreaction, now the court avoids sending cases to the Constitutional Council, especially when the court delivers an interpretation of a given legal statute. After back and forth disputes between the Court and the Council, however, the Court of Cassation has had to admit that, in certain circumstances, its interpretation of a legal statute, delivered in the context of a cassation procedure, may be contrary to the Constitution. In cases where European Union law is at stake in addition to the French Constitution, the Court of Cassation has tried to send the litigants' constitutional complaints (CPQ) not to the Constitutional Council but directly to the European Court of Justice. However, the ECJ has replied that the

---

[24] 31 March 1998, *Rheinhard and Slimane Kaïd*, Case n°21/1997/805/1008 and 22/1997/806/1009.

[25] Boré and Boré (2015), pp. 549–550.

[26] Ibid., pp. 39–40.

CPQ complaints of litigants should be resolved first by the French Constitutional Council before sending them to the ECJ itself.

Moreover, the President of the Court of Cassation has expressed the opinion that if there were fewer cases, the court could regain its traditional influence by concentrating on the most relevant cases.[27] At the moment, more than half of the court's caseload corresponds to the task of checking possible errors incurred in the decisions of the Courts of Appeal. The reason why such a large proportion of its caseload ends up being devoted to that error-monitoring task is the idea that the Court of Cassation should perform a disciplinary role (*mission disciplinaire*) vis-à-vis the lower courts.[28] Assigning such a role to the Court of Cassation, in reality, is not required by French legislation. It is more a widespread notion coming from French legal culture. In fact, some of the judges of the court apparently do not entirely agree with this disciplinary role anymore. Instead, some would like the court to concentrate on cases that are relevant for the uniform interpretation of the law and legal development. A court focused on resolving leading cases as such, they think, would be in a better position to provide more detailed explanations for the reasons behind each judgment.[29]

Additionally, the former President of the Court of Cassation, Louvel, has declared that the court does not apply the principle of proportionality even though this is now a generally accepted principle. Traditionally, the court resolves its cases by applying specific rules of law, in which the grounds for the judgment contain a strict, concise and clear chain of reasoning. The court tends to avoid resolving cases by applying relatively vague legal standards such as the principle of proportionality.[30] Exceptionally, the court would apply this principle only in cases concerning, for example, the balance between the freedom of the press and the right to privacy. But the general practice of avoiding the principle of proportionality is starting to create problems for the French Court of Cassation. The reason is that the ECtHR, and sometimes the ECJ too, now invokes the principle of proportionality to overrule judgments delivered by the court. One example is *Henrioud v France* of 5 November 2015,[31] in which the ECtHR indeed overruled the Court of Cassation, arguing that the French court did not apply the principle of proportionality when it should have done so.

In this case, the Court of Cassation dismissed an application on international child custody because the appealing party did not send a copy of the Court of Appeal's judgment as notification to his opponent. The reason the Court of Cassation took this decision was due to an (excessively) formal and strict interpretation of Article 979 of

[27]See Louvel (2015), p. 13; Louvel (2016), pp. 4–5.

[28]On the *mission disciplinaire,* Cadiet (2012), p. 58; Charruault (2012), pp. 23–25.

[29]On this discussion see Cassia (2015); Deumier (2015), p. 1720; Fattaccini (2015), p. 1734; Fricéro (2015), p. 753; Gautier (2015), p. 902; Guinchard et al. (2015), p. 278; Haftel (2015), p. 1378; Jamin (2015a), pp. 1641–1647; Jamin (2015b); Jeuland and Simiand (2015); Rebeyrol (2015), p. 954; Théry (2015), p. 1731.

[30]On the debate about the principle of proportionality and human rights see Tsakyrakis (2009) and Khosla (2010).

[31]No. 21444/11 Procedures 2016, No.15 (Fricero).

the *Code de procédure civile*. That article establishes a deadline for the appellant party to submit copies of the lower court's decision, under the sanction of declaring the cassation appeal inadmissible *ex officio*. The ECtHR held that the decision of the Court of Cassation infringed the principle of proportionality: dismissing an entire case in a sensitive matter, such as international child custody, is a sanction excessively severe compared to the mere fact that a litigant failed to file some copies. Consequently, the ECtHR ruled against the French state.

Based on these and similar cases, one may ask what changes are needed. One necessary change could be that, in the future, the Court of Cassation indeed should control proportionality in the complaint of all legal rules. Implementing an *ex officio* control of the proportionality principle within cassation proceedings may avoid further censures from the ECtHR. In fact, nowadays the Court of Cassation is taking steps towards a more proactive control of this principle. For instance, the court invoked the proportionality principle in a case involving marriage annulment. The case pertained to a man who married his daughter-in-law following the death of his son. After 20 years of an apparently happy marriage, however, the former wife of the man brought an action to nullify the marriage on the grounds of incest. The Civil High Court and the Court of Appeal both found in favour of the former wife. These two courts agreed with the pleading of incest and, consequently, annulled the marriage. The Court of Cassation, on the contrary, revoked the decision of the first and second instances. In a way that departed from its previous practice of avoiding any application of broad principles; here the Court of Cassation indeed considered that, given the facts of the case, annulling the marriage appeared to be disproportionate and, furthermore, contrary to Article 8 of the European Convention on Human Rights (right to privacy).

Legal scholars (still) in favour of maintaining the judicial syllogism criticise the principle of proportionality and emphasise the necessity of a close supervision over how the courts will apply this principle. They hold that a strict application of the principle of proportionality is only possible if four criteria are met:

1. 'Necessity' of a given measure—i.e. a sanction;
2. 'Suitability' of the measure to its intended goal;
3. 'Balance' of the conflicting interests, given the facts of the case;
4. 'Certainty' in the maintenance of (current) legal relationships.

Other legal scholars, even less optimistic about the principle of proportionality, consider that the application of these broad and substantive criteria are in conflict with the Court of Cassation's traditional approach to legal reasoning, characterised by strict and formal criteria instead. Moreover, they argue, the Court of Cassation would become, in practice, an inferior court under the ECtHR. The application of the principle of proportionality would also take a considerable amount of the court's time. The court would need detailed information about the facts of the case in order to achieve a proper balance between the conflicting interests at stake. Since applying the principle of proportionality depends on such facts in detail, some legal scholars consider that the court would deviate from the tradition of adjudicating on points of law exclusively, and would now adjudicate on points of fact too. The court's practice of deciding exclusively based on judicial syllogisms would come to an end, they say. Furthermore, a group of legal scholars[32] holds that, as a result of these trends, France would no longer be a proper 'civil law' country—in the orthodox view of a legal system characterised, among other things, by the supposed absence of judge-made law. Under the argument of taking into account the detailed facts of the case (as the principle of proportionality so requires), they argue that the Court of Cassation may abstain from applying a given piece of legislation and, thus, it can apply a new rule. Behind this process of checking the proportionality of legal rules in each current case, the authors conclude, the Court of Cassation would be surreptitiously creating law, resembling in this way the judge-made law of common law legal systems.

The former President of the Court of Cassation has highlighted the link between these matters and the question as to how cases should be selected before full cassation review, that is to say, access filters.[33] First, applying the four aforementioned criteria of the principle of proportionality—i.e. necessity, suitability, balance and certainty—will require more detailed explanations for the grounds in support of each judgment, more details when compared to the current conciseness of the legal syllogism. Second, nowadays the general public has higher expectations as regards the justification of the judgments of the court. As a result, the former President of the Court argued, the number of cassation cases heard by the court should be reduced in order to be able to satisfy these higher standards of reasoning per judgment. The number of cases should be reduced also because the court should concentrate on resolving important cases only. In one way or another, therefore, these various problems finally converge in the question of whether or not to introduce access filters, a mechanism for the selection of cases that can be litigated before the court.

How should this filter mechanism be designed and implemented? A working group of the court has studied the access filters of foreign legal systems. The US Supreme Court and the UK Supreme Court, for instance, indeed have access filters that grant the Supreme Court itself the discretional power to select its own cases.[34] In the German appeal system, part of the filtering process is performed by the Courts of Appeal. In Germany, the Court of Appeal selects the cases that should be sent to the Supreme Court for final review.[35] These two filtering models, however, have been criticised in France for different reasons. First, the filtering mechanisms of the US Supreme Court and the UK Supreme Court are criticised as being 'aristocratic' since only a few 'privileged' cases are heard and resolved by the Supreme Court. According to French legal culture, the Supreme Court should remain, quite the contrary, more 'democratic' in the sense of potentially being accessible to all

[32]Jestaz et al. (2014), p. 2061.

[33]In general, on filtering at the *Cour de cassation* see Amrani-Mekki and Cadiet (2005).

[34]On filtering in the US Supreme Court and the UK Supreme Court see Marcus (Chapter "A Happy-Go-Lucky Story: The American Supreme Court and Overload Problems") and Sorabji (Chapter "The Supreme Court of the United Kingdom and the Court of Appeal in England and Wales: Sharing the Appellate Load"), respectively, in this volume.

[35]On filtering in Germany see Stürner (Chapter "Sharing Responsibility: The German Federal Court of Justice and the Civil Appellate System") in this volume.

citizens. Second, the German model, in which the Court of Appeal itself decides which of its own cases could be further appealed, raises criticism from the point of view of the principle of impartiality. The judges on the panel that delivers the judgment and the judges who choose which judgments may be appealed should not be the same. To solve the impartiality problem of the German access filter model, the Presidents of the French Courts of Appeal suggest implementing a separate commission of appellate judges that should be in charge of filtering the cases that may reach the Court of Cassation. This commission would be 'separate' in the sense that the appellate judges filtering cases for access to the Court of Cassation should not be the same judges as the ones who drafted the appealed judgment.

However, judges of the Court of Cassation and the Courts of Appeal are not the only stakeholders in the reform of access filters in France. Another interest group is the lawyers. As previously mentioned, the French judicial system contemplates a special bar of lawyers that have a legal monopoly to plead cases before the Court of Cassation.[36] This special bar of cassation lawyers are lobbying against reforms aimed at introducing access filters. The reason for lobbying against them is that such access filters are seen by these lawyers as a danger to the exercise of their profession.

Furthermore, the problems of the Court of Cassation are not entirely unrelated to similar problems at the Courts of Appeal. In fact, nowadays the Courts of Appeal appear to be overburdened themselves.[37] Like the domino effect, therefore, a reform at the Court of Cassation in these matters may trigger a similar reform at the Courts of Appeal. The Courts of Appeal also need a mechanism to screen out a portion of cases coming from the inferior courts. Compared to the urgency of reforms to the Court of Cassation, however, the problems of the Courts of Appeal seem less pressing for the general public and the political actors that may take the initiative of starting a reform.

An important step in the national debate about access filters was a decree of 6 November 2014. That decree was meant to define the real nature of the recently introduced access filters. The decree stated that the access filters are, in reality, an ordinary cassation procedure, but with the difference that the judgment may omit the grounds for the decision.[38] As a result, the previous criterion for screening out cases—i.e. the lack of serious grounds for cassation appeal (*moyens non sérieux*)—was replaced by a new and more widely used filtering criterion based on the (few) prospects of success of the appeal in cassation.[39] The pertinent panel of judges within the chamber of the Court of Cassation has the option of resolving the case with or without providing grounds for the decision, with or without a

[36]Ferrand (2017), p. 193.

[37]On the reform of the French Courts of Appeal see Cadiet and Loriferne (2011).

[38]Baraduc and Boré (2014), pp. 2197–2200.

[39]Boré and Boré (2015), pp. 656–658.

'motivated' judgment. The criterion for not providing grounds is that it is immediately apparent to the panel of judges that the case has no chances of success.[40]

In addition to these modifications to the access filters to the Court of Cassation, the 2004 decree introduced other changes. The reform extended the requirement of representation by a lawyer before the court to all subject matters. Therefore, previous matters that did not require representation by a lawyer, such as labour matters, now require such representation. Both the several reforms on access filters and the extension of the requirement of representation by a lawyer seem to have contributed to the decrease in the court's caseload. In fact, the court received around 25,000 cases per year at the very beginning of the twenty-first century. Today that number is (only) 20,000 cases, implying a reduction close to 20% in two decades.

3 Conclusion

It is likely that in the short term the French Court of Cassation will be subject to reform, either regarding its organisation or its procedure. Mrs. Arens, the new President of the Court of Cassation, has set up a new working group called "Cour de cassation 2030" to prepare a reform.[41] Most likely, a short-track procedure will be introduced, allowing the court to adapt its proceedings to the variety of its incoming caseload and, consequently, to recover its (lost) influence. The grounds for the court's decisions have already been expanded to some degree, especially where the principle of proportionality is at stake. Reforms will be introduced to reduce the number of cases allowed to proceed before the court. According to current practice, around 25% of the cases are already filtered out by way of a refusal at the early stage of the non-admission procedure. The filtering stage, which was meant to alleviate the court's workload, in practice has become demanding to the extent that the amount of work required per case in this preliminary stage is becoming similar to the amount of work required in normal cassation proceedings. Another reform should reduce the length and increase the speed of the filtering stage.

Other kinds of reforms, however, are more disputed among lawyers and scholars in France. For instance, one of the main contested issues is whether the Court of Cassation should continue to exercise its function of monitoring and correcting erroneous decisions of the lower courts (*mission disciplinaire*).[42] On the one hand, some lawyers and scholars are of the opinion that the Courts of Appeal indeed require close supervision. The Courts of Appeal themselves, on the other hand, disagree with that diagnosis since, in their own opinion, the French appellate courts do have the competences needed to check and minimise their own errors. However, it is generally felt that the Courts of Appeal are the weak element in the structure of

[40]*Code de procédure civile*, Article 1014.

[41]Potocki (2020), p. 1944.

[42]Le Bars (2020), p. 1199.

the French judiciary. Increasing the autonomy of the Courts of Appeal in respect of the Court of Cassation does not appear to be a reform in the right direction. This point of the debate, about whether the Court of Cassation should keep close supervision over the Courts of Appeal or not, has become—according to the French idiom—a *cul-de-sac*, that is to say, a dead end.

Seen in a broader historical perspective, the problem of the large numbers of cases before the Court of Cassation is a recurring problem in France, one that is raised every couple of decades. On each occasion a new tool is invented to (try to) address the problem. Today, after 20 years, the same problem arises one more time and, again, a new filtering tool is devised. But the current repetition of this old problem seems to be different because the Court of Cassation now faces a dilemma. On the one hand, the court aims at remaining faithful to its traditional practices and, on the other hand, it aims at recovering its great influence from earlier times. The dilemma appears when we realise that such traditional influence seems to have been lost precisely due to remaining faithful to traditional practices.

These traditions, however, seem already to be fading away in response to current trends. For instance, a statute of 18 November of 2016 moderates (even more) the traditional practice of the Court of Cassation being limited to annulling or quashing the appealed judgment and referring the case to a lower court for a new decision on the merits. With the 2016 reform, the court may deliver a new decision on the merits by itself when 'the good administration of justice so justifies' (Art. L411-3 COJ). As regards the principle of proportionality, a better approach to solve the dilemma between keeping traditions versus regaining influence—in my opinion—may be that the Court of Cassation should develop a strict case law using its 'margin of appreciation' recognised by the ECtHR and the ECJ. A strict application of the proportionality principle should not greatly distort the traditional methodology of reasoning of the court based on judicial syllogisms. In this manner, the court would still be limited to supervising the correct application of the law and the law exclusively (not the facts). The grounds provided by the court in a strict application of the proportionality principle would need to be a little longer indeed, but not much longer. This should not result in a situation where the length of the judgments becomes excessive—a situation present in some common law jurisdictions such as England & Wales.[43] Every Court of Appeal should create a commission that acts as its own filtering stage, aiming at excluding irrelevant cases coming from the courts of first instance. If fewer cases reach the Courts of Appeal, even fewer cases will reach the Court of Cassation. Furthermore, the same commission at every Court of Appeal should be in charge of enforcing the *mission disciplinaire* of their own appeal judgments. At the Court of Cassation simple cases of routine supervision of the lower courts should not be mixed with complex cases that raise a serious matter on a point of law.

[43] Andrews (2017), p. 42; Blom-Cooper (2009), pp. 160–161.

References

Amrani-Mekki S (2005) Les textes organisant la non-admission des pourvois en cassation en droit français. In: Amrani-Mekki S, Cadiet L (eds) La sélection des pourvois à la Cour de cassation. Economica, Paris, pp 19–31
Amrani-Mekki S, Cadiet L (eds) (2005) La sélection des pourvois à la Cour de cassation. Economica, Paris
Andrews N (2017) The Supreme Court of the United Kingdom: a selective tribunal with the final say in most matters. In: Van Rhee CH, Fu Y (eds) Supreme courts in transition in China and the West: adjudication at the service of public goals. Springer, Cham, pp 37–52
Baraduc E, Boré L (2014) La simplification de la procédure devant la Cour de cassation: À propos du décret n° 2014-1338 du 6 novembre. La Semaine Juridique 49:2197–2200
Bell J (2001) French legal cultures. Butterworths, London
Benvenisti E, Downs GW (2009) National courts, domestic democracy, and the evolution of international law. Eur J Int Law 20(1):59–72
Blom-Cooper LJ (2009) Style of judgments. In: Blom-Cooper LJ, Dickson B, Drewry G (eds) The judicial House of Lords 1876–2009. Oxford University Press, Oxford, pp 145–163
Boré J, Boré L (2015) La cassation en matèrie civile, 5th edn. Dalloz, Paris
Boulet-Sautel M (1990) La cassation sous l'Ancien régime. In: Association des Magistrats et Anciens Magistrats de la Cour de cassation (ed) Le Tribunal et la Cour de cassation 1790–1990. Litec, Paris, pp 1–24
Cadiet L (2012) Civil procedure. In: Berman GA, Piccard E (eds) Introduction to French law. Wolters Kluwer, Alphen aan den Rijn
Cadiet L, Loriferne D (eds) (2011) Le réforme de la procédure d'appel. IRJS Editions, Paris
Cassia VP (2015) Filtrer l'accès au juge de cassation? Recueil Dalloz 24:1361–1362
Charruault C (2012) Remarques sur la mission disciplinaire du juge de cassation. In: Ordre des Avocats au Conseil d'Etat et à la Cour de Cassation (ed) Le Juge de Cassation en Europe. Dalloz, Paris, pp 23–26
Couchez G (2004) Procédure civile, 13th edn. Armand Colin, Paris
Deumier P (2015) Accès à la Cour de cassation et traitement des questions jurisprudentielles. Recueil Dalloz 30:1720–1731
Elliott C, Jeanpierre E, Vernon C (2006) French legal system, 2nd edn. Pearson, Edinburgh
Fattaccini C (2015) L'intensité du contrôle de cassation. Recueil Dalloz 30:1734–1737
Ferrand F (2017) The French Court of Cassation: on the threshold of a quiet revolution? In: Van Rhee CH, Fu Y (eds) Supreme courts in transition in China and the West: adjudication at the service of public goals. Springer, Cham, pp 175–206
Fricéro VN (2015) L'avenir de la Cour de cassation: La vision originale du Club des juristes. La Semaine Juridique 26:1258–1260
Garapon A, Papadopoulos I (2003) Juger en Amérique et en France: culture juridique française et common law. Odile Jacob, Paris
Garlicki L (2007) Constitutional Courts versus Supreme Courts. Int J Const Law 5(1):44–68
Gautier PY (2015) Eloge du syllogisme. La Semaine Juridique 36:1494–1497
Gillet JL (2012) L'Arrêt de la Cour de cassation. Motivation, Style et Structure. In: Hourquebie F, Ponthoreau M-C (eds) La motivation des décisions des cours suprêmes et cours constitutionnelles. Bruylant, Brussels, pp 167–181
Gonod P (2014) Le Conseil d'Etat et la refondation de la justice administrative. Dalloz, Paris
Guinchard S, Ferrand F, Moussa T (2015) Une chance pour la France et le droit continental: La technique de cassation, vecteur particulièrement approprié au contrôle de conventionnalité. Recueil Dalloz 5:278–286
Haftel B (2015) Libres propos sur l'avant-projet de réforme de la Cour de cassation et la fonction du juge. Recueil Dalloz 24:1378–1383
Heringa AW, Kiiver P (2012) Constitutions compared. An introduction to comparative constitutional law, 3rd edn. Intersentia, Cambridge

Hortala S (2020) La réforme de la rédaction des décisions de la Cour de cassation. La Semaine Juridique 37:999–1001
Jamin CH (2015a) Cour de cassation: Le fil de la pelote. Recueil Dalloz 29:1641–1647
Jamin CH (2015b) Cour de cassation – une question de motivation. La Semaine Juridique 29:1403–1405
Jestaz PH, Marguenaud JP, Jamin CH (2014) Révolution tranquille à la Cour de cassation. Recueil Dalloz 36:2061–2070
Jeuland E, Simiand G (2015) Casanova à la Cour de cassation, force normative et anonymisation des arrêts. La Semaine Juridique 29:1430–1438
Khosla M (2010) Proportionality: an assault on human rights? A reply. Int J Const Law 8(2):298–306
Lasser M (2004) Judicial deliberations. A comparative analysis of judicial transparency and legitimacy. Oxford University Press, Oxford
Le Bars T (2020) Proposition de lecture du rapport sur les 'accassations disciplinaires' en matière civile. La Semaine Juridique 45:1199–1200
Louvel B (2015) Réflexions à la Cour de cassation. Recueil Dalloz 23:1326–1327
Louvel B (2016) Regards d'universitaires sur la réforme de la Cour de cassation. La Semaine Juridique 1-2:4–5
Mathieu B (2011) Le Conseil Constitutionnel: 'Legislateur positif' ou la question des interventions du juge constitutionnel français dans l'exercice de la fonction legislative. In: Brewer-Carías AR (ed) Constitutional courts as positive legislators: a comparative law study. Cambridge University Press, Cambridge, pp 471–496
Montesquieu CS ([1747] 1998) De l'esprit des lois, Book XI, Chapter 6. Voltaire Foundation, Oxford
Potocki A (2020) Penser ensemble la Cour de cassation de demain. Recueil Dalloz 34:1944
Rebeyrol V (2015) Une réforme pour la Cour de cassation? La Semaine Juridique 37:1583–1590
Roussillon H, Espulgas P (2015) Le Conseil constitutionnel, 8th edn. Dalloz, Paris
Stone Sweet A (1992) The birth of the judicial politics in France. The Constitutional Council in comparative perspective. Oxford University Press, New York
Théry PH (2015) Cours suprêmes: Essai – manqué – de typologie et de definition. Recueil Dalloz 30:1731–1734
Troper M, Grzegorczyk C, Gardies JL (1991) Statutory interpretation in France. In: MacCormick N, Summers RS (eds) Interpreting statutes. A comparative study. Darthmouth Publishing, Aldershot, pp 171–211
Tsakyrakis S (2009) Proportionality: an assault on human rights? Int J Const Law 7(3):468–493
Weber JF (2010) La Cour de cassation. La documentation française, Paris
Wijffels A (2013a) Late-medieval and early-modern France. In: Wijffels AA, Van Rhee CH (eds) European Supreme Courts. A portrait through history. Third Millennium Publishing, London, pp 62–73
Wijffels A (2013b) France from the revolution to the present. In: Wijffels AA, Van Rhee CH (eds) European Supreme Courts. A portrait through history. Third Millennium Publishing, London, pp 74–85

Finding a Cure or Simply Relieving Symptoms? The Case of the Italian Supreme Court

Federico Ferraris

Abstract For more than 20 years the Italian Supreme Court (*Corte di Cassazione*) has been in a state of crisis because of the high number of cases it must review and the paucity of resources, both human and material, allocated for the examination of each appeal. The national legislator has intervened several times in the last 10 years to introduce a sort of petition screening and 'filter' tool to basically limit the decision in a public hearing to questions of law relating to important individual values only and, at the same time, divert all other petitions to a simplified decision by way of chamber proceedings. Nonetheless, the crisis the court faces remains serious, and a more courageous reform—perhaps even one which would eliminate the right to 'unconditional' access to the court guaranteed by the Italian Constitution—is clearly needed.

1 The Italian Supreme Court and Its Performance

The 2020 World Bank Group *Doing Business* report places Italy at the 122th position in the ranking of 190 countries with regard to the time and cost of business litigation while other leading Member States of the European Union earn higher positions. Among the factors that are commonly identified as the cause of the malfunctioning of Italian justice is certainly the excessive number of cases the courts have to deal with, a situation which of course does not spare the highest judicial body, the *Corte di Cassazione* (Court of Cassation), that is to say, the Italian Supreme Court.[1] Over the last decade, the average number of petitions filed annually

[1]Author's note: In this contribution, I refer to the *Corte di Cassazione* as the Italian Supreme Court and the highest judicial body in civil and criminal matters in the Italian judicial system, to be distinguished from the *Corte Costituzionale* (the Constitutional Court), which is the highest judicial body in matters of constitutional law.

F. Ferraris (✉)
University of Milan-Bicocca, School of Law, Milan, Italy
e-mail: federico.ferraris@unimib.it

P. Bravo-Hurtado, C. H. van Rhee (eds.), *Supreme Courts Under Pressure*, Ius Gentium: Comparative Perspectives on Law and Justice 83,
https://doi.org/10.1007/978-3-030-63731-6_3

with the court reached 89,000 (51,000 criminal petitions and 38,000 civil petitions).[2]

Leaving aside the immediate impact on the *management* of appeals (in terms of time—the disposition of a case often takes up to 3.5 years[3]—and cost of proceedings), this massive demand has serious consequences for the court's *functioning*. As observed by several prominent scholars, the court's case law has become a sort of 'supermarket' where the parties may always find a decision that best suits their own particular interests.[4] In addition to this, reports often show that a large number of conflicts occur between the different chambers of the court[5] and that there are many decisions whose scope is so narrow that it is hard to understand the different positions and roles played by the court in the appellate system, even though it has been called upon to deal with a question of law pertaining only to the challenged decision.[6] As a result, the very conception of the highest body of the Italian judicial system is put at risk: because of its nature and functions, the court is expected to ensure both the necessary synthesis of positions and interests expressed from time to time by individuals and society *and* the correct course in the development of national law.

2 One Court and Two Different Functions

The situation just described, together with the increased need for tools with which to relieve the overburdened Italian Supreme Court, requires some—although brief—considerations about the role played by the court in the Italian judicial system. Indeed, an 'effective' case-selection technique must take into account the scope of the goal pursued by the court, so that the anticipated reduction in caseload will allow judges to devote more time and energy—and thus improve consistency—to

[2]See Report on the State of the Administration of Justice 2019.

[3]See the *2019 Report*, p. 114.

[4]See Chiarloni (2002), p. 6; Taruffo (1991), p. 103.

[5]The Supreme Court consists of six civil chambers and seven criminal chambers. In particular, with regard to civil litigation, the first three chambers were established in 1923. Article 19 of Law No. 533 of 11 August 1973 added a fourth chamber devoted to labour cases. By Decree of 19 June 1999, No. 61, the Tax Chamber, or the Fifth Chamber, was instituted following the introduction of the appeal against the decisions issued by the Regional Tax Commissions. The Sixth Civil Chamber, also called the 'filter division,' was introduced by Law No. 69 of 18 June 2009. In addition, the Court can decide cases *en banc* (Joint Chamber) when it has to resolve conflicts that have occurred within the chambers and/or major issues of particular importance. It also rules on all questions concerning jurisdiction and conflicts of jurisdiction as well as on the appeals against disciplinary sanctions issued by the Superior Council of Magistrates or the National Bar Association.

[6]See, e.g., the reports provided by Moneta (1992), pp. 1245ff.; idem (1993); idem (1995).

performing their specific functions.[7] In this regard, the 'general rule' requires that when the court carries out a 'public' function—that is, ensuring the development of national law—case-selection mechanisms are necessary to limit its review to the most relevant issues that can implement legal principles in a super-individual perspective; vice versa, when the court carries out a 'private' function—where the goal is to check the decision-making process of the lower court—the same use of case-selection mechanisms appears inconsistent with a court responsible for verifying the correctness of the challenged decision. Yet, as far as the Supreme Court is concerned, such a distinction (and its consequences), as we are going to explain, cannot adequately fit the double, seemingly contradictory role assigned to the court by the various provisions governing its functioning. More in detail, pursuant to Article 65(1) of the Law on the Judiciary, the court 'as a supreme organ of justice, ensures the observance and uniform interpretation of the law, the unity of national law, respect for the limits of the various jurisdictions, governs conflicts of jurisdiction and powers, and performs other tasks conferred by law.'[8]

Such a temperament, which is generally referred to in Italy as *nomofilachia*,[9] means that the main function of the court is the protection of the interests of society, and this comes from the need to uphold different fundamental principles governing the judicial system. On the one hand, it stands as a consequence of the general equality principle provided by Article 3 of the Italian Constitution, since, in determining once and for all the meaning of a rule, the court ensures the equal treatment of citizens under the law;[10] on the other hand, it enhances other relevant principles, such as the predictability of decisions, the efficiency of the process and, last but not least, the authority of the court itself. Indeed, a consistent case law production allows the parties to anticipate within a reasonable time the outcome of their dispute; lower courts can count on 'well-packaged' and 'ready-to-use' principles, thus saving time and energy to address new issues; and, finally, an institution that resolves conflicts of interpretation and develops clear and defined rules can increase the impact of its (although non-binding) precedents in the inferior courts.

The existence of a 'public' character within the Supreme Court's duties can also be acknowledged from several provisions of the Code of Civil Procedure (hereinafter, CCP). Here we recall Article 384 CCP and the related power to lay down the principle of law to be applied by the judge in the subsequent referral judgment (following cassation of the challenged decision), which is perhaps the main instrument by which the court gives the rules that are subject to its own attention a certain and precise interpretation. We recall also Article 363 CCP, which allows the court to provide the principle of law—following the request by the Public Prosecutor—when

[7]See Silvestri (2001), p. 105.

[8]Author's note: All translations are mine.

[9]See Calamandrei (1920); Fazzalari (1960); more recently see Denti (1987); idem (2004), pp. 106ff.; Mazzarella (2003); Panzarola (2005); Ricci (2009a), pp. 571ff.; Taruffo (1988), pp. 237ff.; Taruffo (1990), pp. 349ff.; Taruffo (1991); Verde (2008), pp. 1ff.

[10]See Calamandrei and Furno (1958), p. 1056; more recently see Proto Pisani (2002), p. 504.

the appeal has not been brought within the proper time limits, has been abandoned, or when the decision cannot be challenged in front of the Supreme Court, but also by its own motion in cases where the appeal is declared inadmissible and the question decided is at the same time considered to be of a particular importance. In such cases, too, the court exercises its duty to provide future litigants with a correct interpretation of certain legal issues, in light of their special relevance and potential extensive application. We recall Article 374 CCP as well, which allows each chamber to send back to the Joint Chamber a petition in the event of a disagreement with the principle of law previously issued by the Joint Chamber on the same issue, and which has been provided in order to prevent conflicts within the court and to improve the forthcoming interpretation of the law.

While the Supreme Court is thus called upon to play a leading role in promoting national law, thereby approaching the common law perspective where the Supreme Court is placed 'outside' the system of appeals, at the same time there are many elements that make the court a body in charge of dealing with the correctness of the lower court proceedings and the parties' interests in a 'right' decision. Reference here is made to the constitutional guarantee pursued by Article 111(7) of the Italian Constitution, which states that the final appeal (to the Supreme Court) against judgments is 'always admitted'. The original purpose of the provision was to strengthen the principle of effectiveness of judicial protection, as established in Article 24 of the Constitution, by filling gaps in the legislation where no other recourse for review of a particular decision previously issued had been provided for. Over time, though, this guarantee made litigants aware of the fact that they could always count on a further chance to have an unfavourable judgment reversed; it also had a significant impact on the effectiveness of the decision-making process of the court and on the possibility to limit in some way the court's docket. Indeed, in providing all citizens unconditional access to the Supreme Court, the constitutional principle appears to represent a threat to the court's capacity to carry out the functions laid down in Article 65 of the Law on the Judiciary. In fact, the court ends up deciding an alarming average of 30,000 civil appeals per year, which makes it virtually impossible to preserve the consistency of legal interpretation and also serves as a serious obstacle to any efforts to set up a case-selection mechanism for the management of appeals.

Additionally, in the Code of Civil Procedure, besides the provisions which tend to ensure the 'public' role of the court, it is not difficult to discover other provisions that, at the same time, relate to its 'private' role, meaning the role it plays for the protection of the parties to the case at hand. One example is the power of the court, pursuant to Article 384 CCP, to decide appeals on the merits when no further factual findings are needed. If it is true that the aim here is to fulfil the need for procedural economy, it is equally true that in this way the court ends up acting as a court of 'third instance.'[11] Moreover, the various provisions preventing first appeals against certain judicial measures, thus allowing an appeal to the court of last resort only,

[11] See Consolo (1990), pp. 440ff.; Consolo (2007), pp. 297ff.

together with the power of the parties to agree in filing a petition directly with the Court of Cassation against a judgment delivered by the court of first instance, complete the picture, creating the legitimate expectation of a further degree of adjudication that the parties can always count on.[12] In this perspective, the idea of *nomofilachia* is 'configured as the subject matter of an individual right relating to a particular (challenged) decision rather than as a way to protect the integrity of the rule of law.'[13] In other words, what really matters is not so much the violation of the law, but rather the injury caused to a specific subjective individual right, so that the clarification of a particular principle stands as an 'occasion' for restoring 'justice' in the case at hand.

3 Overburdened Docket: Consequences, Internal Solutions ...

As shown by the statistics mentioned in the previous section, over the years the Supreme Court has acted more like a court of third instance rather than as a guardian of the correct and uniform interpretation of the law. Of course, such behaviour has produced significant disadvantages, which should be taken into account when trying to describe and understand the crisis facing the court. First, such 'hypertrophic' decision-making strongly reduces the impact of each judgment of the court since, in most instances, it is impossible to extend the principle of law provided by the court beyond the individual case to which it refers. Second, the greater specificity of the decisions turns the court into an 'entropic' institution, called upon year after year to deal with issues which, in most cases, have already been disposed of several times. Third, the excessive workload of the court not only results in different interpretations of the same principles between different chambers, but also puts at risk the 'uniform interpretation' duty laid down in Article 65 of the Law on the Judiciary: indeed, ensuring the harmonisation of thousands of judgments per year, not to mention the huge number of decisions issued in previous years, clearly is an impossible task. Additionally, such 'confusion' has significant effects on the inferior courts, which are likely to remain somewhat disoriented in the face of the 'changing principles' of the Supreme Court, thus enhancing the risk of conflicting decisions on the merits.

Of course, over time, many initiatives have been taken in reaction to this unsustainable situation. On this subject, before considering the latest legislative reforms, it is important to recall an internal mechanism developed by the judges of

[12]It should be noted that a reform of first appeal judgments (Law No. 134 of 7 August 2012) has provided for a sort of filter so that the court of appeal can issue an order declaring the petition inadmissible anytime the appeal prima facie does not show a reasonable chance of being granted on the merits (Article 348 *bis* CCP). In such cases, the first instance judgment can be challenged at the Supreme Court.

[13]See Taruffo (1988), p. 238; in the same terms see Denti (1987), pp. 26f.; Verde (2008), p. 19; Ricci (2009a), p. 578.

the court themselves which—through an extensive use of the chamber proceedings and their simplified character—has produced several positive effects on the management of appeals. The reference here is to the so-called 'Unified Structure,' established in 2005 by First President of the Supreme Court Nicola Marvulli (in cooperation with Vincenzo Carbone, President-in-Office) for the preliminary examination of all petitions with a view to identifying those which should be declared inadmissible or immediately adjudicated on the merits in light of a 'manifest' solution.

Briefly, the decree stated that each chamber would provide the Unified Structure with a number of judges sufficient to form a judicial panel (i.e. a president and four justices) and that to this same body 20 magistrates belonging to the 'Massimario' Office[14] would also be assigned. Once a petition was filed, the action should be sent to the Unified Structure which would ascertain, through a summary examination, whether or not it was possible to define the appeal in the simplified forms of the chamber proceedings provided by Article 375 CCP (i.e. in the case of a petition being inadmissible or where a 'manifest' solution could be found). Finally, all other appeals—which could not be defined by way of the chamber proceedings—should be transmitted to the competent chamber and provided with a specific classification (in terms of identification of the legal questions raised) prepared by the 'Massimario' Office, which could simplify the work of the chamber.

This procedure created by the court and its internal organisation produced some encouraging results if we consider that in 2008, for the first time, the difference between the number of appeals decided and the number of petitions filed was reversed, thus bringing the balance back into a reasonable working condition.[15]

[14]The institutional task of the 'Massimario' Office consists in the systematic analysis of the case law in order to create the conditions for useful and shared information, internal and external, which in turn appears to be fundamental for the best exercise of the 'public' function of the Court. In particular, the Office is involved in:

- Reading, selecting and extracting brief 'legal principles' (*massime*) from civil and criminal judgments;
- Drafting, in addition to the above priority activity, of concise 'decision-making news' limited to the most important decisions, to be published on a specific website;
- Reporting of conflicts, their resolution and the interpretative guidelines of the case law, as well as the most important legal reforms;
- Drawing up reports on appeals assigned to the Joint Chamber for the purpose of resolving conflicts or presenting major issues of particular importance;
- Drafting information sheets and reports at the request of the President, for appeals concerning matters of particular relevance assigned to the ordinary chambers;
- Periodic reports on decisions concerning the main guidelines provided by the Supreme Court.

[15]See the statistics provided by the 2008 Report on the State of the Administration of Justice 2018.

4 ... and External Interventions: The 2009 and 2016 Legislative Reforms

With Law No. 69 of 18 June 2009, the Italian legislator appears to have accepted the idea (usually thought of as belonging to common law systems) that any reforms to the Supreme Court procedures must necessarily aim at reducing the number of petitions filed with the court, so as to prevent judges from devoting time and resources to ruling on matters which have nothing to do with the duties of the court. The point, therefore, was that Italy too should begin to consider—without fear or prejudice—some sort of 'filter' mechanism for appeals in cassation.

In point of fact, we must be very clear when talking about the 'Italian style' of case selection, in the sense that the 2009 reform does not provide the Supreme Court with any discretion in selecting cases to be decided on the merits (which is instead the essence of the common law filters). The new provisions simply establish a sort of 'fast track' for all those appeals that exhibit characteristics that justify a faster disposition of the case. More in detail, according to the new set of rules (Articles 360 *bis*, 375, 376, 380 *bis* CCP and Article 65 *bis* of the Law on the Judiciary), all petitions filed with the court are subject to a preliminary screening whose purpose is to uncover cases where the appeal is inadmissible and thus justifies a simplified decision, thereby saving the time and energy involved in the 'ordinary' management of cases and allowing the judges to reallocate their limited resources to the most important issues.[16]

Apparently, the category of 'inadmissibility' is the 'core business' of the legal reform which identifies further reasons, not already present in existing law, in the new Article 360 *bis* CCP that justify a 'fast track': these reasons, however, are not connected to any 'defects of the pleadings... which are the consequence of the non-existence or of the misuse of the right of appeal'[17] and which prevent the same discussion of the petition, but rather to the merits of the case. In particular, according to Article 360 *bis* (1) CCP, the petition is inadmissible when 'the challenged decision has ruled on the issue following well-established case law of the court and the examination of the grounds for appeal does not provide elements which can confirm or reverse such precedents.' Such a category of 'inadmissibility' is perhaps the most prominent element of the 2009 reform: it emphasises the 'public' function of the Supreme Court, especially with regard to the 'uniform interpretation' of the law, and this function (*rectius*, its result) is taken as a parameter with which to assess the merits of the appeal. Accordingly, where the appealed judgment has correctly applied the principles drawn up by the court, the plaintiff—unless he can prove they should be somehow overruled—must accept the outcome reached by the

[16]Actually, the preliminary examination is not limited to the identification of the different cases of 'inadmissibility': in fact, pursuant to Article 380 *bis* (1), which in turn recalls Article 375(5) CCP, the Court (*rectius*, the special chamber responsible for the screening) can also decide the case on the merits whenever the appeal is manifestly founded or unfounded.

[17]See Luiso (2017), p. 350.

lower court judge. Thus the appeal would be considered to be 'useless' and, therefore, disposed of by the court through an inadmissibility statement.

A second parameter of inadmissibility provided by Article 360 *bis* (2) CCP imposes inadmissibility of the appeal whenever 'the alleged violation of the principles of due process is clearly unfounded.' This provision was immediately criticised for its succinct boundaries by scholars who questioned its *ratio* and capacity to relieve the overloaded docket of the court.[18] Leaving to the next section several considerations on the effectiveness of this parameter, here we should point out that it does not appear to provide the court with any specific powers: in fact, the same result (i.e. the dismissal of the case) could have been achieved by way of a statement of 'manifest' unfoundedness pursuant to Article 375(5) CCP.[19]

With regard to the procedure that has to be followed, the screening of all petitions filed with the court[20] is carried out by a specialised body—the Sixth Chamber, commonly referred to as the 'Inadmissibility Chamber' or 'Filter Chamber,' which replaced the former Unified Structure—composed of judges belonging to the ordinary chambers, as provided by the new Article 67 *bis* of the Law on the Judiciary, who are called upon to serve temporarily on the basis of turnaround criteria. Law No. 197 of 25 October 2016, which recently amended the 2009 reform and addressed its technical difficulties, provides for two different stages. The first (necessary) stage is conducted by the Filter Chamber, which is responsible for a summary screening in which it tries to uncover cases of inadmissibility of appeal or determine the possibility of immediately defining a petition 'manifestly' unfounded (or founded) on the merits. The second stage could eventually take place before the other chambers of the court (of course, provided that the appeal is not disposed of by the Special Chamber). More in detail, if the outcome of the first examination points to elements which suggest that the petition should be decided on by the Filter Chamber, the appeal is then briefly discussed (following the applicable rules of the chamber) and, if the tentative opinion is confirmed, the chamber issues an order, thus closing the judgment. Vice versa, in the event that—after the discussion of the petition—there is no evidence of the elements which may justify an early decision on the appeal, the petition is reassigned to the competent chamber of the court for subsequent discussion and decision on the merits.

Moreover, the same 2016 reform—in its attempt to speed up Supreme Court proceedings—substantially overturned the usual relationship between the chamber proceedings (in particular cases) and the public hearing (as a rule), meaning that today each chamber deals with and decides cases by way of an order issued within

[18] See Balena (2009), pp. 755f.; Bove and Santi (2009), p. 67; Consolo (2009), p. 740; De Cristofaro (2013), p. 262; Fornaciari (2013), §4; Raiti (2010), p. 435.

[19] See Silvestri (2010), p. 421.

[20] Except those petitions the First President of the Supreme Court says have to be decided by the Joint Chamber in light of the particular importance of the legal issues involved.

the chamber proceedings,[21] unless weighty reasons that justify a public examination of the appeal in light of the 'particular relevance of the question of law the court has to rule on' exist (Article 376 CCP).

In this way, the Italian legislator has established a 'double track' in managing final appeals, depending on their 'public' or 'private' relevance. Where the scope of review is limited to the confirmation or reversal of the decision below, a simplified judicial order (which provides for a simpler explanation of the grounds, including references to the case law of the Supreme Court) is considered more than sufficient for the purpose. On the other hand, where broader issues are at stake, each chamber may opt for a discussion of the appeal in a public hearing and a ruling by way of a judgment.

5 Effectiveness of the Solution

In spite of the attempts by the Supreme Court to maximise the effects of the new reforms through the exercise of its managerial duties,[22] the situation described by the First President in his report on the state of the administration of justice in 2020 shows that much remains to be done. It is true that some improvements have been achieved, since at the end of 2017 the number of pending cases was substantially the same as in the previous year, with an increasing rate in the total number of cases disposed of by the court.[23] In spite of that, the number of petitions filed with the court rose to 117,033 in 2019, which amounts to an increase in the total number of pending cases.[24]

There are two explanations for this disappointing result. The first has to do with the objective difficulties in applying the new rules; the second is the specific (social) context in which the new rules are applied. As to the first, the way the new parameters of inadmissibility are structured is unclear, sometimes contradictory and ultimately unable to provide for a real reduction of the caseload. Thus, for example, as for the requirement laid down in Article 360 *bis* (1) CCP, it is difficult to

---

[21] See Briguglio (2017), pp. 301ff.; Carratta (2017); Costantino (2017), pp. 7ff.; Panzarola (2017), pp. 269ff.; Punzi (2017), pp. 1ff.; Sassani (2017), pp. 35ff.

[22] Emblematic, e.g., is the composition of the Sixth Chamber: despite the fact that the provision which created the new chamber (Article 65 *bis* Law on the Judiciary) stated that it should be composed of magistrates belonging to the other chambers only, the Court has tended to repeat the positive experience provided by the Unified Structure by way of a progressive specification of the activities required by law. Thus, in accordance with the number of ordinary chambers, five different sub-chambers have been created within the special division, each coordinated by a presiding judge, whose duty is to screen the petitions that would, *ratione materiae*, be assigned to one of the chambers of the Court (of course, in the event that they pass the preliminary examination).

[23] See *2019 Report*, p. 46.

[24] See *2019 Report*, pp. 46–47, which underlines, *inter alia*, the increasing number of cases related to human rights protection.

identify precisely when it is right to assess the existence of a 'consolidated case law'; and at risk is the very consistency of the rule, for it allows the petition to pass the screening simply in the event that the appeal is capable of 'confirming' the challenged case law.

Much greater problems are raised by the second parameter provided by Article 360 *bis* (2). In fact, if the criterion mentioned earlier were applied to all the procedural rules that contribute, as a whole, to promoting the due process of law, that would turn the provision into something useless because merely switching the outcome from an unfounded decision (which is what would have happened before the legal reforms) to a sub-type of an inadmissible one would not add anything to the existing powers of the court or, above all, to the underlying need for the reform.[25] On the other hand, a restrictive perspective,[26] which takes into account only the procedural complaints that could directly affect constitutionally protected values, would be forbidden by Article 111(7) of the Constitution and its guarantee of appeal on the basis of a 'breach of law,' which must be referenced not only to substantive law but even to procedural provisions.[27]

As far as the procedure is concerned, even though it has recently been reformed, the most critical point appears to be the workload of the new chamber, called upon to examine all the petitions, deal with all the cases of inadmissibility and decide on the merits those appeals whose solution is manifest: needless to say, the huge number of cases on the docket that the court has to deal with should have suggested a more structured solution.

6 'Tips' from the Outside

In establishing the new rules governing the Supreme Court proceedings the Italian legislator has apparently followed the French experience—probably the only one in Europe which seems to better preserve the principles set by the Constitution[28]—where access to the *Cour de cassation* is somehow 'governed' by the creation of special panels of judges (*formations restreintes*) within each chamber of the court (composed of three magistrates, including the President of the Chamber and the

[25] See Ricci (2009b), p. 135; Bove and Santi (2009), p. 67; De Cristofaro (2013), p. 262; Fornaciari (2013), §11; Raiti (2010), p. 435.

[26] See Salmè (2009), p. 441; Rordorf (2010), pp. 142f.

[27] See Graziosi (2010), pp. 56ff.; De Cristofaro (2013), p. 260; Poli (2010), p. 374; Raiti (2010), p. 434; Silvestri (2010), p. 421.

[28] Indeed, apart from the English system based on permission to appeal, other major European systems (e.g. those of Spain and Germany) provide for a system based on the predetermination of a specific *summa gravaminis* required to challenge a decision or on the satisfaction of certain parameters which, although predetermined, require the exercise of some discretional power by the court; all such elements appear to be incompatible with the 'universal' access granted by the Italian Constitution.

judge appointed as rapporteur) (Article 1012 Civil Procedural Code (CPC)) which are required to summarily examine each petition filed with the court. If the reporting judge positively evaluates the possibility of reaching a decision of 'non-admission' (Article 1013 CPC), he drafts his own report, where the relevant reasons are explained, followed by a special meeting of the panel, and a subsequent decision. On the other hand, if the rapporteur is convinced that there are no statutory requirements (Article 1014 CPC) for such a declaration, the appeal is then assigned to the same chamber in its ordinary composition for a subsequent hearing on the merits.

As to the grounds which can convince the *formation* to declare the case inadmissible, Article 1014 CPC provides for two different elements which must be taken into account. The first, *irrecevabilité*, refers to those defects strictly connected to the essential aspects of the right to appeal and which must be disposed of—similar to the inadmissible or unfounded cases provided for in the Italian Code of Civil Procedure—by way of a decision certifying the impossibility of proceeding further in the examination of the petition.[29] The second—the appeal does not appear prima facie *fondé sur un moyen sérieux de cassation*—seems to be a rule that can be given many different meanings. However, as noted by scholars, it appears that the 'non-admission' decision is usually issued in the case of a petition that is clearly unfounded, but also in all circumstances that do not reveal any super-individual matter that can justify the performance of a 'public' function by the court.[30]

The French system thus focuses on a 'fast track' to dispose of appeals which, because of the lack of legal requirements or because of the questions submitted, cannot be further discussed on the merits. This is, in essence, the same principle adopted by the Italian legislator in setting up the new approach to access to the Supreme Court, but with some significant differences. Indeed, even if the procedure followed by the *formations restreintes* recalls the activity of the Sixth Chamber, the fact is that in the French approach *more* than one body (one for each chamber) carries out the preliminary screening. As noted earlier, in the Italian approach, the creation of a *single* chamber with the task of uncovering those appeals which appear clearly unfounded and, at the same time, detecting the various cases of inadmissibility of the petition produces an unavoidable overload and a consequent delay in case management, which in turn impacts on the activity of the other chambers of the Supreme Court. Moreover, sharing the screening power within the whole Court is something very important in light of a correct and uniform interpretation of the parameters of Italian legislation that grant access to the court.

As far as the reasons that justify dismissal of the case are concerned—and in particular the reason related to 'serious grounds for cassation'—if they facilitate the role the court intends to play, they will have too much effect on the parties' rights, even recognising that usually the decisions of 'non-admission' are not provided with any grounds. It is therefore preferable to have a model which tries to define, ex ante,

[29]See Amrani Mekki and Cadiet (2005), pp. 105ff.

[30]Canivet (2002), pp. 2195ff.; Vigneau (2010), pp. 107ff.

the *moyen sérieux* that every appeal must present in order to justify a final examination on the merits.

7 Conclusion

Understanding that the ‘filter’ at the doors of the Italian Supreme Court is nothing more than a procedure which *intends* to rationalise the management of appeals, separating those with defects (or characteristics) that justify the disposition of the case in a simplified manner from those deserving a more thorough examination, leaves one with the feeling that the recent legal reforms are contradictory in nature. As often happens in Italy, the impression is that successful identification of the problems and malfunctions of institutional bodies is followed by unsuccessful choices and actions which do not resolve the issue at stake, and perversely end up making matters worse.

It is time to face reality. If we really want the Supreme Court to come out of its state of crisis, we should start thinking about changing our conception of the final instance appeal as an unassailable guarantee, if necessary by way of interventions relating to Article 111 of the Constitution. In our view, the best tool for detecting and correcting defects in the decisions rendered in the courts remains the first appeal and the related possibility to challenge all aspects of the case, both of fact and of law, within the judgment. It is difficult to understand why a further appeal, whose grounds are exclusively provided by the legislator and limited to questions of law—and most of all characterised by numerous ‘procedural intricacies’—can better protect citizens who complain about a violation of their rights.[31] In this regard, it is therefore important for Italian lawyers to stop thinking of the first instance judgment as merely a sort of ‘general test’ before the appellate phase and, at the same time, to re-evaluate the first appeal and recognise the beneficial possibilities it holds for the parties.

[31] Accordingly, we express some doubts about the reform mentioned here of the first appeal, which has introduced even there a sort of ‘filter’ which allows the court of appeal to dispose of all those petitions which do not present prima facie ‘a reasonable likelihood of being adjudged on the merits’ (Article 348 *bis* CCP). The need for reducing caseload cannot really be the only engine of procedural reforms, for it is necessary, once again, to intervene having a clear idea of the role of the Supreme Court and, more generally, of the role the appellate system is required to perform; only in this way will it be possible to establish an organic design that ultimately ensures that efficiency and legitimacy which the legislator has recently lost sight of.

References

Amrani Mekki S, Cadiet L (eds) (2005) La sélection des pourvois à la Cour de cassation. Economica, Paris

Balena G (2009) La nuova pseudo-riforma della giustizia civile (un primo commento della legge 18 giugno 2009, n. 69). Giusto processo civ:749–826

Bove M, Santi A (2009) Il nuovo processo civile tra modifiche attuate e riforme in atto. Milano, Hoepli

Briguglio A (2017) Le nuove regole sul giudizio civile di cassazione: Per i singoli casi normali e per i casi a valenza nomofilattica. La scelta 'fior da fiore' di una Suprema Corte ristretta nei limiti dell'art. 111. Giust civ 2:301 340

Calamandrei P (1920) La Cassazione civile. Bocca, Milano

Calamandrei P, Furno C (1958) Cassazione civile. Nuovo digesto italiano 2:1056–1075

Canivet G (2002) La procédure d'admission des pourvois en cassation. Recueil Dalloz 28:2195–2201

Carratta A (2017) Le più recenti riforme del processo civile. Giappichelli, Torino

Chiarloni S (2002) Ruolo della giurisprudenza e attività creative di nuovo diritto. Riv dir proc 56 (1):1–16

Consolo C (1990) Un codice di procedura civile 'seminuovo'. Giur it 11(1):429–449

Consolo C (2007) Sul 'processo di cassazione in funzione di una decisione tendenzialmente sostitutiva pur se nomofilattica'. Riv trim dir proc civ 1:297–316

Consolo C (2009) Una buona 'novella' al c.p.c.: La riforma del 2009 (con i suoi artt. 360 bis e 614 bis) va ben al di là della sola dimensione processuale. Corriere giur 6:737–743

Costantino G (2017) Note sulle 'misure urgenti per la definizione del contenzioso presso la Corte di cassazione'. Foro it 5(1):7–17

De Cristofaro M (2013) Sub art. 360 bis. In: Consolo C (ed) Codice di procedura civile commentato. IPSOA, Milano

Denti V (1987) Sub art. 111. In: Branca G (ed) Commentario della Costituzione. Zanichelli, Bologna

Denti V (2004) La giustizia civile: Lezioni introduttive. Il Mulino, Bologna

Fazzalari E (1960) Il giudizio civile di cassazione. Giuffrè, Milano

Fornaciari M (2013) L'inammissibilità del ricorso per cassazione ex art. 360 bis c.p.c. Riv trim dir proc civ 67(2):645–675

Graziosi A (2010) Riflessioni in ordine sparso sulla riforma del giudizio di cassazione. Riv trim dir proc civ 64(2):37–65

Luiso FP (2017) Diritto processuale civile, II - Il processo di cognizione. Giuffrè, Milano

Mazzarella A (2003) Analisi del giudizio civile di cassazione. Cedam, Padova

Moneta G (1992) La cassazione civile e i suoi contrasti di giurisprudenza del 1990. Contr e impresa 92:1245–1260

Moneta G (1993) Mutamenti nella giurisprudenza della Cassazione civile. Ottocento-sessantasette casi di contrasto nel quinquennio 1988–1992. Cedam, Padova

Moneta G (1995) Conflitti giurisprudenziali in Cassazione. I contrasti della Cassazione civile dal settembre 1993 al dicembre 1994. Cedam, Padova

Panzarola A (2005) La Cassazione civile giudice del merito. Giappichelli, Torino

Panzarola A (2017) La Cassazione civile dopo la l. 25 ottobre 2016, n. 197 e i c.d. Protocolli. Nuove leggi civ comm 2:269–368

Poli R (2010) Il c.d. filtro di ammissibilità del ricorso per cassazione. Riv dir proc:363–384

Proto Pisani A (2002) Lezioni di diritto processuale civile. Jovene, Napoli

Punzi C (2017) La nuova stagione della Corte di Cassazione e il tramonto della pubblica udienza. Riv dir proc 72(1):1–12

Raiti G (2010) Note esegetiche a prima lettura sul 'filtro' in Cassazione secondo la legge di riforma al codice di rito civile, n. 69 del 18 giugno 2009. In: Alpa G (ed) Le modifiche al codice di procedura civile. Esi, Napoli, pp 419–430

Report on the State of the Administration of Justice 2008. http://www.cortedicassazione.it/cassazione-resources/resources/cms/documents/RelazionePPresCarbone2007.pdf. Accessed 25 May 2019

Report on the State of the Administration of Justice 2019 by the First President of the Court of Cassation. http://www.cortedicassazione.it/cassazione-resources/resources/cms/documents/Relazione_Primo_Presidente_Cassazione_Cassazione_2020.pdf. Accessed 29 May 2020

Ricci GF (2009a) La Suprema corte tra funzione nomofilattica e tutela dello jus litigatoris. Il problema alla luce del controllo di motivazione. Riv trim dir proc civ 1(2):571–601

Ricci GF (2009b) Il Ricorso per cassazione – La riforma del giudizio di cassazione tra funzione nomofilattica e tutela dei diritto di difesa. Prev Forense 2:131–145

Rordorf R (2010) Nuove norme in tema di motivazione delle sentenze e di ricorso per cassazione. Riv dir proc 65(1):134–145

Salmè G (2009) Il nuovo giudizio di cassazione. Foro it 132(11):437–444

Sassani B (2017) Giudizio sommario di cassazione e illusione nomofilattica. Riv dir proc 72(1):35–40

Silvestri E (2001) Corti supreme europee: Accesso, Filtri, Selezione. In: Le Corti supreme. Atti del convegno svoltosi a Perugia il 5–6 maggio 2000. Giuffrè, Milano, pp 105–116

Silvestri E (2010) Le novità in tema di giudizio di cassazione. In: Taruffo M (ed) Il processo civile riformato. Zanichelli, Bologna, pp 409–430

Taruffo M (1988) La Corte di Cassazione tra legittimità e merito. Foro it 111(5):237–244

Taruffo M (1990) La Corte di Cassazione e la legge. Riv trim dir proc civ 40(2):349–385

Taruffo M (1991) Il vertice ambiguo. Saggi sulla Cassazione civile. Il Mulino, Bologna

Verde G (2008) In difesa dello jus litigatoris (sulla Cassazione come è e come si vorrebbe che fosse). Riv dir proc 63(1):1–20

Vigneau V (2010) Le régime de la non-admission des pourvois devant la Cour de cassation. Recueil Dalloz 2:102–120

Back in Focus: Case Overload and Case Selection Standards in the Spanish Supreme Court

Marco de Benito

Abstract This contribution describes the evolution of the Spanish Supreme Court and cassation appeal with a focus on the techniques used to control the court's caseload. The Supreme Court was created in 1812 and remained the highest court from 1836 to 1978, when the Constitutional Court, which individuals and companies can access directly for further protection of their rights, was established. Similarly, Spanish cassation appeal was conceived in 1812; it saw the light of day, as a full-fledged French-type cassation appeal, in 1838; and it found its own particular form, restricting the *renvoi* to procedural errors, in 1855. In 2000 and 2011, in view of the court's backlog, cassation was reformed to adopt a German-inspired 'cassational interest' standard as an access filter, together with a high monetary threshold. Albeit non-discretional and quite narrowly defined, the introduction of this standard helped put the court's caseload under control. Also important was the reinforcement of the Technical Cabinet, a body of qualified jurists that assists the Supreme Court in granting or denying leave to appeal. In 2007, a 'special constitutional transcendence' standard, to be discretionally appreciated, was adopted as an exclusive filter to access the overburdened Constitutional Court. This has inspired proposals to turn the 'cassational interest' standard into a similarly open-ended, discretional filter of access to the Supreme Court.

1 Overview of the History of the Supreme Court

1.1 The Constitution of Cádiz (1812)

The establishment of the Supreme Court in Spain went hand in hand with the advent of the liberal state.

M. de Benito (✉)
Jean Monnet Chair of European Civil Procedure, IE University, Madrid, Spain
e-mail: marco.debenito@ie.edu

P. Bravo-Hurtado, C. H. van Rhee (eds.), *Supreme Courts Under Pressure*, Ius Gentium: Comparative Perspectives on Law and Justice 83,
https://doi.org/10.1007/978-3-030-63731-6_4

The Bourbon dynasty, installed in Spain in 1707, had inherited from the Habsburg monarchy a 'polysynodial' system of government based upon a series of royal councils coexisting at the highest echelons of the political and legal system. These councils represented the supreme governmental, administrative and judicial authority in their respective areas.[1]

This centuries-old system collapsed in the wake of the Napoleonic invasion in 1808. New institutions had to be improvised in the form of the genuinely popular *Juntas*, soon coordinated by a national *Junta Suprema Central*. One of the main tasks of the *Junta Central*, apart from coordinating the conduct of war, was to spearhead far-reaching political reform.[2]

In 1810, the *Junta Central* convened a universal meeting of the *Cortes*, the long inactive national representative body. Representatives elected throughout the monarchy, including all overseas territories, met in 1811 at the only site which had evaded French control: an island within the territory of the vibrant, liberal city of Cádiz.

With its constituting powers having been established, discussions regarding a constitution were immediately undertaken.[3] The creation of a Supreme Court was proposed and accepted. In 1812, the Constitution was proclaimed. Among the functions of the Supreme Court, according to the Constitution, was 'to hear nullity appeals [*recursos de nulidad*] filed against the judgments given in final instance, for the precise effect of correcting the process and sending it back to the lower court.' It would, however, take a few years for this nullity appeal to take on its definitive configuration.

The creation of the Supreme Court was one of a series of important elements in a plan to liquidate the judicial system of absolutism and construct an entirely new order based upon an independent judiciary made up of irremovable and responsible judges; the separation of governmental, legislative and judicial functions; and the principle that everyone was to be judged by a court previously constituted according to law.[4]

1.2 The Establishment of Cassation Appeal (1838)

Such a Supreme Court was incompatible with the old royal councils. As a consequence, in the two decades that followed its creation, the liberal Supreme Court and

[1]See generally, on the organisation of justice in absolutist Spain, Escudero (2012), pp. 777ff. See also Sáinz (1992), pp. 70ff.; Garriga (2006).

[2]See generally Tomás y Valiente (1983), pp. 437ff.; specifically on the *Junta Central* see Artola (2000), pp. 205ff.

[3]See Moreno (1989), pp. 28ff. A selection of the most important parliamentary speeches, particularly in connection with the nullity appeal, can be found in Fairén (1969b).

[4]See Moreno (1989), pp. 50ff.; Escudero (2012), pp. 943ff.

the main absolutist councils were alternately dissolved and reinstated—inheriting each other's caseload.[5] The year 1834 marked the definitive transition to the liberal state. The Supreme Court was definitively established in 1836.[6]

In 1838, a procedural decree regulated the *recurso de nulidad* announced in the 1812 Constitution, which had not yet been effectively applied. It was this decree of 1838 that established a full-fledged cassation in Spain.[7] The first nullity judgment was given and published in 1839.

The decree made nullity appeals available for both infringements of substantive law (including case law) and a limited number of procedural vices. Virtually all judgments rendered in the second instance of plenary declaratory proceedings were open to appeal; only petty claims were excluded. Once the party posted the required deposit or bond, the appeal had to be admitted on a preliminary basis, without room for judicial discretion. A panel of seven judges then decided on the nullity appeal. For the first time[8] they were bound to state the reasons for their judgments, which would be published in the official gazette.

If the alleged grounds for nullity were found to exist, the original French system of *renvoi* was followed: the judgment was quashed and the file returned to the lower court. In cases involving misapplication of substantive law, the lower court would decide again on the merits through a larger panel of seven new judges. In cases involving nullity on procedural grounds, new lower court judges would resume the case. In no case would it be possible to file a second nullity appeal.

The minutes of the legislative debates leading to the 1838 decree reflect a remarkable knowledge of legal history and comparative law. Its proponents proved to be fully aware of the aims and nature of the technique of cassation.[9] One of the priorities of the 1838 reformers was the basic liberal tenet of ensuring an application of the law that was uniform[10] and, therefore, equal for all. Equally highlighted was the public interest in allowing the formation of an authoritative body of repeated, consistent decisions (*doctrina legal* or simply *jurisprudencia*) in order to supplement and clarify the laws, thus providing further legal certainty (the codification process was by then still incipient).[11] In the words of a distinguished jurist two decades later:

[5]See Moreno (1989), pp. 58ff., 88ff.

[6]See ibid., pp. 167ff., 232ff.

[7]See ibid., pp. 258ff.

[8]In Castile it was traditionally forbidden to give reasons; the prohibition was extended to all Spanish territories in 1778. See Sáinz (1992), pp. 132ff.

[9]See Moreno (1989), pp. 261ff., quoting the parliamentary speeches of Bravo Murillo and Pacheco in the congressional records of 24–28 January 1937.

[10]Article 244 of the Cádiz Constitution already established the principle of procedural uniformity by declaring that 'the laws will set out the order and formalities of the procedure, which shall be uniform in all courts, and neither the Parliament nor the King can dispense with them' ('*Las leyes señalarán el orden y las formalidades del proceso, que serán uniformes en todos los tribunales, y ni las Cortes ni el Rey podrán dispensarlas*').

[11]See Moreno (1989), pp. 261ff.

> Are there today as many doubts on positive law as before this period [starting in 1834]? No, because case law is increasingly equal in the different parts of the Monarchy; because the unity of case law, by completing the unity of [positive] law, ends up bringing about the unity of the law [legal system].[12]

1.3 The Definitive Shape of Spanish Cassation (1855–1881)

In the codification process that followed,[13] the most important milestone was the 1855 Civil Procedure Law.[14] This code introduced two changes that determined the shape of Spanish cassation until today.[15] On the one hand, the French model was adopted (*recurso de casación*). On the other hand, the original French system of *renvoi* was partially abandoned: in cases involving misapplication of substantive law, the Supreme Court would not only quash the *bad* judgment, but also issue the *good* one—originally in a separate judgment, later in the same document—without remitting the case to the lower court.

For that purpose, there would be two court chambers (*Salas*): the first for substantive law issues (without *renvoi*) and the second for procedural infringements (with *renvoi*). The change was motivated by pragmatic[16] reasons: since the Supreme Court was fully integrated into the ordinary judicial structure, remitting the case back to the lower court was perceived as pointless and cumbersome.[17] The change was likewise more in line with the century-old Spanish tradition of last resort appeals.[18] The Spanish cassation appeal would never abandon this hybrid, pragmatical approach.

The application of the 1855 regime gave rise, in the eyes of contemporary observers, to an exponential growth in the number of appeals, an 'agglomeration of colossal proportions.'[19] In the 18 years from 1838 to 1856, the Supreme Court had ruled on 172 *recursos de nulidad*, plus 139 ordinary appeals for denial of leave to appeal by the lower court. In contrast, in the 1857 to 1859 triennium 454 *recursos de casación* and 77 appeals for denial of leave were filed. Different solutions were

---

[12] '*Existen hoy tantas dudas sobre derecho constituido como antes de este período? No, porque la jurisprudencia va siendo igual en las diferentes partes de la monarquía; porque la unidad de la jurisprudencia, completando la unidad de la ley, concluye por producir la unidad del derecho*' (Pedro Gómez de la Serna at the Royal Academy of Jurisprudence and Legislation, 1855, in Lorente et al. 2012, p. 207).

[13] See generally Tomás y Valiente (1983), pp. 524ff.; Lorente (2007).

[14] See generally Lasso (1998), pp. 57ff.; Fairén (1969a).

[15] On the key changes of the 1855 regime in a historical perspective see Lasso (1971), pp. 140–146.

[16] A comparative consideration of the more pragmatic Spanish cassation vis-à-vis the more dogmatic French and—to a lesser extent—Italian ones can be found in Vázquez (1979, 2010).

[17] Banacloche and Cubillo (2012), p. 359.

[18] See De la Plaza (1944).

[19] '*Una aglomeración de colosales proporciones*' (Lasso 1971, p. 140). The author explains the key changes of the 1855 regime in a historical perspective on pp. 140–146.

proposed to avoid backlog: the reinstatement of *renvoi* to the lower court; the establishment of a *summa gravaminis* or monetary threshold; the setting up of a chamber to rule on preliminary admission—either with discretionary powers or subject to rules; or the splitting of the civil division of the Supreme Court into two chambers. The latter was finally enacted in 1864, but in 1870 the division was re-unified as a 'guarantee of the unity of case law.' In turn, the same 1870 reform eliminated the grounds based on the denegation of a means of evidence—since it did not affect the prevailing public interest—and abolished the appeal for denial of leave to appeal by the lower court.[20]

The year 1870 also saw the enactment of the Organic Law on the Judiciary (*Ley provisional sobre organización del Poder Judicial*),[21] which organised Spanish justice for more than a century, surviving several political regimes of opposite ideologies virtually intact. The Supreme Court was to be composed of 33 judges, including those making up the criminal and administrative divisions.[22]

The 1878 Civil Cassation Law established a chamber (*Sala de admisión*) solely devoted to the preliminary admission of cassation appeals, modelled after the French *Chambre des requêtes*. It would not take root, however, and would be eliminated in 1893.[23]

In 1881, a new Civil Procedure Law amended some procedural aspects, but left the basic tenets of the 1855 regime unchanged.[24] Following the same pragmatic approach, it redistributed the grounds for cassation in two lists depending on whether or not the consequence of a successful cassation appeal would be remanding of the case to the lower court or not. Thus, a first article set forth the grounds for cassation for 'infringement of the law or case law' (*infracción de ley o de doctrina legal*), which included errors *in iudicando* and those *in procedendo* that affected only the decision and, therefore, could be corrected by the Supreme Court itself without remanding the case to the court *a quo*. The following article listed the grounds for the so-called cassation for a 'breach of form' (*quebrantamiento de forma*), which entailed the *nullity* of the procedure and, therefore, could not be corrected by the Supreme Court, thus necessitating quashing of the judgment and *renvoi* to the lower court.

The 1881 law[25] brought stability to civil cassation. Strictly speaking, no amendments were made to the regime of civil cassation until 1984, apart from an indirect, relatively minor increase in the threshold to access cassation in 1966.

As regards the organisation of the Supreme Court, the 1870 Organic Law on the Judiciary achieved similar permanence and was only affected by the changes

---

[20]Lasso (1998), pp. 98ff., 104ff.

[21]See generally Escudero (2012), pp. 949ff.

[22]Lasso (1998), pp. 104ff.

[23]Lasso (1998), pp. 106ff. See also generally on the 1878 law Lasso (1971), pp. 150–160.

[24]For a summary of the main tenets of Spanish cassation see Lasso (1971), pp. 168–175.

[25]See generally, on the background and elaboration of this law, Lasso (1998), pp. 129ff., as well as Lasso (1971), pp. 160–167.

brought about by the 1978 Constitution, and then superseded by a new Organic Law on the Judiciary in 1985, and by two minor adjustments which took place in 1938 when the Supreme Court was reorganised into four divisions—civil, criminal, administrative and labour—and in 1945 when a division was added for military cases. The five divisions still exist today.

1.4 The Passing of the Crown (1978)

Only the 1978 Constitution, currently in force, altered the system of last resort appeals through the introduction of the Constitutional Court and the individual constitutional protection appeal (*recurso de amparo*, literally 'shelter' appeal).[26] The 1978 Constitutional Court and *amparo* follow closely the model of the German *Bundesverfassungsgericht* (1949) and *Verfassungsbeschwerde* (1951).

So far, the very *raison d'être* of the Supreme Court was precisely to be *supreme*. It is not surprising that the passing of the crown to the Constitutional Court plunged the Supreme Court into a profound identity crisis.[27] Indeed, the introduction of the Constitutional Court and the individual constitutional protection appeal weakened the unifying force of the cassation appeal. Since fundamental rights permeate private law and civil litigation,[28] cassational doctrine no longer suffices to provide a complete, accurate picture of the interpretation of the law on a given subject; the case law of the Constitutional Court needs to be taken into consideration as well.[29] In a way, *amparo* operates like a cassation's cassation, which means four instances: two ordinary and two extraordinary instances.[30]

1.5 A Monetary Threshold (1984–1992)

Besides the Constitutional Court, strictly speaking, no amendments were made to the regime of civil cassation until 1984 and 1992. By the early 1980s, the increase in the Supreme Court's caseload had become a serious problem. Reforms in 1984 and 1992 aimed at controlling it.[31]

---

[26]Both had been adopted, but hardly tested in practice, during the Second Republic (1931–1936); see Oliver (2010).

[27]See Ortells (2007) and Ramos (2007). On the tension that the new situation created between the two courts see De la Oliva and Díez-Picazo (1996).

[28]Constitutional rights can be violated in civil litigation in a wide variety of ways; for a detailed account see Montero and Flors (2008), esp. at pp. 49ff.

[29]See generally Catalina (2010); more specifically on the relationship between the two courts in this regard see Pizzorusso (2004), pp. 34ff.; Xiol (2004), esp. at pp. 86ff.

[30]See Pizzorusso (2004), pp. 38ff.

[31]De la Oliva et al. (2001), p. 297.

The 1984 reform introduced a *summa gravaminis* or monetary threshold to access cassation, regardless of the type of proceedings. Until then there was an implicit threshold of €3000; the new, explicit threshold was set at the equivalent of €18,000.[32]

As the reform failed to produce any noticeable effect in limiting the Supreme Court's caseload, in 1992 other relatively minor reforms were made with the same aim. Firstly, the threshold was doubled to the equivalent of €36,000. Secondly, the court could deny leave if the appeal was 'manifestly unfounded.' Thirdly, errors in the evaluation of documentary evidence were excluded from cassation appeal. Fourthly, the number of judges hearing a regular appeal was reduced from five to three. Finally, it would now be possible to decide without calling the parties to a hearing.[33]

Perhaps surprisingly, the number of cassation appeals doubled in spite of these measures.[34] By the end of the century, the court accumulated delays of between 5 and 8 years to decide cassation appeals.

1.6 'Cassational Interest' As the Central Standard (2000)

In 2000 (effective 2001), a whole new Civil Procedure Law was enacted. In light of the limited success of the previous measures to alleviate a seriously overburdened Supreme Court, a radical solution was approved: to abolish centralised cassation appeal on procedural grounds and to assign it to the 17 regional high courts, with the rather flimsy safeguard of the appeal 'in the interest of the law,' in the hands of the public prosecutor and other public or semi-public institutions (and outside the hands of the parties), who would have been in charge of taking to the Supreme Court the fragmented lines of case law that the regional high courts would have produced.[35] Only at the last minute, due to political circumstances, was the change left without effect and replaced by a regime that, in spite of its provisional character, has been in force until today.

The provisional regime of cassation in the new Civil Procedure Law[36] featured two types of appeals: 'cassation,' now solely on substantive grounds, and what is called the 'extraordinary appeal for procedural infringement.'

As regards the effects of the appeal judgment, the old, distinctive Spanish system remained in place: quashing the judgment and simultaneously rendering a new one if

---

[32]See generally De la Oliva (1985), pp. 9–19; Gutiérrez de Cabiedes (1985), esp. at pp. 110ff.

[33]See generally Martínez-Calcerrada (1993). On the different selection techniques used in Spain in the last few decades see Ortells (2010).

[34]López (2002), pp. 43ff., 58ff.

[35]For a concise explanation of the originally intended system see Banacloche and Cubillo (2012), pp. 360ff. See also De la Oliva (2010a).

[36]See generally Banacloche and Cubillo (2012), pp. 362ff.

there is a misapplication of substantive law (through 'cassation' appeal *stricto sensu*); quashing and *renvoi* back to the lower court if there is a procedural error (now through the so-dubbed 'extraordinary appeal for procedural infringement').

What was really innovative, however, was the selection of complaints that would be subject to cassation: firstly, all complaints for the protection of fundamental rights; secondly, those with a considerably high *summa gravaminis* (€150,000, from the previous €36,000); and thirdly—and most importantly—any complaint featuring 'cassational interest.'

The standard of 'cassational interest' constituted the most ambitious innovation carried out in 2000.[37] However, the standard never intended to operate fully as a *Generalklausel*—a relatively open, flexible standard of discretional construction.[38] The authors of the law were careful to give the 'cassational interest' standard a precise, narrow meaning: 'cassational interest' exists where the judgment at hand has: (*a*) contradicted the Supreme Court's case law; or (*b*) ruled on points on which the case law from the provincial courts is contradictory; or (*c*) applied a recent statute.

The civil division of the Supreme Court, in a controversial collective decision adopted in 2000, announced that it would interpret the three grounds—fundamental rights, monetary threshold and 'cassational interest'—as mutually exclusive remedies: (*a*) if the case was *principaliter* about fundamental rights protection, cassation appeal would always be allowed; (*b*) if the type of procedure in the first instance had been determined *ratione valoris*, i.e. based on the amount in dispute, cassation appeal would only be allowed if the value of the case was above €150,000, even if 'cassational interest' existed—a low or undetermined amount thus constituting an insurmountable obstacle; and (*c*) 'cassational interest' would be the only test for procedures *ratione materiae* to access the Supreme Court even if they were for an amount in excess of €150,000. Although this interpretation proved severely restrictive and was universally condemned,[39] it had the side effect of bringing the Supreme Court's caseload under control.

The new regime and its questionable interpretation by the Supreme Court were not the only factors to control the backlog. In 1985, a Technical Cabinet (*Gabinete técnico*), a body of seasoned judges and other jurists permanently or provisionally appointed to assist the Supreme Court, particularly in the granting or denying leave to appeal, was established.[40] However, it would not be until the 2000s that its staff was seriously reinforced. The role of this efficient, dedicated group of lawyers proved essential to alleviating the Supreme Court's backlog.

---

[37] See De la Oliva et al. (2001), pp. 6. See generally, on the genesis of the standard, De la Oliva et al. (2001), p. 831; López (2002), pp. 106ff. For a thorough study of the standard itself see López (2002).

[38] This was a fully deliberate decision based on prudential reasons: see De la Oliva (2010a), p. 122; De la Oliva (2010b), pp. 71–72.

[39] See De la Oliva et al. (2001), pp. 1–8.

[40] See Ortells (2010), pp. 73ff. A detailed analysis of the procedure of *admisión* (the equivalent of permission to appeal) can be found in De Castro and González (2010).

In 2011, the legislature clarified the law so as to prevent the Supreme Court's contested interpretation and, in passing, increased the threshold significantly, from €150,000 to €600,000. The selection criteria were set as follows: (*a*) if the case is about fundamental rights protection, cassation appeal could always be brought; (*b*) the same if the amount in dispute is higher than €600,000; and (*c*) for any other proceedings, determined either *ratione valoris* or *ratione materiae*, the claimant must establish 'cassational interest' to access the Supreme Court.

This system, currently in force, has generally been praised for having reached an acceptable balance. On the one hand, the *ius constitutionis*—the public interest in the uniformity of case law, formulated as 'cassational interest'—has become central in the majority of cases, and a low or undetermined amount is no longer incompatible with it. On the other, the *ius litigatoris*—the private interest in the adequate application of the law to the particular case—is given priority only exceptionally, in cases of fundamental rights and economically relevant cases.

1.7 A Constitutional Certiorari (2007)

In the 1978 Constitution, the Constitutional Court was entrusted with the task of not only providing a body of decisions to interpret the constitutional provisions (the *ius constitutionis* or public purpose of *amparo*), but also to actually provide a remedy against violations by the courts of the fundamental rights enshrined in the Constitution (the *ius litigatoris* or private purpose of *amparo*). Over time, however, the active exercise by the Constitutional Court of its powers to quash judgments encouraged the lodging of a massive number of constitutional protection appeals (around 10,000 per year, with 96% denied leave in 2006), which placed the Constitutional Court on the brink of collapse.

In 2007, a radical solution was given: the violation of a fundamental right (private purpose) remained a necessary but no longer a sufficient requirement for admission; the claimant needed to establish also why the court's decision would have 'specific constitutional importance' (*especial trascendencia constitucional*; public purpose); and the Constitutional Court would be free to deny leave without citing reasons. Thus, a discretionary notion of 'specific constitutional importance' became the centrepiece of the *amparo* regime.[41] The technique of limiting access through *Generalklauseln* was inspired both by the 'cassational interest' of the Civil Procedure Law 2000 and by the German experience, where similar standards were set out to limit access to the Constitutional Court in 1996 and to the Supreme Court in 2001. However, the German qualifying standard of 1996, albeit focusing on the public purpose,[42] also included a subjective safeguard for cases in which not hearing the

[41]See, for an explanation and critical assessment of the reform, Espinosa (2010).

[42]The *grundsätzliche verfassungsrechtliche Bedeutung* of § 93a(1) of the *Bundesverfassungsgerichtsgesetz*.

Table 1 Supreme Court: Case Backlog 1995–2002

Backlog	1995	1996	1997	1998	1999	2000	2001	2002
Incoming	2800	3007	3399	3668	4184	4484	5342	
Decided	2163	2061	2338	2451	2532	2875	4617	
...on the merits					1106	1080	1238	1260
Pending	6042	6998	8049	9266	10,914	12,523	15,079	13,367

appeal would prove particularly detrimental to the appellant regardless of any objective or public interest.[43] In 2007, Spain's legislature went a step further and chose to focus exclusively on the public purpose.

1.8 Legal and Statistical Overview

As a result of the developments just described, four levels of protection exist for regular civil cases: first instance, ordinary appeal, cassation appeal and constitutional protection appeal. Access to the last two is, of course, limited. The discrete substantive or procedural grounds for appeal remain necessary requirements, but they are no longer sufficient to access the Supreme Court or the Constitutional Court. In both cases additional requirements must be met, which are set out in the form of standards: 'cassational interest' (more narrowly defined) and 'special constitutional transcendence' (more openly defined). As regards civil cassation, the public 'cassational interest' (*ius constitutionis*) is counterbalanced by automatic leave to appeal where it concerns (*a*) proceedings for the protection of constitutional rights and (*b*) proceedings for an amount in excess of €600,000, in which cases the private interest of the party prevails. In the case of the constitutional protection appeal, objective public interest is always a necessary condition, without any private or subjective counterbalance.

The critical caseload situation of the Supreme Court during the first decade of the new century, with appeals taking more than 5 years, and exceptionally up to 8, is now under control. Appeals are decided in approximately 1 year. Tables 1, 2 and 3 illustrate the various stages in this regard.[44]

As can be seen, the number of cases decided came to the point of surpassing the incoming cases, thus putting an end to the previous backlog (although a worrying trend is noticeable in more recent years). This is particularly remarkable considering that the last decade has witnessed a noticeable increase in litigiousness: the number of lawsuits in all jurisdictions was 33% higher than during the 10 years prior; in civil litigation, the number of lawsuits more than doubled.

[43] § 93a(2)b in fine of the *Bundesverfassungsgerichtsgesetz*.

[44] Sources: Annual reports of the General Council of the Judiciary (2000–2010) and the Supreme Court (2010–2018).

Table 2 Supreme Court: Case Backlog 'Update' 2003–2010

Update	2003	2004	2005	2006	2007	2008	2009	2010
Incoming	5453	4873	4251	3603	3519	3560	3510	3642
Decided	5180	5472	5907	5572	6784	6625	5422	4603
...on the merits	1269	1254	1032	1340	1339	1154	828	790
Pending	14,751	14,152	12,496	10,527	7262	6424	4512	3551

Table 3 Supreme Court: Case Backlog 'Control' 2011–2018

Control	2011	2012	2013	2014	2015	2016	2017	2018
Incoming	4591	4238	3579	3904	4284	5781	5974	6822
Decided	4839	3597	3953	2947	3188	4271	3759	4603
...on the merits	1242	792	821	758	734	802	699	734
Pending	3326	3984	3628	4614	5286	6806	9021	10,482

As for the Constitutional Court, the *recursos de amparo* or constitutional protection appeals soon became the main source of work. In 1980, 218 constitutional protection complaints were granted leave; in 1990, 2910; in 2000, the number of new appeals reached 6792.[45] In 2006, 13,883 constitutional protection appeals—compared to 37 constitutionality issues—were awaiting leave, which only 4% obtained.

In 2008 (the year following the 2007 reform), denials of leave slightly increased to 98.39%, and they have remained at similar figures to date. The Constitutional Court renders approximately 100 *amparo* judgments per year on average, as shown in Table 4 below.[46]

1.9 Almost a Revolution (2014)

On 4 April 2014, the Council of Ministers approved a draft bill presented by the Minister of Justice to reform the Organic Law on the Judiciary. Although in October it was decided not to send the draft bill to the Congress, it is worth making a brief reference to it, as it included significant amendments to the regime of cassation appeals, some of which were based on the text drafted by a commission of experts including justices of the Supreme Court.

The terms of the reform proposed were profound and far-reaching. First and foremost, cassation would solely serve the public function of creating and unifying jurisprudence, without any reference to the private interest of the party. The monetary threshold would have altogether disappeared; only cases for the protection of fundamental rights would be allowed unrestricted access to the Supreme Court.

[45]Montero and Flors (2008), p. 356.

[46]Source: Annual reports of the *Tribunal Constitucional*.

Table 4 Constitutional Court: Number of Appeals 2009–2019

Period 2009–2019	2009	2010	2011	2012	2013	2014	2015	2016	2017	2018	2019
Incoming	10,848	9041	7192	7294	7573	7878	7369	6774	6381	6977	7621
. . . of which *amparo* appeals	10,792	8948	7098	7205	7376	7663	7203	6685	6286	6918	7554
Decided	16,022	10,546	6931	8041	6665	7409	8.765	7822	6322	6842	6575
. . . of which on *amparo*	15,693	10,110	6584	7472	6012	6882	8513	7596	6186	6721	6494
. . . of which on the merits	177	91	145	124	87	109	96	88	53	55	117

At the same time, the notion of 'cassational interest' was formulated in a remarkably open-ended manner in the draft bill:

> Article 44. It lies with the appellant to establish the existence of cassational interest justifying, in accordance with the circumstances of the particular case, a ruling of the Supreme Court.

The draft project proposed by the commission of experts—not the subsequent draft bill, though—set forth a list of cases that would have 'cassational interest':

- The dispute concerns the validity of a provision of a general nature;
- There is no case law on the issue, it is insufficient or unclear or it does exist but has been deliberately disregarded in the contested judgment;
- There are well-founded reasons for a jurisprudential shift;
- The litigious question is, for any reason, of general interest.

With or without the list, 'cassational interest' was in the bill a truly open-ended *Generalklausel*, along the lines of the 'special constitutional transcendence' introduced in 2007 for the *recurso de amparo* before the Constitutional Court. Similarly, in the original draft the Supreme Court would evaluate the standard discretionally and without the need of providing reasons.

Some final remarks must be made about the pre-legislative intention to turn Spanish private law into a full-fledged system of precedents, even as we put aside any doubts as to the constitutionality of such a proposal. The binding nature of Supreme Court case law would have been reinforced by the possibility for any court to raise *incidenter* prejudicial issues with the Supreme Court when case law is not clear. Even more surprisingly, a sort of *stare decisis* principle would have been introduced whereby the judgments of each court would bind the same court as precedents applicable to any future similar decisions. And this was not just a rhetorical declaration: departing from those precedents would in itself constitute a breach of the constitutionally enshrined right to effective legal protection and, as such, might result in access the Supreme Court and the Constitutional Court. These provisions would have altered the century-old system of sources of law to include judicial precedent among them.

1.10 Towards a New Stability?

Leaving extravagant aspects aside, the reform, even if trumped, called for what was perhaps a natural evolution of a genuine trend, whose landmarks were the introduction, in 2000 and 2007, respectively, of the 'cassational interest' and 'special constitutional transcendence' standards of access to the Supreme Court and the Constitutional Court. The turning of 'cassational interest,' already the centrepiece of cassation, into an open-ended, discretional standard, counterbalanced by unrestricted access to the Supreme Court for the protection of fundamental rights, maybe was just anticipating the culmination of that trend.

The technique of general clauses or standards has allowed for a reasonable management of the caseload of the two courts of last resort which were on the verge of being overwhelmed. More importantly, this has not occurred by arbitrarily sacrificing the rights of the parties, but as a result of a—more or less rushed—process of reflection on the real functions of last resort appeals in contemporary societies[47] and the particularities of the Spanish legal system.

Organic reforms such as more judges, special chambers or smaller sections would in all likelihood fail to keep pace with the intense litigiousness of contemporary society, or prove downright counterproductive for the purposes of issuing clear, unified legal criteria. Likewise, procedural restrictions such as absolute monetary thresholds, excluded types of proceedings, high deposits or charges for filing, even if successful, would sacrifice important legal sectors—proceedings with just one instance, exequatur, monitory or summary proceedings—and might jeopardise the principle of equality.

In large part, refocusing on legal certainty through legal interpretation—which also serves the principle of equality by ensuring, through authoritative precedent, that like cases are treated alike[48]—means going back to the roots. It is true, however, that doing so exclusively and discretionally would mean entrusting the justices of the Supreme Court with an immense responsibility. So far, the risk of case overload has been very successfully managed; taking that further step may seem unnecessary at best.[49]

2 Particular Aspects

Having offered this historical overview, we are now in a position to directly address some additional, more specific questions.

2.1 *Composition of the Supreme Court and the Cassation Procedure*

The Supreme Court is composed of five ordinary divisions (*Salas*), each of them with a different number of justices or *Magistrados*: First Division, Civil (ten justices); Second Division, Criminal (15 justices); Third Division, Administrative (33 justices); Fourth Division, Labour (13 justices); Fifth Division, Military (eight

[47]As suggested by Calamandrei (1945), p. 428. Fairén (1969b), p. 199, highlights as well the 'historical relativity' of cassation appeal.

[48]See Taruffo (2015).

[49]De la Oliva (2011), p. 259.

justices). The President and Vice President are also *Magistrados* with jurisdictional functions, adding up to 81 justices in total.

The justices in each division work ordinarily through chambers or sections (*Secciones*) made up of five judges. The civil division, for example, is divided into two sections, without any specialization as regards cassation appeals. In important cases, the justices gather in plenary session (*Pleno*) to render the judgment.

The so-called Technical Cabinet (*Gabinete técnico*) assists the justices, particularly in the granting or denying of leave. The Cabinet is made up of 71 clerks (*letrados del Gabinete técnico*), of which 12 judges in secondment and 59 jurists, of which two judges and 18 jurists serve in the civil division. The *letrados* are not inexperienced clerks, but seasoned, specialised jurists—mainly seconded judges—with at least 10 years of experience. This body of qualified jurists operates collegially, following the instructions of the president of the respective division, while not serving as individual clerks to individual justices.

Unlike in other countries, in Spain no special bar of lawyers exists to act before the Supreme Court. Once admitted to any of the local bar associations (*Colegio de abogados*), Spanish attorneys can practise their profession anywhere in the national territory and before any courts, of any hierarchy or area of law, thus including the Supreme Court and the Constitutional Court.

As explained in Sect. 1 above, the requirements and criteria to access the Supreme Court are basically as follows:

1. If the amount in dispute is €600,000 or less, the claimant must establish 'cassational interest' to access the Supreme Court. 'Cassational interest' exists where the judgment *a quo*:
   - Contradicts the Supreme Court's case law, or
   - Rules on points on which the case law from the provincial courts is contradictory, or
   - Applies a recent statute, which has been in force for less than 5 years.
2. If the amount in dispute is in excess of €600,000, or if the proceedings were *principaliter* for the protection of fundamental rights, the claimant enjoys unrestricted access to the Supreme Court and need not, therefore, establish 'cassational interest.'

To assess these criteria, there is no separate preliminary selection committee. A section of three justices, one of them the president of the division, meets once or twice a week to grant or deny leave to cassation. Previously, the *letrados del Gabinete técnico* will have prepared and circulated a report on each particular case. During the meeting the respective *letrados* briefly present each case and assist the *Magistrados* in their deliberation by answering any questions they may have on the case.

The provisional regime set forth in 2000 made leave to the appeal on procedural grounds dependent on whether it complied with the conditions required for the appeal on substantive grounds. This immediately gave rise to interpretation problems, since the appeals were not designed to be combined (the procedural appeal was intended for the regional high courts). In order to be granted leave, the judgment at hand must meet the requirements for substantive cassation: either to have been rendered in a procedure for the protection of fundamental rights or to present the required quantitative threshold, even if the appeal is solely for procedural reasons. The situation will, perhaps, be better understood by considering the cases where the two appeals are filed jointly: in order to decide whether or not to grant leave to appeal, the requirements for substantive cassation are examined first; if these are not met, both appeals—also the procedural appeal—are rejected; if they are met, then the procedural appeal is decided before the substantive appeal, for logical and practical reasons. This situation was and remains inadequate: it is a provisional solution envisaged only for the practical joint handling of two instruments that were conceived as different in nature.

Once leave has been granted, the relevant section—or the whole civil division gathered in plenary session—will decide on the alleged errors of a substantive or procedural legal nature. All the justices participate in the deliberations, but a single *ponente* is delegated the task of writing the judgment.

The Supreme Court will only review points of law. Manifestly irrational evaluation of evidence or application of the law, or the lack of true reasoning, are considered to fall within this category.

The judgment will have different consequences depending on the procedural or substantive nature of the appeal:

1. In case of procedural errors, the judgment is quashed and sent back to the lower court (in classic terminology, only the *iudicium rescindens* is given);
2. In case of substantive errors, a new judgment is rendered (following the same terminology, a *iudicium rescissorium* is given alongside a *iudicium rescindens*).

Tables 1–3 above show the actual figures, but it is safe to think of a rough average of 4000 incoming cases per year and another 4000 decided cases, of which around 800 are judgments on the merits, including those remanding the case back to the lower court and those containing a new decision.

2.2 Case Overload Problems

In the 1990s and 2000s, the Supreme Court faced a serious case overload problem. The most obvious symptom was a significant backlog, with a delay at times of more than 5 years (up to 8 during the peak) to decide a cassation appeal.

As soon as the case overload increased in the 1990s, the backlog was unanimously denounced. At that time Spain was signalled on several occasions by the European Court of Human Rights for undue delays, mainly in criminal proceedings. Also, the 'barometer' of the General Council of the Judiciary (*Consejo General del Poder Judicial*), a survey to assess the public perception of the justice system, showed a steady increase in the concern over delays (from 55% in 1983 to 61% in 1992). A renovated General Council of the Judiciary launched in 1996 a wider consultation to both central state institutions and the general public: delays appeared to be one of the main concerns in all cases. The Ombudsman reported that 18% of the complaints recorded referred to delays, mainly in the civil and administrative orders. Legal scholars reflected on that state of affairs and engaged in a lively debate on the possible solutions and the very purpose of the Supreme Court and cassation appeal.

The General Council of the Judiciary then drafted a White Book, published in 1998, which presented the situation in clear terms and advanced the following two proposals to remedy it:

1. To adopt the 'cassational interest' as a filter to access the Supreme Court, together with an increased monetary threshold above which 'cassational interest' would be presumed to exist, and
2. To reinforce, mainly with career judges on secondment, the personnel of the Supreme Court's Technical Cabinet, in order to assist the justices in the evaluation and drafting of denials of leave.

Ms. Margarita Mariscal de Gante, then Minister of Justice, was not a professional politician but a career judge, as well as a fine jurist and a purposeful reformer. She decided to include the General Council's proposals in the text of the new Civil Procedure Law, enacted by the Parliament in 2000. Ms. Mariscal de Gante also agreed and made possible for the Supreme Court to create new positions in the Technical Cabinet, as requested by the General Council in the White Book.

Finally, the Supreme Court itself, in principle with little capacity to solve its own case overload problems, contributed to updating the backlog by expeditious means, through the previously mentioned 2001 collective agreement of the Supreme Court, which arbitrarily restricted—by way of an anticipated interpretation unrelated to any particular case—the legal criteria for access in connection with the new 'cassational interest' standard.

As part of the effort to 'update' (i.e. reduce) the backlog, the number of decisions—mainly denials of leave—accelerated in the 2000s. That did not mean, though, that there was not enough time to analyse each case in depth. It may be true—it is hard to provide an accurate, overall assessment—that the quality, level of detail and internal consistency of the judgments did not reach historical peaks in those years, during which the primary concern was to reduce the backlog; but they surely did not vary greatly. The key to reducing the workload was not to issue significantly more judgments on the merits, but rather to deny leave to a higher number of appeals and to do so at a higher pace. And this increase in the denials of leave was possible, as mentioned, thanks to a combination of factors:

1. The new 'cassational interest' access filter;
2. An exceedingly restrictive interpretation of the legal criteria for access in connection with the new 'cassational interest' standard, based on a questionable, self-standing collective agreement adopted by the Supreme Court in 2001 (an arbitrary interpretation aimed only at excluding cases), and
3. A *Gabinete técnico* reinforced with personnel and focused on the case overload challenge.

The result was remarkably successful. The number of decided cases surpassed that of incoming cases, and in a few years the backlog was reduced. From that point on, the number of incoming and decided cases has remained proportional, with no significant delays. And the figures seem to have remained relatively stable, in particular in view of the general increase in litigiousness, particularly intense in civil litigation.

The transition was smooth. Albeit the Spanish Constitution of 1978 never included any right of access to the Supreme Court, by 2000 there was some sense of entitlement to access to the Supreme Court, particularly among practising attorneys. However, the public function of cassation, if newly underlined, had always been there. Also, the new law did not entirely eliminate the private component, which continued to prevail in cases involving fundamental rights and high amounts at stake. These factors contributed to a fluid, uneventful transition.

Court fees and budget considerations did not play a significant role in the process. Court fees disappeared in 1985, when justice became fully state-funded. With time, this did create a sense of entitlement towards free access to justice. In 2002, not without criticism, a tax for the filing of certain procedural briefs was introduced for legal persons. The amount varied from €300 for ordinary declaratory proceedings to €800 for an ordinary appeal and €1200 for a cassation appeal. The number of cassation appeals did not decrease noticeably. In 2012, the government proposed extending the payment of court taxes to individuals, but the measure encountered stark social, professional and scholarly reaction and had to be withdrawn in 2015. As regards budget considerations, on the one hand, 2000 was generally a good year for state revenue; on the other hand, Spain was determined to be in the founding group of the euro and the government imposed a policy of strict financial discipline in the administration.

As explained in Sect. 1 above, cassation appeal was designed as a means to create a body of decisions that would supplement and clarify statutory law. This was perceived as its most important function. The best legal minds of the early nineteenth century stressed the important role of cassation in the shaping and unfolding of the law. At the same time, each of these decisions would result in the correction of a judgment by a lower court. The relatively limited litigiousness of society allowed for the public interest to be realised along with the private interest, while correcting the particular cases, as had been done traditionally. Even though the public function was always considered to be the most characteristic and meaningful, the hybrid, pragmatical nature and function of Spanish cassation was generally accepted for more than a century.[50]

The overburdening of the Supreme Court in the last decade of the twentieth century prompted reflection on the original ends of cassation; the number of seminars and publications on the topic increased noticeably. That reflective process allowed the appeal to be reformulated around the 'cassational interest.' In a way,

[50]Indeed, soon the *ius litigatoris* came to be understood as a natural and integral part of Spanish cassation together with the *ius constitutionis*: see Buendía (2006) and Delgado (2009).

the challenge posed by case overload made the Supreme Court return to its pristine ends.

2.3 *Case Overload Solutions*

2.3.1 Increasing Capacity

The most obvious answer to the case overload challenge is to increase the capacity of the court by adding more judges; giving judges more law clerks to assist them; dividing the court into smaller units; allowing the relevant division to operate in panels of five or three judges; etc. All of these measures have been tried in Spain at one point or another.

The Supreme Court was created in 1812 with an undetermined number of justices. At first it was composed of 16 justices, seven of which in the civil division. The number of justices was doubled in 1864, when two chambers were created (but reunited in 1870). Some years later the civil division reached its maximum number in history: 16 justices. The addition of the administrative and labour divisions in the twentieth century required further increases. Today the number of judges is stable at 79 justices, including the ten justices of the civil division.

Another remedy for curing the mid-century backlog, which was favoured by a majority of reformers, was to set up a *Sala de admisión*, a chamber to rule on preliminary admission—either with discretionary powers or subject to rules. The proposal was dropped at the last minute, but was reinstated and entered into force in 1878. It would not take root, however, and would be eliminated in 1893.

Other solutions were proposed in those central decades of the nineteenth century: to reinstate the *renvoi* (quashing and remanding the case to the lower court also in appeals on substantive grounds) or to establish a *summa gravaminis* or monetary threshold.

Already in the twentieth century, the civil division was authorised to resolve cases not in panels of seven justices, but in panels of five, and in 1992, temporarily, of three.

In the beginning there was in the Supreme Court a body of *relatores*, collaborators devoted to presenting summaries of cases and proposals for decision. This traditional category, which had existed for centuries, disappeared when the *relatores* were united with the *escribanos* to create the unified body of *secretarios judiciales* (analogous to the French *greffiers*). The new *secretarios* inherited, but as a matter of fact discontinued, the functions carried out by the old *relatores*. More than a century later, in 1985, the *letrados del Gabinete Técnico* were created and seemed somewhat reminiscent of those old positions.

2.3.2 Procedural Measures

Procedural reforms can also be introduced to accelerate the process with the court. Oral hearings can be disposed of; different tracks can be created to deal with easy or hard cases in order to save time. Spain has experienced its share of procedural measures as well.

As an early example of purely procedural reforms, the 1870 reform eliminated the grounds based on the denegation of a means of evidence—since it did not affect the prevailing public interest—and abolished the appeal for denial of leave to appeal by the lower court (soon reinstated).

By the early 1980s, the increase in the Supreme Court's caseload had become a serious concern. Reforms in 1984 and 1992 aimed at controlling it. The 1984 reform introduced a monetary threshold to access cassation regardless of the type of proceedings. Until then there was an implicit threshold of €3000; the new, explicit one was set at €18,000. As the reform failed to produce any noticeable effect in limiting the Supreme Court's caseload, in 1992 other relatively minor reforms were introduced with the same aim:

1. The threshold was doubled to the equivalent of €36,000;
2. The court could deny leave if the appeal was 'manifestly unfounded';
3. Errors in the evaluation of documentary evidence were excluded from cassation appeal;
4. The number of judges hearing a regular appeal was reduced from five to three;
5. It would be possible to decide *without* calling the parties to a hearing.

Perhaps surprisingly, the number of cassation appeals doubled in spite of these measures.

2.3.3 Reducing Quantity

Apart from increasing capacity and making the procedure more expeditious, another solution to the case overload challenge entails reducing the number of cases that the court needs to review by means of case filtering or case selection.

In light of the limited success of earlier attempts to alleviate the seriously overburdened Supreme Court, the new Civil Procedure Law 2000 contained a radical solution: to abolish a centralised cassation appeal on procedural grounds and to assign it to the 17 regional high courts. Only at the last minute was the change left without effect and replaced by a regime that, in spite of its provisional character, has been in force until today.

This originally provisional regime was innovative in that it established that only three categories of rulings qualified for cassation at the Supreme Court (previous to the examination of the particular grounds of appeal). Although already mentioned earlier (Sect. 1.6 above), they bear repeating here:

1. All proceedings for the protection of fundamental rights;

2. Those with a considerably high *summa gravaminis* (€150,000, from the previous €36,000), and
3. Any case featuring 'cassational interest.'

The standard of 'cassational interest' has quite a narrow meaning: it exists where the judgment *a quo*:

1. Departed from the Supreme Court's case law;
2. Ruled on points on which the case law from the provincial courts is contradictory, or
3. Applied a recent statute, enacted within the five previous years.

Only the Supreme Court can assess whether these criteria exist in a given case. The role of the lower court has always been limited to examining the existence of external, less important criteria.

It has already been said, but deserves an additional reference in this section devoted to 'reducing quantity,' that in 2000, right before starting to apply the new Civil Procedure Law, the full civil division announced—in a statement disconnected from any particular case—that it would interpret certain aspects of the new cassation regime in a manner that proved severely restrictive and was universally condemned. This interpretation was applied for 10 years and, even if unfair, demonstrated to be effective. This questionable shortcut can only be understood in the light of the overwhelming backlog.

On a separate note, the Civil Procedure Law 2000 set forth the provisional enforcement of judgments as a general rule for any kind of appeals, ordinary or extraordinary. Any first instance judgment would be capable of being provisionally enforced, only against payment of a bond. Provisional enforcement would be unconditional. This measure deterred purely tactical, unfounded appeals lodged with only delaying purposes.

3 Conclusion

Spain offers an example of remarkable success. The technique of access filters through general clauses such as 'cassational interest' has been key to getting the caseload of the Supreme Court under control. How open-ended and discretional these general clauses must be remains dependent on the tradition and degree of trust in the quality and independence of each country's judges. The Spanish example has demonstrated so far that relatively precise access filters, with reasons being provided for each denial of leave, can suffice to manage and revert a critical situation of case overload.

Whether denying leave is discretional or not, and whether with or without reasons, the Spanish example underlines the central importance of a body of qualified clerks. In Spain, this is a unified body of seasoned jurists; in other systems clerks may be less experienced—but perhaps equally qualified—and assigned to each individual judge. What seems vital is that there is no lack of talent and experience assisting the judges in what truly is one of the most conspicuous moments in a nation's legal process.

References

Artola M (2000) Los orígenes de la España contemporánea, vol I. Centro de Estudios Constitucionales, Madrid

Banacloche J, Cubillo I (2012) Aspectos fundamentales del Derecho Procesal Civil. La Ley, Madrid

Buendía A (2006) La casación civil. Estudio doctrinal sobre los fines casacionales. DIJUSA, Madrid

Calamandrei P (1945) La casación civil, vol. II (trans: Sentís Melendo S). Editorial Bibliográfica Argentina, Buenos Aires

Catalina MÁ (2010) El Tribunal Supremo y la tutela de los derechos fundamentales. El recurso de casación y el art. 53.2 de la CE. Tirant Lo Blanch, Valencia

De Castro RM, González J-P (2010) El trámite de admisión del recurso de casación civil en España, según la Sala Primera, de lo Civil, del Tribunal Supremo. In: Bonet J, Martín J (eds) El recurso de casación civil. Aranzadi, Cizur Menor, pp 155–230

De la Oliva A (1985) Panorama general de la reforma de la L.E.C. por la Ley 34/84. Boletín del Colegio de Abogados de Madrid 6:9–19

De la Oliva A (2010a) L'esperienza spagnola della Cassazione civile. Riv Trimest Dirit Proced Civ 64(1):107–125

De la Oliva A (2010b) Spanish Civil Procedure Act 2000: flying over common law and civil law traditions. In: Walker J, Chase O (eds) Common law, civil law and the future of categories. LexisNexis, Markham, pp 63–74

De la Oliva A (2011) Un modelo de casación civil eficaz para el Tribunal Supremo de España. Annuario di diritto comparato e di studi legislativi:249–279

De la Oliva A, Díez-Picazo I (1996) Tribunal Constitucional, jurisdicción ordinaria y derechos fundamentales. McGraw-Hill, Madrid

De la Oliva A, Díez-Picazo I, Vegas J (2001) Comentarios a la Ley de Enjuiciamiento Civil. Civitas, Madrid

De la Plaza M (1944) La casación civil. Revista de Derecho Privado 203:293–304

Delgado J (2009) La historia de la casación civil española: Una experiencia que aconseja no avanzar en el modelo de unificación de doctrina. Revista de Derecho de la Pontificia Universidad Católica de Valparaíso 23:345–367

Escudero JA (2012) Curso de Historia del Derecho. Fuentes e instituciones político-administrativas. Escudero, Madrid

Espinosa A (2010) El recurso de amparo: Problemas antes, y después, de la reforma. InDret 2. http://www.indret.com/pdf/722_es.pdf. Accessed 20 Dec 2019

Fairén V (1969a) Estudio histórico externo de la Ley de Enjuiciamiento Civil de 1855. In: Fairén V (ed) Temas del ordenamiento procesal, vol I, Historia, Teoría general. Tecnos, Madrid, pp 19–111

Fairén V (1969b) La recepción en España del recurso de casación francés. In: Fairén V (ed) Temas del ordenamiento procesal, vol I, Historia, Teoría general. Tecnos, Madrid, pp 195–235

Garriga C (2006) Justicia animada: Dispositivos de la Justicia en la Monarquía Católica. In: Lorente M (ed) De justicia de jueces a justicia de leyes: Hacia la España de 1870. Cuadernos de Derecho Judicial, vol VI. Consejo General del Poder Judicial. Centro de Documentación Judicial, Madrid, pp 59–104

Gutiérrez de Cabiedes E (1985) Caracteres principales de la casación civil en la reforma urgente de la Ley de Enjuiciamiento. Revista de Derecho Procesal 1:65–120

Lasso JF (1971) Evolución histórica de la casación civil en España. Revista de Derecho Procesal Iberoamericana (supplement) 1:127–183

Lasso JF (1998) Crónica de la codificación española, vol 2, Procedimiento civil. Ministerio de Justicia, Madrid

López J (2002) El interés casacional. Civitas, Madrid

Lorente M (2007) De justicia de jueces a justicia de leyes: Hacia la España de 1870. Consejo General del Poder Judicial, Madrid

Lorente M, Martínez F, Solla MJ (2012) Historia legal de la justicia en España (1810–1978). Iustel, Madrid

Martínez-Calcerrada L (ed) (1993) La nueva casación civil. Estudio de la Ley 10/1992, de 30 de abril, de reforma de los procesos civiles. Civitas, Madrid

Montero J, Flors J (2008) Amparo constitucional y proceso civil. Tirant Lo Blanch, Valencia

Moreno L (1989) Los orígenes del Tribunal Supremo, 1812–1838. Ministerio de Justicia, Madrid

Oliver J (2010) El recurso de amparo en la Segunda República Española (1931–1936) y la posterior Guerra Civil (1936–1939). Anuario Iberoamericano de Justicia Constitucional 14:323–346

Ortells M (2007) El Tribunal Supremo español: Un tribunal en busca de identidad. In: Gimeno V (ed) El Tribunal Supremo, su doctrina legal y el recurso de casación. Iustel, Madrid, pp 31–106

Ortells M (2010) La casación en España: Selección de recursos y carga de trabajo del Tribunal Supremo. In: Bonet J, Martín J (eds) El recurso de casación civil. Aranzadi, Cizur Menor, pp 31–86

Pizzorusso A (2004) La posición constitucional del Tribunal Supremo. In: Trillo R, Bacigalupo E, Murillo PL (eds) El Tribunal Supremo en el ordenamiento constitucional. Jornadas en conmemoración del XXV Aniversario de la Constitución de 1978. Tribunal Supremo, Madrid, pp 19–43

Ramos F (2007) ¿Qué hacemos con el Tribunal Supremo? In: Gimeno V (ed) El Tribunal Supremo, su doctrina legal y el recurso de casación. Iustel, Madrid, pp 107–134

Sáinz J (1992) La Administración de justicia en España (1810–1870). EUDEMA, Madrid

Taruffo M (2015) Las funciones de los tribunales supremos: Entre la uniformidad y la justicia. Diario La Ley 8473:1–15

Tomás y Valiente F (1983) Manual de Historia del Derecho español. Tecnos, Madrid

Vázquez JL (1979) La casación civil (revisión crítica). Ediser, Barcelona

Vázquez JL (2010) Ineficacia de la casación bajo el peso de la dogmática. In: Bonet J, Martín J (eds) El recurso de casación civil. Aranzadi, Cizur Menor, pp 231–246

Xiol JA (2004) La posición constitucional del Tribunal Supremo. In: Trillo R, Bacigalupo E, Murillo PL (eds) El Tribunal Supremo en el ordenamiento constitucional. Jornadas en conmemoración del XXV Aniversario de la Constitución de 1978. Tribunal Supremo, Madrid, pp 71–128

Part III
Germanic Legal Tradition

Sharing Responsibility: The German Federal Court of Justice and the Civil Appellate System

Michael Stürner

Abstract When evaluating the role of Supreme Courts the main problem consists in finding the right balance between the goal of doing justice in the individual case and the overarching responsibility of every Supreme Court to clarify and develop the law. The history of reforms of access to the German Federal Court of Justice (*Bundesgerichtshof*) can be seen as a constant attempt to redefine this equilibrium; sometimes one aspect is given more emphasis, sometimes the other. In Germany, traditionally, much weight has been placed on the goal of individual justice. However, in recent decades the collective aspects of *Revision* have been strengthened. The major reform of 2001 not only introduced restrictions on access to the Federal Court of Justice, but also reshaped the entire procedural system, giving more weight to the first instance. This has led to a significant reduction in the caseload of the Federal Court of Justice.

1 Overview of the Supreme Court

The Federal Court of Justice (*Bundesgerichtshof*) is the highest court of ordinary jurisdiction; it is competent to hear both civil and criminal matters. It was instituted on 1 October 1950, its seat in Karlsruhe (§ 123 Judicature Act (*Gerichtsverfassungsgesetz—GVG*)).[1]

[1]For a comparative account of the Supreme Courts in the German-speaking countries cf. Domej (2017).

M. Stürner (✉)
University of Konstanz, Faculty of law, Konstanz, Germany
e-mail: michael.stuerner@uni-konstanz.de

P. Bravo-Hurtado, C. H. van Rhee (eds.), *Supreme Courts Under Pressure*, Ius Gentium: Comparative Perspectives on Law and Justice 83,
https://doi.org/10.1007/978-3-030-63731-6_5

1.1 The Historical Setting

Only a short time before 1 October 1950, on 24 May 1949, the German Constitution, called the Basic Law (*Grundgesetz—GG*), had become law, thereby providing the legal basis for the Federal Court of Justice for West Germany in Article 95(1) *GG*. There was considerable competition between German cities to be chosen as the seat of the newly established court: while Chancellor Konrad Adenauer favoured his hometown, Cologne, where the court would be located in close proximity to the new capital, Bonn, the German Parliament (*Bundestag*) voted in favour of Karlsruhe, the old residence city of the Grand Duchy of Baden. The other candidate cities—Kassel, Hamburg, Brunswick (Braunschweig) and Bamberg—were unsuccessful. One of the criminal panels, the Fifth Senate, was moved to West Berlin in 1952. In the German Democratic Republic, the Supreme Court of the GDR (*Oberstes Gericht der DDR*) had jurisdiction in civil and criminal matters. It was set up in 1949 in (East) Berlin and abolished by the Unification Treaty in October 1990. The initiative to move the seat of the Federal Supreme Court to Leipzig, in the past the seat of the Imperial Court (*Reichsgericht*), faced severe opposition from the judges. Only the Fifth Criminal Senate was moved from Berlin to Leipzig in 1997.

When taking into account the long history of Supreme Courts in Germany, the Federal Court of Justice can look back on a tradition of more than 500 years of administration of justice. Its immediate predecessor, the Imperial Court of Justice (*Reichsgericht*), existed from 1879 to 1945 with its seat in Leipzig and was the successor to the Higher Commercial Court of the Empire (*Reichsoberhandelsgericht*), which had been established in 1871. The main function of the Imperial Court of Justice was to bring legal coherence to the German Empire (founded in 1871), more specifically to ensure the uniform application of a series of new acts, such as the Code of Civil Procedure (*Zivilprozessordnung—ZPO*), the Judicature Act (*Gerichtsverfassungsgesetz—GVG*), the Bankruptcy Act (*Konkursordnung—KO*), the Code of Criminal Procedure (*Strafprozessordnung—StPO*)[2] and, later on, the German Civil Code (*Bürgerliches Gesetzbuch—BGB*) and the Commercial Code (*Handelsgesetzbuch—HGB*), which entered into force on 1 January 1900. The Imperial Court of Justice was abolished by the Allies in 1945, as it was seen as a major proponent of the Nazi regime.[3] In fact, from 1933 to 1945, the court issued numerous politically motivated death sentences. Moreover, it was entangled in Nazi ideology which led to racially motivated judgments in family and contract law even before the regime had formally enacted the Nuremberg Race Laws in 1935.[4]

---

[2]These statutes are commonly referred to as the Imperial Judicial Acts (*Reichsjustizgesetze*). They entered into force on 1 October 1879.

[3]See the account given by the *Bundesgerichtshof (BGH)*, *Neue Juristische Wochenschrift (NJW)*, 1952, p. 937.

[4]See, e.g., Imperial Court of Justice, *Entscheidungen des Reichsgerichts in Zivilsachen (RGZ)*, vol 147, pp. 65, 68, dealing with the duty to respect 'aryan values' in education.

From 1495 to 1806 the Imperial Chamber Court (*Reichskammergericht*), seated in Wetzlar (from 1689), was the highest Court of Justice in the Holy Roman Empire. The court mainly dealt with appeals against the civil judgments of inferior courts.[5] However, as the competence of the *Reichskammergericht* posed a threat to the power of the princes of the empire, they strove to undermine the possibility to appeal against the judgments of the local courts within their territories. Consequently, most of them obtained (in exchange for an adequate counter performance) a *privilegium de non appellando* which banned appeals to the *Reichskammergericht*, thus severely limiting the practical influence of the court.

It may come as a surprise to foreign lawyers that the highest courts are, and almost always have been, located outside the capital city. This can be explained as a consequence of German particularism, in modern times in the guise of federalism. It creates a certain balance of power and is deeply engrained in the DNA of the German justice system.

1.2 The Structure of the Federal Supreme Court

1.2.1 Internal Organisation

There are 133 judges working at the *Bundesgerichtshof* (Civil and Criminal Divisions).[6] The Civil Division of the court has 84 judges; it is divided into 12 senates sitting in panels of five judges, with each senate having predefined competences and specialisations.[7] The First Senate, for instance, deals with intellectual property and copyright law, the Second Senate deals with company law, the Eleventh Senate with banking and capital markets law, etc.[8] As a matter of internal organisation a senate may defer a case to another senate if it finds unanimously that the legal points raised fall under the competence of that senate. Pursuant to Article 101(1) *GG*, '[N]o one

---

[5]See amply Weitzel (1976).

[6]As of 31 December 2016. See the data provided by the Federal Office of Justice (*Bundesamt für Justiz*) at https://www.bundesjustizamt.de/DE/Themen/Buergerdienste/Justizstatistik/Personal/Personal_node.html. Accessed 28 May 2019. Other Federal Supreme Courts: Federal Constitutional Court (*Bundesverfassungsgericht*): 16 judges; Federal Administrative Court (*Bundesverwaltungsgericht*): 55 judges; Federal Finance Court (*Bundesfinanzhof*): 59 judges; Federal Labour Court (*Bundesarbeitsgericht*): 39 judges; Federal Social Court (*Bundessozialgericht*): 42 judges; Federal Patent Court (*Bundespatentgericht*): 107.8 judges (the number combines full- and part-time appointments); Military Court (*Truppendienstgericht*): 12 judges.

[7]There are other senates, such as the Cartel Claims Senate; see the overview at http://www.bundesgerichtshof.de/DE/DasGericht/Geschaeftsverteilung/SachlicheZustaendigkeit/WeitereSenate/weitereSenate_node.html. Accessed 28 May 2019.

[8]See the detailed organisational plan (*Geschäftsverteilungsplan*). https://www.bundesgerichtshof.de/DE/DasGericht/Geschaeftsverteilung/Geschaeftsverteilungsplan2019/Zivilsenate2019/zivilsenate2019_node.html. Accessed 28 May 2019.

may be removed from the jurisdiction of his lawful judge.' As opposed to many other jurisdictions, in Germany the lawful judge must be determined in a random manner to avoid the possibility that cases may be conferred ad hoc on certain judges for political (or other) reasons. Certainly, the degree of specialisation also helps raise the quality of decisions. To ensure uniformity within the 12 senates of the *Bundesgerichtshof* a Grand Chamber (*Großer Senat für Zivilsachen*) will convene to decide on the request of one senate wishing to deviate from the jurisprudence of other senates.[9]

As a matter of fact, mostly senior judges will be appointed as members of the Federal Court of Justice. The law, however, only prescribes that candidates must be at least 35 years of age (§ 125(2) *GVG*). As a general rule, candidates are chosen from within the judiciary.[10] It is rare for external jurists to be selected, one of the reasons being the pension system for judges, which does not welcome career changers. Pursuant to the Law on the Election of Judges (*Richterwahlgesetz—RiWG*), the competent federal minister may appoint judges of the Federal Supreme Courts together with the Judicial Election Committee (*Richterwahlausschuss*) in which the federal states are duly represented (§§ 2–7 *RiWG*). Thus, the appointment of members of the *Bundesgerichtshof* falls within the competence of the Minister of Justice. This process seems to be much less of a political nature than the appointment of judges to the Federal Constitutional Court.

Law professors are hardly ever among the candidates for the Federal Supreme Courts. They sometimes serve as part-time judges at Regional Courts of Appeal (*Oberlandesgerichte*). Even though the courts pay close attention to legal doctrine, it is impossible, under the doctrine of *iura novit curia*, to commission a legal opinion by a legal academic.

1.2.2 Special Bar of Lawyers

Pursuant to § 78(1)(3) *ZPO*, in proceedings before the *Bundesgerichtshof* the parties to the dispute must be represented by an attorney admitted to practise before the court. There are currently only 42 attorneys admitted to the *Bundesgerichtshof*.[11] Those attorneys may not plead before lower courts (§ 172 Federal Lawyers' Act (*Bundesrechtsanwaltsordnung—BRAO*)). These restrictions were set up to maintain a high standard of legal argument before the *Bundesgerichtshof*. Members of the special bar are appointed for life by an election committee which consists of the President of the *Bundesgerichtshof*, the presidents of each of the 12 Civil Senates, the members of the presidium of the Federal Bar Association as well as the presidium of the Bar Association of the *Bundesgerichtshof* (§ 165(1) *BRAO*). The only formal

---

[9] § 132 *GVG*.

[10] Note that this does not hold true for the Federal Constitutional Court, as frequently law professors are appointed as judges.

[11] Source: http://www.rak-bgh.de/. Accessed 28 May 2019.

requirements are a minimum age (35 years) as well as uninterrupted practice as an attorney for at least 5 years (§ 166(3) *BRAO*). There are no sanctions for filing unmeritorious claims to the *Bundesgerichtshof*. It will be in the best interest of each attorney to choose well-founded cases, as their reputation, among other things, builds upon a certain rate of success.

1.2.3 Other Federal Supreme Courts

There are five more Federal Supreme Courts. The Federal Administrative Court, the Federal Finance Court, the Federal Labour Court and the Federal Social Court are Supreme Courts of administrative, financial, labour and social jurisdiction. The existence of these courts is enshrined in Article 95(1) *GG*. Moreover, there is a Federal Patents Court (Article 96(1) *GG*).[12]

As a consequence of such a multitude of Federal Supreme Courts, a Common Senate of the Federal Supreme Courts (*Gemeinsamer Senat der Obersten Gerichtshöfe des Bundes*) was created (Article 95(3) *GG*).[13] The Common Senate deals with overarching legal issues in order to maintain uniformity. It convenes only rarely. One of the cases it decided concerned the admissibility of claim forms filed by way of computer fax.[14]

1.2.4 The Federal Constitutional Court

For constitutional matters, the Federal Constitutional Court (*Bundesverfassungsgericht*) was set up (Article 93(1) *GG*). The court deals with civil cases only exceptionally, namely if, on a constitutional complaint (*Verfassungsbeschwerde*), an individual alleges that one of his or her basic rights (Articles 1–20 *GG*) or other rights as set out in the Constitution have been infringed by a court (or, indeed, any other public authority).[15] The Federal Constitutional Court has shown considerable interest in civil law cases and was therefore dubbed

[12]In total, there are 436 federal judges; see the reference provided in n. 6 above.

[13]The legal basis is the *Gesetz zur Wahrung der Einheitlichkeit der Rechtsprechung der obersten Gerichtshöfe des Bundes* vom 19. Juni 1968 (*Bundesgesetzblatt [BGBl.]*, vol I, p. 661). See generally Schulte (1986).

[14]*Gemeinsamer Senat der obersten Gerichtshöfe des Bundes*, Beschluss vom 5.4.2000, Az. GmS-OGB 1/98 – *Computerfax*, *Entscheidungen des Bundesgerichtshofs in Zivilsachen (BGHZ)*, vol 144, p. 160.

[15]Between 1951 and 2018 229,899 constitutional complaints were filed with the Constitutional Court. The overall success rate, however, is only about 2.3%. A considerable part of all constitutional complaints (56,510 between 1991 and 2018) are directed against court judgments in civil cases. cf. https://www.bundesverfassungsgericht.de/DE/Verfahren/Jahresstatistiken/2018/statistik_2018_node.html. Accessed 28 May 2019.

the 'super court of appeal' (*Superrevisionsinstanz*).[16] The jurisprudence of the court has been influential on the development of private law. In the famous *Lüth* case it endorsed the doctrine of the indirect effect of fundamental rights on private law (*Drittwirkung der Grundrechte*)[17] and, through that, considerably changed private law thinking. Other landmark cases include judgments on the validity of post-contractual non-competition clauses without compensation in commercial agency,[18] and on the validity of oppressive suretyships[19] and contractual freedom in marriage contracts.[20]

However, as the catalogue of rights includes procedural guarantees such as the right to be heard, frequently the constitutional complaint is used by the aggrieved party as a last resort. In order to prevent the constitutional complaint from becoming an extraordinary appeal, the plenary Constitutional Court held in a landmark case that the legislator should enable the ordinary courts to provide redress in cases of violations of the right to be heard.[21] As a consequence, § 321a *ZPO*, which was inserted in 2002 into the Code of Civil Procedure, was amended. That provision gives the aggrieved party the right to object to the *iudex ad quem*.[22]

1.3 The Procedural Setting

1.3.1 The Court System in Civil Matters

The German civil court system consists of four levels. In the first instance, Local Courts (*Amtsgerichte*) or Regional Courts (*Landgerichte*) are competent to hear civil cases, depending on the value of the claim: Local Courts hear cases with an amount

[16]The term has been used by the Constitutional Court itself; cf. *Entscheidungen des Bundesverfassungsgerichts (BVerfGE)*, vol 7, p. 198, § 31: 'So wenig das Bundesverfassungsgericht berufen ist, als Revisions- oder gar "Superrevisions" -Instanz gegenüber den Zivilgerichten tätig zu werden, sowenig darf es von der Nachprüfung solcher Urteile allgemein absehen und an einer in ihnen etwa zutage tretenden Verkennung grundrechtlicher Normen und Maßstäbe vorübergehen.' See Krauß (1987), § 6; Hager (2006), p. 773.

[17]*BVerfGE* 7, p. 198 (*Lüth*).

[18]*BVerfGE* 81, p. 242 (*Handelsvertreter*).

[19]*BVerfGE* 89, p. 214 (*Bürgschaftsfall*).

[20]*BVerfGE* 103, p. 89 (*Ehevertrag*).

[21]*BVerfGE* 107, p. 395 (*Rechtsschutz gegen den Richter*).

[22]§ 321a(1) *ZPO* reads: 'Redress granted in the event a party's right to be given an effective and fair legal hearing has been violated. (1) Upon an objection having been filed by the party adversely affected by the decision, the proceedings are to be continued if:

1. No appellate remedy or any other legal remedy is available against the decision, and
2. The court has violated the entitlement of this party to be given an effective and fair legal hearing and this has significantly affected the decision.

No objection may be filed against any decision preceding the final decision.'

in controversy of up to €5000, whereas for all other cases the Regional Courts are competent.[23] The latter are also competent to hear appeals against decisions of the Local Courts. Higher Regional Courts (*Oberlandesgerichte*) mainly have appellate jurisdiction over decisions by Regional Courts.[24] Finally, the *Bundesgerichtshof* is the final court of appeal in civil (and criminal) matters.[25]

1.3.2 The Types of Appeal

The German Code of Civil Procedure (*Zivilprozessordnung—ZPO*) establishes three regular types of appeal:[26] ordinary appeal (*Berufung*, § 511ff. *ZPO*), appeal on points of law (*Revision*, § 542ff. *ZPO*) and complaint (*Beschwerde*, § 567ff. *ZPO*).[27] In 2001, a major reform of civil procedure was enacted.[28] It entered into force on 1 January 2002, introducing important changes to the appellate system.

According to the (still) predominant opinion in the legal literature, the German Constitution does not guarantee a right of appeal.[29] From the very beginning the Constitutional Court has shared this view.[30] While it is true that there is no explicit provision in the Basic Law conferring a right to a further instance, the constitution does guarantee judicial protection against any act of the public authority (Article 19 (4) *GG*). Clearly, courts of law are part of the public authority.[31] It follows from this, at least in the view of a number of authors, that in principle an appeal must lie against any decision of a court.[32] However, as this would lead to an infinite chain of appeals, it is up to the legislator to set limits, taking into account other constitutional values such as the principle of finality. Restrictions on access to the appellate court must be designed following the principle of proportionality.[33]

While denying such a concept in principle, the Constitutional Court did accept in a plenary decision that the Rule of Law requires a legal remedy against the violation

[23]See §§ 23, 71 *GVG*.

[24]See § 119 *GVG*.

[25]See §§ 133 and 135 *GVG*.

[26]For a brief history of the law of appeals in Germany as well as for further references see Stürner (2002), pp. 7ff.

[27]Furthermore, proceedings may be reopened under very limited conditions; see § 578ff. *ZPO*.

[28]*Gesetz zur Reform des Zivilprozesses* vom 27.7.2001 (*BGBl.* I, p. 1887).

[29]See, e.g., Schmidt-Aßmann (2003), Enders (2016), both with further references.

[30]See, e.g., *BVerfGE* 1, pp. 433, 437.

[31]The (presumably still) predominant opinion, however, takes the rather narrow view that Article 19 (4) *GG* guarantees a legal remedy *by* the judge, not *against* him ('Rechtsschutz durch, nicht gegen den Richter'; see *BVerfGE* 15, pp. 275, 280, *BVerfGE* 49, pp. 329, 340, *BVerfGE* 65, pp. 76, 90). That maxim was coined by Günter Dürig; see Dürig (1958).

[32]See Voßkuhle (1993, 2003); Stürner (2002), pp. 66ff.

[33]For that rationale see Stürner (2002), pp. 79ff.

of the right to be heard.[34] However, the court held that such a remedy may be designed in a way that could be dealt with by the *iudex a quo*, thus leaving unchanged the position taken in earlier decisions.[35]

Appeal (Berufung)

An appeal lies against the final judgments delivered by the court of first instance (§ 511(1) *ZPO*).[36] If the court of first instance was a Local Court, the appeal will be heard by the Regional Court. If a Regional Court was the court of first instance, the appeal will be heard by the Higher Regional Court. Generally, almost every case will be suitable for appellate review. Pursuant to § 511(2) *ZPO*, an appeal shall be admissible if the value of the subject matter of the appeal is greater than €600. Even for cases below that threshold, the court of first instance may grant leave to appeal, namely if the 'legal matter is of fundamental significance or wherever the further development of the law or the interests in ensuring uniform adjudication require a decision to be handed down by the court of appeal' (§ 511(4) *ZPO*). The decision to grant leave is not discretionary, as the statutory requirements just mentioned must be fulfilled. A US-type writ of certiorari is unknown to German civil procedure. Admittedly, at least on the face of it, the difference would be one of degree, as the statutory requirements under German law are relatively broadly construed. Yet, a considerable volume of case law exists to clarify exactly what a question of fundamental significance is. Once those requirements are met, the case has to be dealt with without any discretion.

The appeal has a double focus. First, it may be based on the allegation that the decision handed down was wrongly decided from a legal point of view. Second, the appellant may claim that the factual basis of the decision was wrong (§ 513(1) *ZPO*). However, there is only limited scope of review of fact-finding. As a matter of principle, the appellate court is bound by the facts established by the court of first instance. It is only where 'specific indications give rise to doubts as to the court having correctly or completely established the facts relevant for its decision' that a new fact-finding process will be permissible (§ 529(1)(1) *ZPO*).[37] Moreover, new facts and circumstances may be introduced under limited conditions (§§ 529(1)(2), 531 *ZPO*).[38]

---

[34] *BVerfGE* 107, p. 395: 'Es verstößt gegen das Rechtsstaatsprinzip in Verbindung mit Artikel 103 Absatz 1 des Grundgesetzes, wenn eine Verfahrensordnung keine fachgerichtliche Abhilfemöglichkeit für den Fall vorsieht, dass ein Gericht in entscheidungserheblicher Weise den Anspruch auf rechtliches Gehör verletzt.' This has been reiterated in *BVerfGE* 108, pp. 341, 347.

[35] See the reference in n. 30 above. The legislator reacted soon after the decision, inserting § 321a *ZPO*; see n. 22 above.

[36] For a comparative Anglo-German perspective see Stürner (2002), pp. 106ff.

[37] See Arnold (2013).

[38] § 531(2) *ZPO* reads: '(2) New means of challenge or defence are to be admitted only if they: 1. Concern an aspect that the court of first instance has recognisably failed to see or has held to be

As parties made ample use of their right to challenge court decisions, the appellate courts were flooded with unmeritorious appeals.[39] Consequently, the reform of 2001 introduced a doorkeeper: pursuant to § 522(2) *ZPO*, the appellate court may strike out such appeals if it is satisfied that:

1. The appeal manifestly has no chance of success;
2. The legal matter is not of any fundamental significance;
3. The further development of the law or the interests in ensuring uniform adjudication do not require a decision to be handed down by the court of appeal; and that
4. No hearing for oral argument is mandated.

The court may not decide on these points merely summarily. It will carry out a thorough examination of the merits of the case. Clearly, a certain margin of appreciation remains whether the prospect of success of the appeal is just absent or is manifestly absent.[40] The parties will be informed of the intention of the court to strike out the appeal, and the appellant will get the opportunity to submit his position within a period of time to be set (§ 522(3) *ZPO*).[41] The decision to strike out the appeal will render an oral hearing unnecessary and thus save time and costs.

Immediately after the reform introducing the possibility to strike out unmeritorious appeals the situation was unsatisfactory, as court practice varied considerably. Some courts struck out almost 60% of appeals, others only 20% or so.[42] There was no way to attack the decision of the court. In 2011, the legislator introduced an important change.[43] Pursuant to the new § 522(3) *ZPO*, the unsuccessful appellant may attack the decision striking out the appeal with an appeal on points of law under the same conditions as if a full judgment were handed down by the appellate court. This led to a significant increase in the number of new cases.[44]

insignificant; 2. Were not asserted in the proceedings before the court of first instance due to a defect in the proceedings; or 3. Were not asserted in the proceedings before the court of first instance, without this being due to the negligence of the party.'

[39]Germany was sometimes seen as a *Rechtsmittelstaat* (the term plays with the central notion of *Rechtsstaat*, i.e. a state governed by the Rule of Law; *Rechtsmittel* means 'appeal'): see, e.g., Justizministerium Baden-Württemberg (1999); some commentators ironically referred to the German '*Instanzenseeligkeit*'; cf. Zeidler (1983), p. 253; Sendler (1982), p. 164.

[40]cf. Rimmelspacher (2016).

[41]See Weller (2011).

[42]cf. Greger (2004), p. 813.

[43]*Gesetz zur Änderung des § 522 der Zivilprozessordnung* vom 21.10.2011 (*BGBl.* I, p. 2082), in force since 27 October 2011.

[44]See Sect. 1.5.1 below.

Appeal on Points of Law (*Revision*)

Pursuant to § 542(1) *ZPO*, 'An appeal on points of law may be filed against the final judgments delivered by the appellate instance on fact and law.'[45] Such appeals on points of law will be heard by the *Bundesgerichtshof* (§ 133 *GVG*). The goal of the appellate proceedings is revision, not cassation. This means that in the event of a successful appeal the judgment of the lower court will not just be quashed. The *Bundesgerichtshof* may hand down a decision on the merits, provided that 'the judgment is reversed only due to a violation of the law, in application of the law to the situation of fact as established, and if in light of said situation the matter is ready for the final decision to be taken' (§ 563(3) *ZPO*). Pursuant to § 566(1) *ZPO*, a so-called leapfrog appeal (*Sprungrevision*) may be brought against the final judgments of first instance courts provided that the defendant consents and the appellate court allows the appeal.

In family matters the appeal on points of law is called *Rechtsbeschwerde*; it is regulated in § 70 of the Act on Proceedings in Family Matters and in Matters of Non-contentious Jurisdiction (*Gesetz über das Verfahren in Familiensachen und in den Angelegenheiten der freiwilligen Gerichtsbarkeit—FamFG*). It basically follows the same pattern as *Revision* in civil cases. It will also be heard by the *Bundesgerichtshof*.

Complaint (*Beschwerde*) and Complaint on Points of Law (*Rechtsbeschwerde*)

The Code of Civil Procedure sets up a third type of remedy: the so-called complaint. A complaint may be filed against the decisions delivered by the Local Courts and Regional Courts in proceedings before them as courts of first instance provided that those decisions did not require an oral hearing and did not dismiss a petition concerning the proceedings (§ 567 *ZPO*). The complaint will be dealt with in this contribution only insofar as it concerns access to the *Bundesgerichtshof*, namely in the form of the complaint against denial of leave to appeal (§ 544 *ZPO*: *Nichtzulassungsbeschwerde*) and the complaint on points of law (§ 574 *ZPO*: *Rechtsbeschwerde*).

1.3.3 Restricting Access to the *Bundesgerichtshof*

Clearly, access to the highest instance has to be restricted in order to enable the court to concentrate on those cases which merit closer attention because they raise

[45] Before the reform of 2001 there was no *Revision* against final appellate judgments of the Regional Courts.

important legal issues for society at large.[46] One model confers the power to choose those cases on the Supreme Court (example: the USA).[47] Other models mainly entrust the appellate courts with that responsibility (example: Germany).[48] A third model combines both approaches (example: the UK).[49]

The System as It Was Before 2002

The major reform of civil procedure of 2001 mainly concerned the (ordinary) appeal (*Berufung*), but also brought about some changes to the appeal on points of law. Before that reform, access to the *Bundesgerichtshof* was possible within two different constellations:[50] (*a*) in cases where the value of the claim was below DM60,000 (or €30,000), leave had to be granted by the appellate court (*Zulassungsrevision*); (*b*) where the value of the claim was above that sum, appeal was possible without leave of the court (*Wertrevision*). However, the *Bundesgerichtshof* had the power to dismiss such appeals with a majority of two-thirds of the members of the senate provided that the case did not raise any legal matters of fundamental significance[51] and was obviously unmeritorious.[52] That provision was criticised, as about 80% of all cases did not qualify for an appeal on points of law.[53] The functions of the *Bundesgerichtshof* to clarify and develop the law were not properly served.

Leave to Appeal[54]

By Lower Court The basic assumption is that the appellate court (the *iudex a quo*) has the best knowledge of the case and, consequently, is in a position to evaluate the case's suitability for appellate review. Thus, § 543(1)(1) *ZPO* provides that an appeal on points of law may be lodged only if it is admitted by the appellate court. As a matter of law, not discretion, an appeal on points of law is to be admitted if: (*a*) the legal matter is of fundamental significance or (*b*) the further development of the law

[46]See generally Domej (2014).

[47]28 USC § 1254(1), § 1257(a). See Schack (2011), note 7 with references.

[48]Note, however, that there is a complaint against denial of leave to appeal (§ 544 *ZPO*: *Nichtzulassungsbeschwerde*). See on Appeal Against Denial of Admission (*Nichtzulassungsbeschwerde*) below.

[49]Andrews (2013), Chapter 15. See Article 40 Constitutional Reform Act 2005. http://www.legislation.gov.uk/ukpga/2005/4/section/40. Accessed 28 May 2019.

[50]§ 546 *ZPO* as of 2001. See amply Prütting (1997).

[51]*Nichtannahmebeschluss*, § 554b *ZPO* as of 2001.

[52]cf. *BVerfGE* 54, p. 277.

[53]See *Bericht zur Rechtsmittelreform in Zivilsachen*, C.1.1.1.2. This report can be downloaded at http://gesmat.bundesgerichtshof.de/gesetzesmaterialien/15_wp/Zivilprozessreformgesetz/b_rechtsmittelr_zs-index.htm. Accessed 28 May 2019.

[54]cf. Althammer (2014), pp. 98ff.

or the interests in ensuring uniform adjudication require a decision to be handed down by the court hearing the appeal on points of law (§ 543(2) *ZPO*). The court hearing the appeal on points of law is bound by the decision of the lower court. Those reasons for admittance reiterate the model of the ordinary appeal (§ 511 (4) *ZPO*).[55] They ensure that the public interest in uniform adjudication and clarification of the law will be duly served.[56]

Appeal Against Denial of Admission (Nichtzulassungsbeschwerde) The decision of the appellate court is not final. In cases where leave to appeal is denied by the *iudex a quo* the aggrieved party may lodge a complaint against the denial of leave to appeal pursuant to § 544 *ZPO*. The complainant must set out the grounds on which leave to file an appeal should be granted (§ 544(2)(3) *ZPO*)—these are identical to those set out in § 543(2) *ZPO*.

Consequently, the mere fact that the decision by the appeal court was wrong does not justify the complaint. Even blatantly wrong decisions or violations of fundamental procedural rights will not fulfil the criterion of ensuring uniform adjudication. There will only be fundamental legal significance if the case was decided arbitrarily and a constitutional complaint would be manifestly well founded.[57] The individual interest in receiving a correct judgment ranks lower than the public interest in clarifying and developing the law. A reform act of 2013[58] further strengthened the public dimension of *Revision*: pursuant to § 555(3) *ZPO*, a judgment based on the respondent's acknowledgment (*Anerkenntnisurteil*) shall be handed down only where the claimant has filed a separate petition to this effect; insofar as the law diverges from the basic principle enshrined in § 307 *ZPO*, which mirrors the parties' freedom to dispose of the claim on the merits at stake (*Dispositionsmaxime*). By the same token, pursuant to § 565 *ZPO*, *Revision* may be withdrawn without the consent of the respondent only prior to the time at which the respondent commences oral argument on the merits of the case. The reform can be seen as a reaction to the fact that large corporate respondents (e.g. banks, insurance companies) have tried to drop out of proceedings as soon as they realised that the case was lost, in order to avoid the full judgment (§ 313b(1) *ZPO*).[59] Note that the legislator thereby returned to the law as it stood before the reform of 2001.

The Code of Civil Procedure does not contain any monetary threshold. The old system was done away with in 2001, as the legislator acknowledged that the

[55] See Sect. 1.2.1 above.

[56] cf. *BGHZ* 152, p. 182.

[57] cf. *BGHZ* 152, p. 182.

[58] *Gesetz zur Förderung des elektronischen Rechtsverkehrs mit den Gerichten* vom 10.10.2013 (*BGBl*. I, p. 3786). It entered into force on 1 January 2014.

[59] cf. Winter (2014).

fundamental importance of a case was in no way determined by the value of the claim.[60] However, the old system was somehow conserved by the back door: the transitional provision hidden in § 26(8) of the Introductory Act to the Code of Civil Procedure (*Einführungsgesetz zur Zivilprozessordnung—EGZPO*) provides that the value of the claim (*Wert der Beschwer*) must be above €20,000. Otherwise no complaint will be possible against a denial by the appellate court to grant leave to appeal. That regime was extended to 30 June 2018 and then further extended to 31 December 2019.[61] As of 1 January 2020, the pertinent rule was transferred to § 544 (2)(1) *ZPO* and will from now on apply without any temporal restrictions.

Striking Out Revisions

The *Bundesgerichtshof* may strike out unmeritorious appeals on points of law: pursuant to § 552a *ZPO*, the court shall dismiss by unanimous decision the appeal on points of law admitted by the court of appeal if the court hearing the appeal on points of law is convinced that the prerequisites for admitting the appeal have not been met and that the appeal on points of law has no chance of success. Just as in second-tier appeals[62] the court has to carry out a full-blown examination of the merits of the appeal. A prima facie case of lack of success will not suffice.[63]

1.3.4 Grounds for Appeal (*Revisionsgründe*)

As opposed to the ordinary appeal, the appeal on points of law is restricted to legal matters.

---

[60] *Referentenentwurf eines Gesetzes zur Reform des Zivilprozesses* vom 23.12.1999, pp. 83ff. The full text can be downloaded at http://www.gesmat.bundesgerichtshof.de/gesetzesmaterialien/15_wp/Zivilprozessreformgesetz/RefE.pdf. Accessed 28 May 2019.

[61] The *Zweites Gesetz zur Modernisierung der Justiz* vom 22.12.2006 (*BGBl.* I, p. 3416) extended the sunset clause from 2006 until 2011; the *Gesetz zur Änderung des § 522 ZPO* vom 21.10.2011 (*BGBl.* I, p. 2082) brought about a further extension from 2011 until 2014. The *Gesetz zur Erleichterung der Umsetzung der Grundbuchamtsreform in Baden-Württemberg sowie zur Änderung des Gesetzes betreffend die Einführung der Zivilprozessordnung und des Wohnungseigentumsgesetzes* vom 5.12.2014 (*BGBl.* I, p. 1962) extended that provision until 31 December 2016. The *Drittes Gesetz zur Änderung der Insolvenzordnung und zur Änderung des Gesetzes, betreffend die Einführung der Zivilprozessordnung* vom 22.12.2016 (*BGBl.* I, p. 3147) brought about a further extension until 30 June 2018. The *Gesetz zur Änderung des Gesetzes, betreffend die Einführung der Zivilprozessordnung* vom 21.6.2018 (*BGBl.* I, p. 863) extended the provision unil 31 December 2019. The provision was held to be constitutional; see *BGH Neue Juristische Wochenschrift – Rechtsprechungs-Report (NJW-RR)*, 2003, p. 645.

[62] § 522(2) *ZPO*; see Section Appeal (*Berufung*) above.

[63] See Krüger (2016).

Violation of the Law

Pursuant to § 545(1) *ZPO*, 'An appeal on points of law may only be based on the reason that the contested decision is based on a violation of the law.' § 546 *ZPO* defines a violation of the law as an instance where 'a legal norm has not been applied, or has not been applied properly.' Such mistakes can be wrong applications of substantive provisions, for instance a misguided interpretation of the notion of 'intention' in delictual responsibility pursuant to § 823 of the Civil Code (*BGB*)[64] or a wrong inference drawn from the facts, e.g. the lower court's factual findings do not justify the assumption that the defendant has acted intentionally,[65] or procedural mistakes are under review. A violation of the rules of evidence (e.g. the principle of evaluation of evidence at the court's discretion pursuant to § 286 *ZPO*) could also justify the appeal.

There has to be a causal link between the violation of the law and the judgment of the lower court. It may happen that the *Bundesgerichtshof* finds a violation of the law but nevertheless upholds the judgment appealed against, as the outcome, e.g. denial of the claim, is justified. However, § 547 *ZPO* defines cases in which the decision of the appellate court is always to be regarded as unlawful ('absolute' reasons for an appeal on points of law). Such mistakes are considered to be so grave that leaving them unsanctioned may distort public confidence in the administration of justice. This concerns the following mistakes:

(1) the composition of the court was not compliant with the relevant provisions;
(2) a judge was involved in the decision who, by law, was prohibited from holding judicial office, unless this impediment was asserted by a motion to recuse the judge without meeting with success;
(3) a judge was involved in the decision although he had been recused for fear of bias and the motion to so recuse him had been declared justified;
(4) a party to the proceedings was not represented in accordance with the stipulations of the law, unless it expressly or tacitly approved the litigation;
(5) the decision has been given based on a hearing for oral argument in which the rules regarding the admission of the public to the proceedings were violated;
(6) contrary to the provisions of the Code, the decision does not set out the reasons for the judgment.

Factual Basis

As to the relevant facts, there are, of course, important restrictions. The factual basis of appellate control consists in the findings of the lower court that 'are apparent from the appellate judgment or the record of the session of the court' (§ 559(1) *ZPO*). The

---

[64]The German terminology is *Interpretationsfehler*.

[65]The German terminology is *Subsumtionsfehler*.

Bundesgerichtshof does not embark on a new assessment of factual allegations, it does not elicit evidence. The parties may not introduce new factual allegations even though they may have come into existence after the appellate proceedings before the lower court.[66] The findings of the lower court with regard to factual allegations being true or untrue will be binding for the purposes of the appeal on points of law. The only exception to this rule concerns the situation in which the appellant has challenged the fact-finding process of the lower court by an admissible and justified petition (§ 559(2) *ZPO*).

1.3.5 A Successful Appeal on Points of Law

Pursuant to § 562(1) *ZPO*, to the extent the appeal on points of law is deemed justified, the contested judgment is to be reversed. This also includes factual findings of the lower court, provided that those findings were based on procedural errors. There are two possible ways to go forward:

1. The matter may be remanded to the appellate court, which is to hear it once again and decide on it. The appellate court is to base its decision on the legal assessment on which the reversal of the judgment was based (§ 563(1) and (2) *ZPO*)[67]—a rare instance where German law adheres to the doctrine of binding precedent.[68] That would be the model of cassation;
2. The powers of the *Bundesgerichtshof* go beyond that: in the event the judgment is reversed only due to a violation of the law, the court may decide on the merits in application of the law to the situation of fact as established, and if in light of said situation the matter is ready for the final decision to be taken (§ 563(3) *ZPO*).

1.4 Workflow: Case Management

1.4.1 Preliminary Selection of Cases

The weeding out of unmeritorious cases is done in several stages. Appellate courts and the *Bundesgerichtshof* share the responsibility for that task. The lower court, which probably knows the case best, decides on the admissibility of the appeal. This seems convincing with regard to the further development of the law or the interests

[66]For exceptions see Reichold (2016).

[67]Example: *BGH NJW* 2004, p. 2736: referral to the court of appeal which does not want to follow; judgment is again attacked; see *BGH NJW* 2007, p. 1227. On the point see generally Bartels (2009) and Madaus (2013).

[68]Another concerns decisions of the Constitutional Court, which are binding on all lower courts pursuant to § 31 Act on the Constitutional Court (*Bundesverfassungsgerichtsgesetz – BVerfGG*).

in ensuring uniform adjudication, but may be less so for the question of fundamental legal significance, as this implies errors of law made by the appellate court itself.[69]

However, an appeal lies against the decision of the appellate court not to give leave to appeal (*Nichtzulassungsbeschwerde*). The parties mostly see this as a last chance to get access to the *Bundesgerichtshof*. Consequently, with six out of seven new cases in civil and commercial matters, this is by far the most important type in numbers.

Arguably, the most important filter consists in the need for a special counsel to bring the appeal pursuant to § 78 (1)(3) *ZPO*. As there are only 45 advocates admitted to the *Bundesgerichtshof*,[70] these specialists closely scrutinise every potential case and perform a very useful filter function.

Summary judgments are rendered on the basis of written proceedings (§§ 544(4)(1) and 128(4) *ZPO*), while in other appeals there is an oral hearing. Summary judgments without an oral hearing are usually signed by a two-judge panel,[71] while all other judgments are signed by all five members of the senate.

1.4.2 Inferior Judges/Law Clerks

There are no inferior judges in the formal sense (such as master or registrar in England and Wales). But like every court, the *Bundesgerichtshof* is supported by a court registry.[72] Each senate has its own registry with two or three clerks working there. These clerks of the court registry (*Urkundsbeamten der Geschäftsstelle*) are entrusted with organisational work and inferior juridical tasks such as maintaining files, calculating costs and proofreading draft judgments. However, they are not involved in the case management process, e.g. they do not set time limits.

On the more informal side, the *Bundesgerichtshof* has an academic staff of approximately 50 people (*Wissenschaftliche Mitarbeiter beim Bundesgerichtshof*, colloquially called *Hiwis*),[73] all promising junior judges, who serve a 3-year term before returning to their Local Court or administrative body.[74] It is their task to do the preparatory legal work for the senate. This could consist in an account of the relevant case law to a given legal problem, but not infrequently draft judgments are

[69]See Stürner (2002), pp. 116ff.

[70]In German, *Rechtsanwälte beim Bundesgerichtshof*.

[71]§ 14(1) and (2) *Geschäftsordnung des Bundesgerichtshofs*.

[72]§ 153 *GVG*.

[73]The correct legal terminology would be *Wissenschaftliche Hilfskräfte* (§ 193(1) *GVG*), hence the abbreviation *Hiwi*. See amply Bichlmeir (1971).

[74]The legal basis is § 37 Judiciary Act (*Deutsches Richtergesetz—DRiG*).

prepared.[75] *Hiwis* may attend the deliberations of a senate.[76] Such a term of service could be a springboard for the career of the *Hiwis*, but there are further options, such as *Hiwi* at the Federal Constitutional Court,[77] or on secondment to a federal ministry or a European Union institution.

1.4.3 Writing the Judgment

With regard to the cases going on appeal, the president of each senate allocates a file to one of the judges, the rapporteur (*Berichterstatter*).[78] Each judgment, whether rendered after an oral hearing or not, is given in writing. However, in the case of a decision without an oral hearing (*Beschluss*) the rapporteur may give his account orally, while in all other cases he will do so in writing.[79] When presenting the case to the panel, usually a week or so before the oral hearing, the rapporteur sets out the main lines of the draft judgment, which is then discussed by the full panel.

1.5 Caseload

1.5.1 Intake

In 2002, a peak of 4595 appeals were counted, most of these appeals being lodged under the old system. Afterwards, the numbers declined in a significant manner (Table 1).

In 2018, in 488 cases (13.6%) leave was given by the lower court (*Revisionszulassung*);[80] all the others (3600 cases) were complaints against the denial of leave by the lower court (*Nichtzulassungsbeschwerden*).[81]

The total intake is higher indeed, as a number of other appeals are dealt with by the *Bundesgerichtshof*, especially the appeal on points of law (*Rechtsbeschwerde*, §

[75]In German these drafts are informally called *Vorvotum* (pre-draft), as the drafts prepared by the *Berichterstatter* (rapporteur) will be called *Votum* (draft). These drafts serve as a basis for the decision of the five-member senate.

[76]§ 193(1) *GVG*, but the presiding judge may exclude their presence.

[77]There are around 65 *Hiwis* at the Constitutional Court. They are informally referred to as the 'Third Senate,' making reference to the importance of their work.

[78]§ 140 *GVG* allows for a delegation to the court itself. The *Geschäftsordnung des Bundesgerichtshofs* has a rule on the rapporteur in § 8.

[79]§ 8(1) and (2) *Geschäftsordnung des Bundesgerichtshofs*.

[80]When also counting appeals on the basis of special legislation such as appeals (*Berufungen*) in patent law or complaints on points of law (*Rechtsbeschwerden*) in energy law and in competition law the number of incoming cases amounts to a total of 6743.

[81]Taking into account complaints pursuant to § 544(1) *ZPO* as well as § 522(3) *ZPO*; also considering applications for leapfrog appeal pursuant to § 566(1) *ZPO*.

Table 1 New *Revisionen* and *Nichtzulassungsbeschwerden* (Source: *Annual Report* (*Jahresstatistik*) *2018*)[a]

Senates	2006	2007	2008	2009	2010	2011	2012	2013	2014	2015	2016	2017	2018
I	235	219	212	208	230	236	243	228	271	270	269	229	226
II	297	283	277	295	252	288	382	424	358	382	347	456	455
III	307	321	319	339	259	295	425	548	391	457	605	374	259
IV	326	343	275	248	288	274	422	447	528	560	400	322	326
V	273	216	248	240	275	277	301	314	291	270	306	345	324
VI	273	312	335	352	335	372	553	560	551	711	629	510	518
VII	240	223	259	200	227	257	363	351	306	310	321	292	262
VIII	339	328	351	338	347	375	416	376	357	299	299	289	400
IX	251	227	232	241	214	212	326	297	305	252	252	292	348
X	88	112	77	29	41	82	103	69	66	87	88	84	119
Xa	–	–	–	46	39	–	–	–	–	–	–	–	–
XI	441	590	390	382	464	511	504	478	548	588	792	766	681
XII	209	176	207	210	159	139	156	195	143	161	130	127	121
Kartellsenat[b]	23	38	26	38	29	25	31	31	30	20	37	34	31
Dienstgericht[c]	4	4	7	3	10	-	4	6	6	4	3	2	2
Senat f. LWS[d]	13	12	15	23	10	14	9	24	7	6	10	5	16
Total	**3319**	**3404**	**3230**	**3192**	**3179**	**3357**	**4238**	**4348**	**4158**	**4377**	**4545**	**4127**	**4088**

[a]*Annual Report 2018*. https://www.bundesgerichtshof.de/SharedDocs/Downloads/DE/Service/StatistikZivil/jahresstatistikZivilsenate2018.pdf?__blob=publicationFile&v=3, p. 6. Accessed 28 May 2019

[b]Cartell Claims Senate

[c]Civil Service Senate

[d]Senate for Agricultural Matters (*Senat für Landwirtschaftssachen*)

70 *FamFG*) in family cases. In 2018, there was a total intake of 6117 cases, as opposed to 6316 in 2017 and 6531 in 2016.[82]

Notably, from 2011 to 2012 the number of cases rose from 3357 to 4238. Clearly, this was the result of the newly introduced § 522(3) *ZPO*, according to which the unsuccessful appellant may attack the decision striking out the appeal with an appeal on points of law under the same conditions as if a full judgment were handed down by the appellate court:

- In 2012 there were 623 such appeals (but counting only from 23 March 2012);
- In 2013 there were 987;
- In 2014 there were 995;
- In 2015 there were 1224;
- In 2016 there were 1370;
- In 2017 there were 1251;
- In 2018 there were 1298.

The success rate of this type of appeal is strikingly low: on average, between 2% and 4% are accepted by the *Bundesgerichtshof*.

1.5.2 Judgment on the Merits

In 2015, 4219 civil cases were disposed of (6228 if other appeals are counted):

- In 681 cases (or 16.14%) final judgment ('on the merits') was given;
- In 2085 cases (or 49.42%) leave to appeal was denied (*Erfolglosigkeit der Nichtzulassungsbeschwerde*);
- 1113 appeals against denial to grant leave (*Nichtzulassungsbeschwerden*) (or 26.38%) were inadmissible (*unzulässig*) or were withdrawn;
- In only 249 cases (or 7.08%) the complaint against denial of leave (*Nichtzulassungsbeschwerde*) was successful;
- Only 74 (or 10.12%) of those appeals where leave was given by the lower court (731) were struck out for obviously being unmeritorious (§ 552a *ZPO*).

1.5.3 Evolution of Caseload Over the Years

Table 2 shows that there is an increasing number of cases pending before the *Bundesgerichtshof*. Note the sudden rise from 2011 to 2012. Apart from that the curve is relatively stable.

[82]The number of *Rechtsbeschwerden* was on the decline after a peak in 2010, but seems to have gone up again lately: 1563 in 2018; 1689 in 2017; 1528 in 2016; 1594 in 2015; 1544 in 2014; 1550 in 2013; 1617 in 2012; 1848 in 2011; 1920 in 2010; 1365 in 2009; 1343 in 2008; and 1267 in 2007.

Table 2 Pending *Revisionen* and *Nichtzulassungsbeschwerden*[a]

Senates	2006	2007	2008	2009	2010	2011	2012	2013	2014	2015	2016	2017	2018
I	380	395	378	349	287	273	292	248	296	273	282	243	237
II	310	306	281	324	333	364	444	476	352	363	388	473	436
III	270	298	267	301	260	209	328	414	322	338	405	308	192
IV	427	504	386	339	318	277	386	380	516	535	428	273	262
V	151	162	163	149	180	186	233	248	202	183	199	260	270
VI	211	258	295	338	288	326	440	504	507	676	630	495	503
VII	196	217	249	251	275	304	392	406	424	477	469	434	387
VIII	355	371	392	402	351	281	295	293	240	230	241	232	323
IX	402	398	366	337	326	302	349	356	354	335	358	329	337
X	143	140	140	43	53	109	119	93	82	100	99	108	97
Xa	–	–	–	56	37	–	–	–	–	–	–	–	–
XI	435	524	356	416	467	500	523	483	564	497	746	625	561
XII	290	258	278	282	214	203	182	194	153	163	120	88	101
Kartellsenat	25	37	39	45	28	29	31	24	32	32	44	55	63
Dienstgericht	3	3	6	5	10	2	3	5	7	5	6	1	2
Senat f. LWS	8	6	7	9	7	10	5	19	4	5	7	2	11
Total	**3606**	**3877**	**3603**	**3646**	**3434**	**3375**	**4022**	**4143**	**4055**	**4212**	**4422**	**3926**	**3782**

[a]*Annual Report 2018*, p. 22

2 Overload Problem

2.1 Symptoms of Overload

Arguably, the backlog of cases and the duration of proceedings are the clearest signals of overload. While the backlog is relatively stable at around 4000 cases, the duration varies greatly. It is difficult to provide an average duration of the proceedings before the *Bundesgerichtshof*. The official statistics indicate that slightly more than 50% of all appeals are disposed of in less than 12 months.[83]

These statistics indicate that there is no major overload problem. More specifically, recent years have not shown a reduction in the level of detail in the decisions rendered by the court. To the contrary, it sometimes seems that the *Bundesgerichtshof* gets bogged down in too many details, such as extensive citations of literature and old case law, the reason being the availability of such information in databases.

By the same token, it has not been a strategy of the *Bundesgerichtshof* to create new ways to weed out cases. The court disposes of various means to get rid of unmeritorious cases, above all by striking out unmeritorious appeals on points of law pursuant to § 552a *ZPO*, i.e. appeals which were given leave by the lower court. Similarly, the summary judgments pursuant to § 544 *ZPO* provide for a basis on which the court could get rid of a large number of cases. It has not, however, been argued that the court acts overly restrictive with regard to the granting of leave to appeal, as the following data demonstrate.

Striking out *Revisionen* pursuant to § 552a *ZPO*:

- 2018: 488 appeals with leave, 57 (or 11.68%) struck out;
- 2017: 641 appeals with leave, 48 (or 7.49%) struck out;
- 2016: 679 appeals with leave, 48 (or 7.07%) struck out;
- 2015: 731 appeals with leave, 74 (or 10.12%) struck out;
- 2014: 776 appeals with leave, 37 (or 4.76%) struck out;
- 2013: 715 appeals with leave, 62 (or 8.67%) struck out;
- 2012: 737 appeals with leave, 75 (or 10.18%) struck out;
- 2011: 837 appeals with leave, 116 (or 13.27%) struck out.

Clearly, the jurisprudence of the Constitutional Court prevents the *Bundesgerichtshof* from narrowing down the grounds for appeal. Under § 321a *ZPO*, the right to be heard must always be a ground for review. Rather, already at the level of the first appeal, many courts have established a very restrictive attitude with regard to the granting of leave pursuant to § 522(2) *ZPO*.

---

[83] *Annual Report 2018*, pp. 32ff.

2.2 Crisis and Reform Movement

The last major debate about a crisis in the civil justice system was heard about two decades ago. It resulted in the major reform of 2001. At the moment, the pendulum seems to have swung back in the opposite direction, as the overall case intake in the lower instances is on a steady and significant decline. The role of the *Bundesgerichtshof* is not the focal point of the debate.

Over the last 20 years there has been a steady decline in the number of cases before the civil courts.[84] From 1995 (418,807 new cases) to 2013 (358,792 new cases) the number of cases pending at the regional courts (*Landgerichte*) dropped by 14.33%, between 2004 (439,829 new cases) and 2013 even by 18.42%. The decline is especially significant for large-scale commercial cases which are adjudicated by a specialised division of the *Landgericht*, the *Kammer für Handelssachen*: statistics reveal that the number of cases dropped by 45.7% between 1995 and 2013.[85]

In the Local Courts (*Amtsgerichte*), from 1995 (1,751,448 new cases) to 2013 (1,138,419 new cases) there was a drop of 35% in the number of cases.[86]

While the general situation in Germany has seen the presence of only sectorial consumer ADR mechanisms, notably for insurance, banking and transport cases,[87] concerns have been raised that the litigation landscape may undergo profound changes, as the implementation of the ADR Directive[88] requires Member States to ensure that basically all disputes between consumers and traders concerning contractual obligations stemming from sales or service contracts can be submitted to an ADR entity. The relevant legislation in Germany is the *Gesetz über die alternative Streitbeilegung in Verbrauchersachen* (*Verbraucherstreitbeilegungsgesetz—VSBG*) of 19 February 2016.[89] Leading representatives of the German judiciary have expressed worry that this might entail drastic consequences for the way disputes are settled. President of the *Bundesgerichtshof* Bettina Limperg fears an erosion of the monopoly on adjudication.[90] In a somewhat more optimistic view, Professor Reinhard Gaier, a senior judge at the *Bundesverfassungsgericht*, calls for an enhanced cross-linkage between ADR and state courts.[91] However, a few years

---

[84]See the account given by Wolf (2015).

[85]See Wolf (2015); data provided by Graf-Schlicker (2014), p. 575, indicates that from 2004 to 2012 there was a 32.4% decline in the number of cases disposed of.

[86]See Wolf (2015), p. 1657.

[87]For an overview see Benöhr et al. (2012), pp. 90ff.

[88]Directive 2013/11/EU of the European Parliament and of the Council of 21 May 2013 on alternative dispute resolution for consumer disputes and amending Regulation (EC) No. 2006/2004 and Directive 2009/22/EC (Directive on consumer ADR), O.J. No. L 165 of 18 June 2013, p. 63.

[89]*BGBl.* I, 254, p. 1039. The *VSBG* entered into force on 1 April 2016.

[90]See Limperg (2015), p. 228. See also Roth (2013, 2015), Eidenmüller and Engel (2013), Wagner (2014), Rühl (2014), Meller-Hannich et al. (2014) and Stürner et al. (2014).

[91]See Gaier (2016).

after the entry into force of the *VSBG*, consumer ADR seems not to be a major competitor to litigation before the courts as many businesses are unwilling to accept this dispute resolution mechanism.

The decline in the number of cases in the lower courts suggests that there might also be a reduction in the caseload at the *Bundesgerichtshof* in the future. However, there is no clear evidence in this respect, as the number of cases has been relatively stable in the past decade despite the decline in the number of proceedings in the first instance just shown. There is a certain concern that the *Bundesgerichtshof* does not get the important cases. In that context, an alliance formed by the legal professions and the chambers of commerce and industry has launched an initiative titled 'Law – Made in Germany.'[92] The Federal Ministry of Justice supports this initiative.[93] Its main aim is an information campaign on the advantages of the German legal system.[94] However, without structural reforms such initiatives may not be as convincing as they could be. The federal government basically proposes to confer on the federal states (*Bundesländer*) the power to establish specialised court divisions.[95] A Working Group set up to that end by the *Länder* has made preliminary suggestions to make civil litigation more efficient.[96] The Working Group proposes to set up specialised court divisions for construction disputes, medical malpractice disputes and capital market disputes. Furthermore, it suggests extending the competence of Local Courts (*Amtsgerichte*) to a value of the claim of €10,000. The threshold for the small claims procedure, currently €600 pursuant to § 495a *ZPO*, should be raised to €2000. It remains to be seen whether, and in what form, these ideas reach the parliamentary stage.[97]

2.3 *Caseload and Functions*

The *Bundesgerichtshof* performs a dual role of error control, and clarification and development of the law. The reform of 2001 has brought about a certain turn towards

---

[92] See http://www.lawmadeingermany.de. Accessed 28 May 2019. Partners are: *Bundesnotarkammer*, *Deutscher Anwaltsverein*, *Deutsche Notarverein*, *Bundesrechtsanwaltskammer*, *Deutscher Richterbund*, and *Deutscher Industrie- und Handelskammertag*.

[93] As reiterated in the Coalition Agreement (*Koalitionsvertrag*) of 2013, p. 154; cf. https://www.cdu.de/sites/default/files/media/dokumente/koalitionsvertrag.pdf. Accessed 28 May 2019. cf. also the statement by the German Minister of Justice: Maas (2015).

[94] Commentators are divided as to the viability of the initiative; see Aden (2012) (pro), Wernicke (2014) (pro) and Peter (2011) (con).

[95] See the Coalition Agreement (*Koalitionsvertrag*) (n. 93 above) and the statement by the German Minister of Justice: Maas (2015).

[96] See Hill (2015); Roth (2016), pp. 13ff.

[97] Berlin already introduced a draft bill on 7 July 2015 titled *Entwurf eines Gesetzes zur Modernisierung der Strukturen der Landgerichte*, *Bundesrats-Drucksache (BR-Drs.)* No. 322/15.

the latter.[98] The old system, where the value of the claim was decisive for access to the *Bundesgerichtshof* (*Wertrevision*), led to an increase in the number of such appeals of 145% between 1980 and 1999.[99] This was based on the rationale that such claims have a greater importance just because a large amount of money is at stake. While the value of the claim is still an issue, it has lost considerable weight. As a result, the collective aspect of the final appeal is more important.

3 Overload Solutions

3.1 Increasing Capacity

The structure of the *Bundesgerichtshof*, namely the number of judges, has remained more or less the same for some decades now. Since 1950, though, the number of judges has doubled:

- 1950: 64 judges;
- 1953: 86 judges;
- 1956: 91 judges;
- 1960: 103 judges;
- 1971: 107 judges;
- 1980: 115 judges;
- 1988: 120 judges;
- 1994: 123 judges;
- 2009: 129 judges;
- Since 2016: 133 judges.

By the same token, the number of academic staff (*Hiwis*) has steadily increased. While in 1978 there were 22 *Hiwis*, in 2016 there were around 50, and in 2018 around 60.

3.2 Reducing Quantity

The German civil justice system disposes of a number of access filters designed to weed out cases which do not merit the attention of the *Bundesgerichtshof*.

[98] See *Bundestags-Drucksache (BT-Drs.)* No. 14/4722, p. 66.

[99] See *BT-Drs*. 14/4722, p. 65.

3.2.1 Court Fees

German civil procedure is based on a system of fixed fees. The amount due depends on the value of the claim, on the one hand, and the complexity of the case, on the other. Court fees (*Gerichtskosten*) are relatively low. For a claim of €1000 the standard fee (*Gebühr*) would be €53; for €10,000 the fee would be €241; and for €50,000 the fee would be €3536.[100] This standard fee will be multiplied depending on the procedural stage of the case. A first instance claim will account for three standard fees,[101] which would trigger a total fee of €723 for a claim of €10,000. *Revision* before the *Bundesgerichtshof* accounts for five fees. Those fees have not been raised significantly in recent years. A similar system applies to lawyers' fees.[102]

3.2.2 Restrictions on Access and Other Filters

Restrictions on access have been successfully introduced in recent years. They have already been described earlier.[103] Moreover, a specialist bar exists in Germany. It provides a fairly efficient filter.[104] Lastly, the judgments of lower courts are in principle enforceable even if an appeal is pending (§ 708 *ZPO*). However, in many cases enforcement will only be possible against provision of security (§ 709 *ZPO*).[105]

4 Effectiveness of the Solutions

Commentators have given credit to the reform of 2001 for being fairly effective. A study commissioned by the Federal Ministry of Justice that was published in 2006[106] underlined the following points:

---

[100]See the table set out in Annex 2 to § 34(1)(3) of the Court Fees Act (*Gerichtskostengesetz—GKG*).

[101]See the table set out in Annex 1 to § 3(2) of the Court Fees Act (*Gerichtskostengesetz—GKG*).

[102]See the Act on Lawyers' Fees (*Rechtsanwaltsvergütungsgesetz—RVG*).

[103]See Sect. 1.3.3 above.

[104]See Sect. 1.2.2 above.

[105]§ 709 *ZPO*: 'Provisionally enforceable judgments delivered against security. Other judgments are to be declared provisionally enforceable against provision of security, the amount of which is to be determined by the court. Insofar as a monetary claim is to be enforced, it shall be deemed compliant with the present rule if the amount of the security is specified in a determined ratio to the amount to be enforced in the particular case. Where a judgment upholding a default judgment is concerned, it is to stipulate that enforcement efforts under the default judgment may be continued only against provision of security.'

[106]Hommerich and Prütting (2006).

1. The focus on the first instance proceedings was said to be accepted by parties and judges alike. More than before judges seem to engage in case management decisions pursuant to § 139 *ZPO*;
2. Between 2000 and 2004 there were significantly fewer judgments on the merits in the appellate courts, while the number of decisions striking out unmeritorious appeals pursuant to § 522(2) *ZPO* rose;
3. While the quality of first instance decisions cannot be measured objectively, the ratio of new appeals to contentious judgments in first instance in the same year went down by approximately 10–15% between 2001 and 2004;
4. Judges welcome the possibility to strike out unmeritorious appeals pursuant to § 522(2) *ZPO*;
5. The number of appeals to the *Bundesgerichtshof* declined, but at the same time the number of *Nichtzulassungsbeschwerden* rose.

In 2004, the Association of German Jurists (*Deutscher Juristentag*)[107] made an evaluation of the reform. In particular, the possibility to strike out unmeritorious appeals pursuant to § 522(2) *ZPO* was accepted under the precondition that only clear-cut cases should be envisaged. As to the second appeal, the shift to a leave-based system (*Zulassungsrevision*) was generally welcomed by a large majority. However, many advocated giving greater weight to individual interests when evaluating the 'fundamental significance' of the case pursuant to § 543(2)(1) *ZPO*.

This last point has been raised by other commentators. In the years after the reform of 2001 the *Bundesgerichtshof* was reluctant to accept individual interests as raising issues of fundamental significance as long as the claimant could not demonstrate that the relevant legal question was pertinent to a greater number of cases.[108] Even when a large amount of money is at stake, this does not necessarily entail fundamental significance.[109]

Generally, a steady and significant decline in the number of pending cases in the first instance courts can be witnessed.[110] The reasons for this decline are sometimes said to lie in the rise of ADR, especially arbitration. However, there is no statistical data to prove that. Arbitration is not a mass phenomenon in Germany. The German Arbitral Institute DIS administers only slightly more than 100 cases per year.[111] Another reason may be the low interest rate: While in times of high interest rates a creditor might be tempted not to pay his debts as the interest relating to the judicial

---

107 The history of the *Deutscher Juristentag* dates back to 1860 (see Stürner 2010). A politically and ideologically neutral association, its goal is to contribute to the development of the legal system in all fields of law.

108 See, e.g., *BGHZ* 154, p. 288.

109 See Raeschke-Kessler (2015), p. 823, citing a claim worth €524 million filed with the *Bundesgerichtshof*, which bluntly decided in a two-line judgment that the case did not have fundamental significance.

110 See Sect. 2.2 above.

111 Worldwide: 1322 cases with institutional arbitration in 2012; see Wolf (2015). That accounts for only 3.5% of all commercial cases in Germany in that year (36,324).

proceedings is lower than the late payment interest, low interest rates could entail prompter payment to avoid higher costs in court proceedings.[112]

5 Openness to Transplants

The reform of 2001 is perhaps not the result of great comparative work. However, the explanatory memorandum of the draft reform bill referred to examples of 'good practice' from England, Austria, Switzerland (Zurich), France and Italy to show that the envisaged changes had already been implemented in other jurisdictions.[113] The major development of the 2001 reform was the abolition of the full-blown first appeal where ordinarily a full rehearing of fact and law was undertaken. References were made to Austrian and English law to demonstrate that the focus should instead be on the first instance proceedings.

6 Conclusion

A Supreme Court is part of the judicial system and cannot be viewed isolated from it. If the *Bundesgerichtshof* may be declared to work smoothly with a consistently low level of backlog, this positive evaluation can only be seen as a result of the adequate division of work between the different instances, on the one hand, and the good quality of legal advice, on the other. The solution seems to lie in the right division of work; the adequate distribution of responsibilities. In recent decades a major concern has been to reduce the number of cases. Reforms have often advocated non-contentious solutions for disputes such as the promotion of settlements and ADR in all shapes and forms (mediation, conciliation, arbitration, etc.). There is a growing concern that the judiciary does not live up to the needs of a modern society.[114] In the future the main issue may not be case overload, but rather marginalisation.

References

Aden M (2012) 'Law made in Germany'. Ein Plädoyer für den Export deutschen Rechts und nachhaltige Nachsorge. Zeitschrift für Rechtspolitik (ZRP) 2(1):50–53

Althammer C (2014) Die Zukunft des Rechtsmittelrechts. In: Bruns A, Münch J, Stadler A (eds) Die Zukunft des Zivilprozesses. Mohr Siebeck, Tübingen, pp 87–107

---

[112] See Wolf (2015), p. 1658.

[113] *BT-Drs.* No. 14/4722, pp. 70/71.

[114] See Stürner (2016).

Andrews N (2013) On civil processes, vol I. Intersentia, Antwerp
Arnold S (2013) Zur Überprüfung tatrichterlicher Ermessensspielräume im Zivilprozess. Zeitschrift für Zivilprozess (ZZP) 126:63–81
Bartels K (2009) Grenzen der Bindungswirkung rückverweisender Revisionsentscheidungen. Zeitschrift für Zivilprozess (ZZP) 122:449–464
Benöhr I, Hodges C, Creutzfeldt-Banda N (2012) Germany. In: Hodges C, Benöhr I, Creutzfeldt-Banda N (eds) Consumer ADR in Europe. CH Beck, Hart and Nomos, Munich, pp 73–115
Bichlmeir J (1971) Der juristische Hilfsarbeiter an den deutschen Gerichten. Diss. Erlangen
Domej T (2014) What is an important case? Admissibility of appeals to the Supreme Courts in the German-speaking jurisdictions. In: Uzelac A, Van Rhee CH (eds) Nobody's perfect. Comparative essays on appeals and other means of recourse against judicial decisions in civil matters. Intersentia, Cambridge, pp 277–290
Domej T (2017) Squaring the circle: individual rights and the general interest before the Supreme Courts in the German-speaking countries. In: Van Rhee CH, Fu Y (eds) Supreme courts in transition in China and the West: adjudication at the service of public goals. Springer, Cham, pp 131–148
Dürig G (1958) Article 19(4) at n. 17. In: Maunz T, Dürig G (eds) Grundgesetz-Kommentar. CH Beck, Munich
Eidenmüller H, Engel H (2013) Die Schlichtungsfalle: Verbraucherrechtsdurchsetzung nach der ADR-Richtlinie und der ODR-Verordnung der EU. Zeitschrift für Wirtschaftsrecht (ZIP) 36:1704–1710
Enders C (2016) Commentary on Article 19 GG n. 57. In: Epping V, Hillgruber C (eds) Beck'scher Online-Kommentar zum Grundgesetz, 30th edn. CH Beck, Munich
Gaier R (2016) Schlichtung, Schiedsgericht, staatliche Justiz – Drei Akteure in einem System institutioneller Rechtsverwirklichung. Neue Juristische Wochenschrift (NJW) 19:1367–1371
Graf-Schlicker ML (2014) Der Zivilprozess vor dem Aus? Rückgang der Fallzahlen im Zivilprozess. Anwaltsblatt (AnwBl) 7:573–577
Greger R (2004) Die ZPO-Reform – 1000 Tage danach. Juristenzeitung (JZ) 17(3):805–817
Hager G (2006) Von der Konstitutionalisierung des Zivilrechts zur Zivilisierung der Konstitutionalisierung. Juristische Schulung (JuS) 9:769–775
Hill N (2015) 40 Vorschläge für einen effektiveren Zivilprozess. Deutsche Richterzeitung (DRiZ) 2:46–49
Hommerich C, Prütting H (2006) Rechtstatsächliche Untersuchung zu den Auswirkungen der Reform des Zivilprozessrechts auf die gerichtliche Praxis – Evaluation ZPO-Reform. CH Beck, Munich
Justizministerium B-W (ed) (1999) Rechtsstaat – Rechtsmittelstaat? Stuttgart
Krauß F (1987) Der Umfang der Prüfung von Zivilurteilen durch das Bundesverfassungsgericht. Diss. Erlangen
Krüger W (2016) Commentary on § 552a at n. 2. In: Krüger W, Rauscher T (eds) Münchener Kommentar zur ZPO, 5th edn. CH Beck, Munich
Limperg B (2015) Verbraucherstreitbeilegungsgesetz – wie viel Justiz braucht die Schlichtung. BRAK-Mitteilungen 5:225–228
Maas H (2015) Welt im Wandel – wie das Recht antwortet. Anwaltsblatt (AnwBl) 1:64–69
Madaus S (2013) Die Bindungswirkung zurückverweisender Revisionsurteile. Zeitschrift für Zivilprozess (ZZP) 126:269–294
Meller-Hannich C, Höland A, Krausbeck E (2014) 'ADR' und 'ODR': Kreationen der europäischen Rechtspolitik. Eine kritische Würdigung. Zeitschrift für Europäisches Privatrecht (ZEuP) 1:8–38
Peter AF (2011) Warum die Initiative 'Law – Made in Germany' bislang zum Scheitern verurteilt ist. Juristenzeitung (JZ) 19:939–946
Prütting H (1997) Die Zulassung der Revision. Heymann, Cologne
Raeschke-Kessler H (2015) Schiedsverfahren gegen ordentliche Gerichtsbarkeit: Wie die Ziviljustiz stärken? Anwaltsblatt (AnwBl) 11:822–826

Reichold H (2016) Commentary on § 559 at n. 8. In: Thomas H, Putzo H (eds) ZPO, 37th edn. CH Beck, Munich
Rimmelspacher B (2016) Commentary on § 522 at n. 20. In: Krüger W, Rauscher T (eds) Münchener Kommentar zur ZPO, 5th edn. CH Beck, Munich
Roth H (2013) Bedeutungsverluste der Zivilgerichtsbarkeit durch Verbrauchermediation. Juristenzeitung (JZ) 13:637–644
Roth H (2015) Etabliert EU Verbraucherschutz zweiter Klasser? Deutsche Richterzeitung (DRiZ) 1:24–27
Roth H (2016) Die Zukunft der Ziviljustiz. Zeitschrift für Zivilprozess (ZZP) 129:3–26
Rühl G (2014) Die Richtlinie über alternative Streitbeilegung: Handlungsperspektiven und Handlungsoptionen. Zeitschrift für Zivilprozess (ZZP) 127:61–98
Schack H (2011) Einführung in das US-amerikanische Zivilprozessrecht, 4th edn. CH Beck, Munich
Schmidt-Aßmann E (2003) Commentary on article 19(4) GG. In: Maunz T, Dürig G (eds) Grundgesetz-Kommentar, 42nd edn. CH Beck, Munich
Schulte M (1986) Rechtsprechungseinheit als Verfassungsauftrag: Dargestellt am Beispiel des Gemeinsamen Senats der obersten Gerichtshöfe des Bundes. Duncker & Humblot, Berlin
Sendler H (1982) Zum Instanzenzug in der Verwaltungsgerichtsbarkeit. Deutsches Verwaltungsblatt (DVBl):157–165
Stürner M (2002) Die Anfechtung von Zivilurteilen. CH Beck, Munich
Stürner M (2016) Litigation in the 21st century: How attractive is the German civil justice system? Tijdschrift voor Civiele Rechtspleging (TCR) 4:145–147
Stürner M, Gascón Inchausti F, Caponi R (eds) (2014) The role of consumer ADR in the administration of justice. New trends in access to justice under EU Directive 2013/11. Sellier, Munich
Stürner R (2010) 150 Jahre Deutscher Juristentag – Ein Jubiläum und eine Festschrift. Juristenzeitung (JZ) 17:797–802
Voßkuhle A (1993) Rechtsschutz gegen den Richter. Zur Integration der Dritten Gewalt in das verfassungsrechtliche Kontrollsystem vor dem Hintergrund des Art. 19 IV GG. CH Beck, Munich
Voßkuhle A (2003) Bruch mit einem Dogma – Die Verfassung garantiert Rechtsschutz gegen den Richter. Neue Juristische Wochenschrift (NJW) 56(31):2193–2200
Wagner G (2014) Private law enforcement through ADR: wonder drug or snake oil? Common Mark Law Rev (CML Rev) 51:165–194
Weitzel J (1976) Der Kampf um die Appellation ans Reichskammergericht. Zur politischen Geschichte der Rechtsmittel in Deutschland. Böhlau-Verlag, Vienna
Weller M (2011) Rechtsfindung und Rechtsmittel: Zur Reform der zivilprozessualen Zurückweisung der Berufung durch Beschluss. Zeitschrift für Zivilprozess (ZZP) 124:343–376
Wernicke S (2014) 'Law made in Germany': Von der Selbstvergewisserung zum rechtspolitischen Ziel der 18. Legislaturperiode. Zeitschrift für Rechtspolitik (ZRP) 2:34–37
Winter T (2014) Revisionsrücknahme und Anerkenntnisurteil in dritter Instanz. Neue Juristische Wochenschrift (NJW) 67(5):267–269
Wolf C (2015) Zivilprozess versus außergerichtliche Konfliktlösung – Wandel der Streitkultur in Zahlen. Neue Juristische Wochenschrift (NJW) 68(23):1656–1661
Zeidler W (1983) Rechtsstaat'83. Deutsche Richterzeitung (DRiZ):249–257

Access to the Austrian *Oberster Gerichtshof*: Attempts to Strike a Balance Between Adequate Workload and Adequate Review

Florian Scholz-Berger

Abstract Since the enactment of the Austrian Code of Civil Procedure of 1898, the role and function of the Austrian Supreme Court (*Oberster Gerichtshof*) has changed. Instead of safeguarding individual rights by securing the correct decision in individual cases, currently the main purpose of the court is described as providing guidelines for the development and uniform application of the law. The changed role of the court is clearly reflected in today's rules on access to the court. The reason for the change in its role was partly triggered by the need for effective restrictions on access in the 1980s. Then, the court faced an overburdening caseload that could not sufficiently be met by means of the traditional access filters which were in force at that time. The history of reforms in the last four decades can be described as an on-going attempt to keep the caseload of the court at a reasonable level without causing too drastic restrictions in terms of access to Supreme Court review. Today there are about 2800 appeals to the Austrian Supreme Court per year; about 1000 require a decision on the merits.

1 The Oberster Gerichtshof

1.1 Introduction

The *Oberster Gerichtshof* (Supreme Court, hereinafter *OGH*) is one of the three highest courts in Austria. It has jurisdiction in civil and criminal matters, while the *Verfassungsgerichtshof* acts as a Supreme Court for (certain) constitutional matters, and the *Verwaltungsgerichtshof* for administrative matters (its core competence is to hear appeals against decisions of administrative courts).[1]

[1] cf. Kodek (2008), p. 221; Scholz (2014), pp. 111ff.

F. Scholz-Berger (✉)
University of Vienna, Faculty of Law, Vienna, Austria
e-mail: florian.scholz@univie.ac.at

P. Bravo-Hurtado, C. H. van Rhee (eds.), *Supreme Courts Under Pressure*, Ius Gentium: Comparative Perspectives on Law and Justice 83,
https://doi.org/10.1007/978-3-030-63731-6_6

Article 92(1) of the *Bundes-Verfassungsgesetz* (Austrian Federal Constitution)[2] provides that the *OGH* is the sole highest court for civil and criminal matters in Austria. Nevertheless, this does not mean that recourse to the *OGH* has to be allowed against every decision of a lower court. Article 92(1) only requires that access to the Supreme Court has to be guaranteed when certain criteria are met and that there must be no further remedy to another court after a decision of the *OGH*.[3]

Particularly the latter aspect has been the subject of recurring discussions in recent decades. Some have demanded the introduction of a German-style constitutional complaint[4] that would enable parties in proceedings before ordinary courts[5] to apply to the *Verfassungsgerichtshof* when they claim that their constitutional rights are infringed by a last instance decision of an ordinary court.[6] However, the legislator did not pursue this idea. Instead, it was decided to introduce a remedy against unconstitutional laws that had been applied in civil and criminal proceedings. This proposed remedy, the so-called *Gesetzesbeschwerde*, was initially conceived as conditional upon the existence of a (final) decision by an ordinary court of final instance. However, this solution was strongly rejected by the *OGH* and its judges, who claimed that such a solution would jeopardise legal certainty and due process.[7] Although a *Gesetzesbeschwerde* should only allow the scrutiny of the respective statute and not of the court decision itself, the *OGH*'s criticism was to a large extent motivated by the fact that another court could have been called upon after the decision of the court of final instance. Therefore, the Austrian Parliament in 2013 finally adopted a compromise and introduced a version of *Gesetzesbeschwerde* that allows an application by the parties (only) after the first instance decision has been rendered and only when an appeal is made to the court of second instance at the same time.[8] This complicated construction makes this new remedy very hard to handle, not only for courts, but also for the parties.[9]

This episode from recent history serves as a good example of the importance members of the ordinary judiciary, especially judges of the *OGH*, attach to the equality of all three highest courts and to the principle that the *OGH* is the exclusive Supreme Court in civil and criminal matters.

---

[2]*Bundesgesetzblatt* (Federal Legal Gazette, hereinafter *BGBl*) 1930/1.

[3]Mayer and Muzak (2015), Article 92, n. I; Mayer et al. (2015), marginal number 19.

[4]For the German situation see Stürner (Chapter "Sharing Responsibility: The German Federal Court of Justice and the Civil Appellate System") in this volume.

[5]In accordance with the terminology of the Constitution and the common usage in Austrian academic literature, 'ordinary courts' refers to courts that have jurisdiction in civil and criminal matters, the final instance being the *OGH*.

[6]See Scholz (2014), pp. 119ff.

[7]See, e.g., Ratz (2013) and Rohrer and Kuras (2012).

[8]See Scholz (2014), pp. 121ff.

[9]Grabenwarter and Musger (2015), p. 562; Scholz (2014), p. 150.

1.2 A Brief History of the OGH

In its modern form the *OGH* was established in 1848.[10] Back then it served as the Supreme Court for the entire Habsburg monarchy. After World War I, when the Republic of Austria was founded, the role of the *OGH* as the highest court in civil and criminal matters was confirmed in 1918 and 1919.[11] Finally, the Austrian Constitution of 1920 secured this position in Article 92 mentioned above.[12] In 1939, the *OGH* was abolished and its competences were taken over by the German *Reichsgericht* in Leipzig.[13] The *OGH* was re-established in 1945 and gained additional competences in 1987 when jurisdiction in labour and social security matters was comprehensively integrated into the system of ordinary courts.[14]

The foundation for the modern system of appeal to the *OGH* was laid in 1898 when the *Zivilprozessordnung* (Austrian Code of Civil Procedure, hereinafter *ZPO*),[15] the famous work by Franz Klein, came into effect. Since then, these rules, which can still be found in § 502ff. of the *ZPO*, have been subject to numerous amendments, the most important being the *Zivilverfahrensnovelle* 1983,[16] *Erweiterte Wertgrenzennovelle* 1989[17] and *Erweiterte Wertgrenzennovelle* 1997.[18] [19] In addition to the procedural rules in the *ZPO* and the *Jurisdiktionsnorm* (*JN*) (Statute on Jurisdiction),[20] the organisation and functioning of the *OGH* is governed by the *Bundesgesetz über den Obersten Gerichtshof* (*OGHG*) (Federal Law on the Supreme Court)[21] and the *Geschäftsordnung des Obersten Gerichtshofs* (Internal Rules of Procedure of the Supreme Court).

[10] Danzl (2001), p. 43. At that time it was named *Oberster Gerichts- und Kassationshof*; its predecessor, the *Oberste Justizstelle* (Supreme Judicial Agency), which had been the Supreme Court and the Ministry of Justice at the same time, had been in existence since 1749 (Leonhard 1950, p. 164).

[11] Danzl (2001), p. 45.

[12] Forgó-Feldner (2012), pp. 21ff.

[13] Leonhard (1950), p. 205.

[14] See Ballon (1987), p. 349; Rechberger and Simotta (2017), marginal number 1245.

[15] *Reichsgesetzblatt* (Imperial Legal Gazette) 1895/113.

[16] *BGBl* 1983/135.

[17] *BGBl* 1989/343.

[18] *BGBl* I 1997/140.

[19] See Sect. 2.3 below.

[20] *BGBl* 1895/111.

[21] *BGBl* 1968/328.

1.3 *Organisation of the* OGH

Currently, the *OGH* consists of 60 full-time judges (including a president and two vice presidents), 42 of whom sit in civil and commercial matters (including employment and social security cases).[22] As a general rule, decisions are taken by a panel (senate) of five full-time judges (*Einfacher Senat*).[23] In employment and social security matters, the senate consists of (only) three full-time judges and two lay judges.[24] If a senate of five judges concludes that its decision on a legal question of fundamental importance would depart from the established case law of the *OGH* or from the last relevant decision by an enlarged senate, or if the case law of the *OGH* with respect to such a question is divergent, an enlarged senate (*Verstärkter Senat*) of 11 judges has to be assembled.[25] § 7 of the *Bundesgesetz über den Obersten Gerichtshof* lists a number of matters which are decided by a panel of only three members. Predominantly, this is the case when the *OGH* does not decide on an appeal against the decision of a lower court, but—as the first and only instance—on certain procedural matters.[26]

The civil judges of the *OGH* sit in ten permanent senates of five judges.[27] Each senate is headed either by a senior judge called *Senatspräsident* or by one of the two vice presidents. Each of the remaining judges (*Hofräte*) is assigned to at least one senate. The allocation of cases to the respective senates follows from a combination of two principles. First, each senate is competent for certain matters, such as insolvency (third senate) or intellectual property law (fourth senate). The remainder of cases—'general' civil matters—is distributed among all ten senates following a complex system that aims at a balanced distribution of the workload among the judges.[28]

In addition to the ten 'full' or 'ordinary' civil senates,[29] there are three additional 'special' senates with only very narrow competences. One of these senates exclusively decides on appeals in antitrust cases, while another one is competent for certain matters in respect of arbitration proceedings.[30] Judges serve on the special senates in addition to their duties in ordinary senates.

---

[22]cf. http://ogh.gv.at/de/ogh/geschaeftsverteilung. Accessed 25 May 2020. cf. also Oberhammer (2014), p. 170.

[23]§ 6 *OGHG*.

[24]§ 11(1) *Arbeits- und Sozialgerichtsgesetz* (Act on Procedure in Employment and Social Security Matters, *BGBl* 1985/104).

[25]§ 8 *OGHG*.

[26]e.g. the designation of a competent court in cases where international or European law stipulates that Austrian courts have jurisdiction but national law does not provide a rule for local jurisdiction.

[27]See http://ogh.gv.at/de/ogh/geschaeftsverteilung. Accessed 25 May 2020.

[28]http://ogh.gv.at/de/ogh/geschaeftsverteilung. Accessed 25 May 2020. cf. Kodek (2012), p. 102.

[29]Kodek (2012), p. 100.

[30]Since 2013 (see the 2013 Amendment to the Austrian Arbitration Act—'SchiedsRÄG 2013,' *BGBl*. I 118/2013), the *OGH* has jurisdiction regarding actions for setting aside an arbitral award

Each case that is brought before the *OGH* is assigned to one of the *Hofräte* of the respective senate who acts as a rapporteur and—usually—prepares a draft for the decision.[31] The decision is eventually taken by majority vote of the senate after non-public deliberations.[32] Usually, only the rapporteur and the senate chair know the entire file before the decision; all of the other members of the senate have to rely on the report of the rapporteur.[33]

It should be pointed out that the *OGH* only has a very limited number of legal support staff. Most of these staff are young judges (from first instance courts) who usually serve at the *OGH* for a limited period of time. They provide some assistance, e.g. by summarising files and undertaking research, but they never take part in the actual drafting of the court's decision; this is exclusively done by the members of the *OGH*.[34] In recent years the number of such support staff has increased,[35] but is still relatively low in comparison to other highest courts.

1.4 *Access to the* OGH

As a general rule, the *OGH* handles remedies against decisions of second instance courts. This contribution will focus on this general rule and, thus, the role of the *OGH* as a court of third instance. Further, it will mainly take into consideration the rules governing procedure in general civil and commercial matters; when it seems necessary for the sake of comparison, and only then, references will be made to the special provisions for labour and social security cases and for cases which are handled under the Non-Contentious Proceedings Act (*Außerstreitgesetz*).[36]

---

and for declarations of the existence or non-existence of an arbitral award, as well as for proceedings regarding the constitution of the arbitral tribunal; cf. Oberhammer and Koller (2012), pp. 84ff.

[31] cf. § 6 *OGHG* and Kodek (2012), p. 105.

[32] Even though § 509(2) *ZPO* provides for the possibility of a public hearing before the *OGH*, this hardly ever happens in civil cases; cf. Kodek and Mayr (2018), marginal number 1100.

[33] Kodek (2012), p. 105.

[34] Kodek (2012), p. 103.

[35] Since 2014, there has been one full time staff member for each of the civil senates; see Oberster Gerichtshof 2015, Tätigkeitsbericht für das Jahr 2014, p. 5. https://www.deroberstegerichtshof.at/media/2016/09/ogh_taetigkeitsbericht_2014-web.pdf. Accessed 25 May 2020. These staff, however, assign only half their time to the preparation of decisions; the other half is reserved for the documentation of the *OGH*'s case law on the internet.

[36] *BGBl* I 2003/111.

1.4.1 Short Introduction to the Austrian Court System and Appeal Procedure

The following brief outline of the Austrian court system and second instance proceedings in civil cases might help to understand the legal framework for third instance remedies: jurisdiction for first instance proceedings lies either with a district court (*Bezirksgericht*) or with a regional court (*Landesgericht*).[37] Claims are to be filed with district courts when the value in dispute does not exceed €15,000 and—irrespective of the amount in dispute—in some matters such as family law and tenancy law.[38] Regional courts act as courts of first instance in all other cases;[39] further, they hear appeals against first instance decisions of district courts. In cases where a regional court has decided at first instance, one of four higher regional courts (*Oberlandesgerichte*) decides on the appeal.

A characteristic feature of the Austrian appellate system is the strict prohibition of new factual allegations and new evidence in second instance proceedings (*Neuerungsverbot*).[40] The only purpose of appeal proceedings is to examine the fact-finding process and the application of the law by the lower court, not to provide the losing party with an opportunity to retry the case.[41] As a consequence, second instance proceedings are usually conducted in writing.[42]

1.4.2 Remedies Against Appeal Decisions

Depending on the kind of lower instance decision, there are different kinds of appeals to the *OGH*.[43] Decisions on the merits are usually rendered as *Urteil* (judgment), while the form for procedural decisions is *Beschluss* (court order). The remedy against an *Urteil* of the second instance is called *Revision*, its counterpart for the case that the first and second instance have decided in the form of *Beschluss* is *Revisionsrekurs*. I will mainly outline the rules regarding *Revision*, which is the most frequent kind of remedy and—at least when it comes to access filters—the 'role model' for the others.

Revision can only be based on certain grounds, which are enumerated in § 503 *ZPO*. These include procedural errors and wrong legal assessment. Factual issues are generally excluded from review by the *OGH*; only a discrepancy between

---

[37] Note that in Vienna there is a special district court and a regional court exclusively for certain commercial matters.

[38] § 49(1) *JN*; cf. Rechberger and Simotta (2017), marginal number 273.

[39] § 50(1) *JN*.

[40] Oberhammer and Domej (2010), p. 271; Rechberger (2016), marginal number 131.

[41] Oberhammer (2015), p. 259.

[42] See, e.g., Kodek and Mayr (2018), marginal number 1074; Rechberger and Simotta (2017), marginal number 1103.

[43] See for an overview Bajons (1999), p. 27.

the findings of fact in the judgment of the lower court and the case record (*Aktenwidrigkeit*) can be brought forward in the *Revision*.[44] In regard to procedural errors, it should be noted that, according to the case law of the *OGH*, *Revision* is not admissible if it is based on an error in the first instance proceedings and the second instance has already denied the existence of the error.[45]

Remedies to the *OGH* are subject to a combination of access filters.[46] Pursuant to §§ 502 and 528 *ZPO*, *Revision* and *Revisionsrekurs* to the *OGH* are only admissible when the decision of the case depends on the answer to a question of law which is of significant importance for ensuring the uniformity of the law, legal certainty or the development of the law. In addition to this criterion, which draws on the importance of the legal question, *Revision* to the *OGH* is also limited on the basis of the value in dispute. Appeal to the Supreme Court is always inadmissible if the value of the matter of the second instance decision does not exceed €5000.[47] If the amount lies between €5000 and €30,000, *Revision* is only admissible if the second instance court affirms the existence of an important question of law and grants *Revision* on these grounds (§ 502(3) *ZPO*). If the court of second instance does not grant *Revision* and the value exceeds € 30,000, the parties can launch a so-called extraordinary *Revision* and call upon the *OGH* to reverse the negative decision on admissibility. The application of the party has to include the request for *Revision* itself and the request to overturn the second instance decision on admissibility. If the *OGH* grants the latter, the court can proceed to consider the *Revision* on the merits.

Note in this context that the *OGH* can always overturn an *affirmative* decision of the second instance to grant *Revision* and thus reject an application of the party on the grounds of the absence of a significant question of law.

2 The High Caseload of the *OGH* and Attempts to Reduce It

2.1 Symptoms of Overload and Historical Reasons for It

Since the *OGH* is a relatively old Supreme Court, the problem of high workload also has a rather long history. Actually, there have been calls for reform and attempts to handle the always-increasing caseload almost since the time the court was

[44]cf. Domej (2017), p. 144.

[45]See, e.g., Rechberger and Simotta (2017), marginal number 1116; see in more detail in Sect. 2.5 below.

[46]There is only one exception to this rule: when there has been an appeal against a judgment of a first instance court and the court of second instance has—instead of again taking a decision on the merits of the case—rendered a court order by which it has for formal reasons rejected the claim itself or the appeal, appeal to the *OGH* is allowed regardless of the value in dispute and the existence of an important question of law (§ 519 *ZPO*).

[47]§§ 502(2) *ZPO* and 528(2)(1) *ZPO*.

established.[48] Without going into all of the details of those more than 150 years, it should suffice to say that the problem probably reached a new dimension shortly after the 'new' *ZPO* came into effect in 1898. By then, the rules on *Revision* provided for literally unlimited access to the *OGH*, the only exception being cases with a very small amount in dispute.[49] In the decades to come—starting as early as 1907—the legislator launched a number of reforms aiming to at least put a stop to the constant increase in the workload of the Supreme Court.[50]

For almost seven decades the attempted solutions were more or less limited to establishing and raising the value limits for access to the *OGH*. Although the value limits had been raised several times in the 1970s, the workload still increased in the following years, so that it became clear that there had to be a major reform in order to keep the Supreme Court functional.[51] The workload of the civil judges had increased by about 50% in only 10 years; in 1982, every judge on a civil panel was assigned more than 120 cases for drafting; thus, the average time for appeal proceedings as well as the backlog had grown severely.[52]

As in most reform discussions before and after, it soon became clear that a significant increase in the number of judges—which was, and still is, already quite high compared to other states—would not be an appropriate measure.[53] First, the government could not—or at least did not want to—provide sufficient funds, and, second, there was the fear that an increase in the number of judges would jeopardise the unity and quality of the court's case law. Each additional senate would mean a further impediment to the internal coordination of the court; further, especially in a small country such as Austria, there is only a limited number of the most highly qualified judges who could be considered for a position on the Supreme Court.[54] Thus, it was clear almost from the outset that the proposed reform would aim at a further restriction of access to the *OGH* by expanding the system of access filters.

Of course—and this is also a feature of almost every reform discussion in this context—there were always also critics of (further) restrictions on access to the third instance, because they saw such measures as a threat to access to justice in general and to the Rule of Law.[55]

---

[48]See Leonhard (1950), p. 182.

[49]Danzl (2001), p. 49; Lovrek and Musger (2019), marginal number 25.

[50]For a detailed account of these reforms see Danzl (2001), pp. 53ff.

[51]Danzl (2001), p. 71.

[52]See Petrasch (1983), p. 170; Danzl (2001), p. 71.

[53]See Fasching (1980), p. 66; Danzl (2001), pp. 71ff.; for a divergent opinion see Fichtenbauer (1989), p. 335; of course, this does not mean that the number of judges has not increased over the years; for a detailed account of the development in the number of judges see Danzl (2001), p. 46; Felzmann et al. (2009), p. 32; see also Sect. 3.1 below.

[54]Wurzinger (1984), p. 176.

[55]See (in regard to the 1989 reform process), e.g., Arnold (1989), p. 523; Fichtenbauer (1989), pp. 534ff.

2.2 Important Question of Law Instead of Value Limits?

In regard to access filters, there had for some years been voices in favour of a fundamental change—away from value limits and towards a new kind of filter. It was argued that only a system of leave to appeal (like that in effect in Germany by that time) could ease the workload of the Supreme Court permanently without perpetuating the 'unfair' discrimination between high and low value cases.[56] Originally, that change had been proposed by the *OGH* itself, but in the course of the reform discussion, members of the court voiced their doubts because they saw the risk that the abolition of value limits and the need to decide on whether to allow appeal or not would in the end increase their workload instead of reducing it.[57]

2.3 Combination of Access Filters

As a result of a controversial discussion, in 1983 the new access filters were finally combined with the existing ones.[58] Thus, in principle, appeal stayed absolutely inadmissible below a certain value (which differed depending on whether the court of second instance had departed from the first instance decision or not) and was always allowed above a much higher value.[59] In between those two limits a new 'qualitative' kind of filter was imposed: appeal should only be admissible if the decision of the case depended on a significant question of law (*Grundsatzrevision*). It was up to the lower appellate court to decide whether this was the case and, thus, whether it would allow appeal to the *OGH* or not (*Zulassungsrevision*). If leave to appeal was denied, the parties could launch a so-called extraordinary appeal to the *OGH*, a combination of leave to appeal and appeal itself.[60]

Since the reform of 1983 only led to a very short term decrease in the workload of the *OGH*,[61] there was another major reform in 1989[62] which made the criterion of the 'significant question of law'—and thus the need for leave to appeal—a general requirement for *Revision* in all cases and abolished unlimited access to the *OGH* in high value cases.[63] Additionally, it abolished the discrimination between the appealability of confirmative and divergent decisions of the second instance court.[64] These

---

[56]See, e.g., Wurzinger (1984), p. 177.

[57]Reindl (1984), pp. 45, 54.

[58]*Zivilverfahrensnovelle 1983*, see n. 16 above.

[59]See, e.g., Petrasch (1983), p. 172; Reindl (1984), p. 54; Wurzinger (1984), p. 182.

[60]See in detail Sect. 1.4.2 above.

[61]Danzl (2001), p. 79.

[62]*Erweiterte Wertgrenzennovelle 1989*, see n. 17 above.

[63]See, e.g., Petrasch (1989), p. 745.

[64]See, e.g., Danzl (2001), p. 81; note, however, that this distinction is still the foundation of an important access filter for remedies against second instance court orders (*Revisionsrekurs*). Pursuant

modifications also helped to simplify the system of *Revision* and made it—at least to some extent—more understandable and manageable.[65]

As a result of this reform, the *OGH* had to handle a lot of extraordinary appeals, because the law provided for this remedy in all cases in which the court of second instance had negated the existence of a significant question of law and, thus, had denied leave to appeal. Although the *OGH* could (and still can) theoretically reject extraordinary appeals without giving any reasons, the file still had to be reviewed by a judge who had to prepare a report to the panel,[66] so that the high number of such cases meant a significant workload for the members of the court after all.

Therefore, in 1997 the system of leave to appeal was once again taken one step further,[67] which—for the time being—put an end to the development outlined above. The main feature of this last major reform was that the possibility of extraordinary appeal to the *OGH* was restricted and only applied in cases where the value in dispute exceeded a certain limit.[68]

About 12 years later, in 2009, the value limits for access to the *OGH* were raised again and were fixed at the current amounts outlined in the overview above.[69] The aim of this latest reform was not only to adapt these sums after more than a decade of inflation, but also—once again—to further ease the workload of the *OGH*.[70]

2.4 Other Measures Against Overload

In addition to the ongoing modification of access filters, there also was a parallel development which I have not mentioned so far. Starting in 1983, a number of rules were established that aimed at easing the workload of the judges by lowering the formal standards for the reasons that are provided for the judgment.[71] For example, the decision only has to give an account of the submissions by the parties and the factual basis for the decision to the extent that is absolutely necessary in order to understand the legal reasoning of the court.

Moreover, if the *OGH* affirms the ruling of the second instance court because it deems its reasoning correct, it suffices to state this fact in the reasons for the judgment. As far as it concurs with the appeal decision, the ruling of the *OGH*

---

to § 528(2)(2) *ZPO*, a second instance decision that has affirmed a first instance court order in its entirety can in general not be remedied by means of *Revisionsrekurs*.

[65] See Petrasch (1989), p. 746 with further references; however, the system remained rather complex, which still leads to practical difficulties; see Sect. 3.2 below.

[66] See, e.g., Zechner (2005), marginal number 33.

[67] *Erweiterete Wertgrenzennovelle 1997*, see n. 18 above.

[68] For a more detailed description of the current system see Sect. 1.4.2 above.

[69] Section 1.4.2 above.

[70] See Mayr (2009), p. 563.

[71] § 503(3) *ZPO*; see Fasching (1990), marginal number 1958.

does not give any reasons for its own decision; § 510(3) *ZPO* further names certain grounds for *Revision* that can be dismissed by the *OGH* without any reasons given.[72]

2.5 Other Mechanisms

The workload of a Supreme Court is usually not only restricted through rules that explicitly aim at restricting access to supreme judicature by ruling out less important cases on the grounds of various access criteria. In fact, there are other mechanisms as well that have at least the effect of limiting the scope of review by the highest court or pose impediments for parties who intend to seek review by such a court.[73]

One example for such a mechanism is the fact that an error in the first instance proceedings cannot be brought forward before the *OGH* when it has already been rejected by the second instance.[74] The *ZPO* explicitly stipulates this limitation only for nullities (*Nichtigkeiten*: certain severe procedural errors), but the case law of the *OGH* has extended it to all sorts of procedural errors.[75]

3 Effectiveness of Current Measures

Almost 40 years after the reform of 1983 and more than 20 years after the last major legislative step in 1997, it still remains unclear whether the measures adopted in the course of the reform process described above have been effective or not. While some (mainly judges of the *OGH*) claim that the reforms have 'failed' and that the workload of the court is still unacceptably high,[76] others are of the opinion that an effective filtering system is in place already and that access to the *OGH* should not be restricted further.[77] Most probably, there is no definite answer to the question, since it depends on how one quantifies the success of such measures and—of course—on the expectations towards the work of a Supreme Court. Hence, in the following section I am going to look at a number of different factors that could be indicators for how well the current system of access to the *OGH* works, namely the development of the workload in numbers, the 'usability' of the rules on access to the *OGH* and, most importantly, the question whether they enable the court to fulfil its specific functions.

---

[72]See Lovrek (2019), marginal numbers 19ff.; see also Fasching (1990), marginal number 1958, who criticises this rule as far as it applies to the handling of procedural errors.

[73]See Domej (2014), pp. 277ff.

[74]Section 1.4.2 above.

[75]See, e.g., Rechberger and Simotta (2017), marginal number 1116; this solution is, however, criticised by academia.

[76]See, e.g., Danzl (2001), p. 98; Zechner (2005), marginal number 61.

[77]See, e.g., Mayr (2009), p. 566.

3.1 Development of Workload and Duration of Proceedings

The following data are intended to give an impression of the development of the workload of the *OGH* during recent years. Most certainly, the development of the workload cannot be attributed solely to changes in the rules on access to the *OGH*. Clearly, there are many factors that influence the numbers of complaints filed with a Supreme Court. Further, it has to be noted in this context that there is a general decrease in civil litigation before the Austrian courts.[78]

In 1996, the year before the last big reform, there were 4162 appeals (*Revision, Revisionsrekurs* and *Rekurs* together) to the *OGH*, 2059 ordinary appeals and 2103 extraordinary appeals.[79] In 2008, the total number was 3093 appeals (1524 ordinary and 1569 extraordinary).[80] In 2018, several years after the latest adjustment of value limits in 2009, this number is even lower at 2844 appeals (1492 ordinary and 1352 extraordinary).[81] Interestingly, this number is—or at least seems to be—quite similar to the number in 1982, the year before the first major reform, when the *OGH* handled 2933 appeals.[82] Of course, the major difference is that back then the Supreme Court had to consider all applications on their merits, while today it can (and has to) reject (ordinary as well as extraordinary) remedies as inadmissible when they do not pose a significant question of law,[83] which can be done in a simplified procedure for extraordinary remedies. Some data for 2018 might help to illustrate the importance of this mechanism: in that year, 34% of all ordinary and 83.4% of the extraordinary remedies were found to be inadmissible by the *OGH*; in total, more than 1000 applications reached a decision on the merits.[84]

Undoubtedly, it has to be taken into consideration that the rejection of an extraordinary remedy also has to be prepared by a judge and needs to be sanctioned by the entire panel and that all courts—including the *OGH*—have to handle increasingly more complex cases.[85] Still, the numbers above indicate that the reforms did

---

78 See, e.g., Fuchs (2019) and Nogratnig and Zeiringer (2019).

79 Danzl (2001), p. 94. According to the counting-method as applied by the *OGH* in its annual statistics, those extraordinary remedies that lead to a decision on the merits are counted as ordinary remedies; this method was also used in this paragraph.

80 Oberster Gerichtshof 2009, Tätigkeitsbericht für das Jahr 2008, p. 7. https://www.deroberstegerichtshof.at/media/2016/09/taetigkeitsbericht2008.pdf. Accessed 25 May 2020.

81 Oberster Gerichtshof 2019, Tätigkeitsbericht für das Jahr 2018, p. 10. https://www.ogh.gv.at/media/ogh_taetigkeitsbericht_2018.pdf. Accessed 25 May 2020.

82 Note, however, that this was before jurisdiction in social security matters was comprehensively included in the system of ordinary courts; see Sect. 1.2 above.

83 See Sect. 1.4.2 above.

84 Oberster Gerichtshof 2019, Tätigkeitsbericht für das Jahr 2018, pp. 10 f. https://www.ogh.gv.at/media/ogh_taetigkeitsbericht_2018.pdf. Accessed 25 May 2020.

85 See, e.g., Oberster Gerichtshof 2019, Tätigkeitsbericht für das Jahr 2018, p. 10. https://www.ogh.gv.at/media/ogh_taetigkeitsbericht_2018.pdf. Accessed 25 May 2020. Oberster Gerichtshof 2019, Tätigkeitsbericht für das Jahr 2018, p. 11. https://www.ogh.gv.at/media/ogh_taetigkeitsbericht_2018.pdf. Accessed 25 May 2020.

succeed in stemming the ongoing increase in workload for the *OGH*[86] and so most probably brought a measure of relief after all. This decrease in workload is even more remarkable in light of the above-mentioned fact that the *OGH* gained additional competences for employment and social security matters in 1987. As regards the workload of the individual judge, it further has to be pointed out that the increase of competences in 1987 was accompanied by the creation of six additional positions for judges at the *OGH*.[87]

Recent numbers on the duration of proceedings before the *OGH* do not indicate a significant backlog. For example, the average duration of civil cases (excluding social security and employment matters) was 3.9 months in 2015, 3.4 months in 2016 and 3.8 months in the years 2017 and 2018.[88] In 2015, the number of decisions on remedies in such matters equalled 104.9% of newly raised remedies; in 2016, the percentage was 102.9%, in 2017 98.1% and in 2018 99%.[89]

3.2 'Usability' of the System

As mentioned earlier, the system of access to the *OGH* has become increasingly complex in the course of the various reforms. This is mainly caused by the fact that the legislator has traditionally achieved the respective modifications to the Code of Civil Procedure by adding exceptions, counter-exceptions and cross-references to existing rules.[90] All this has led to a set of rules that only a few specialists can fully understand.[91] Thus it happens quite often that the *OGH* has to deal with inadmissible appeals only because lawyers and lower courts have misunderstood the rules on access to the third instance. In such cases the decision of the *OGH* commonly contains an explanation of the relevant provision (*Rechtsbelehrung in Beschlussform*).[92]

[86]In the opinion of Zechner (2005), marginal number 15, this is the only achievement of the reforms which, according to him, have failed to eliminate the overload of the Supreme Court.

[87]See Danzl (2001), p. 46; in recent years, there has been another slight increase in the number of judges which, however, did not have a significant impact on the civil section of the court.

[88]All numbers according to BIS-Justiz (annual statistics on the justice system, provided by the Austrian Federal Ministry of Justice).

[89]All numbers according to BIS-Justiz (annual statistics on the justice system, provided by the Austrian Federal Ministry of Justice).

[90]See Danzl (2001), p. 49; Geroldinger (2012), p. 65.

[91]See Fasching (1998), p. 25.

[92]See Zechner (2005), marginal number 16, with further references.

3.3 *Effectiveness in Relation to the* OGH*'s Function*

As I have pointed out previously, there is a dispute as to whether the current rules on access to the *OGH* have resulted in an 'appropriate' caseload or not. The answer to this question depends—at least to some extent—on how one defines the function of the *OGH*. As Jolowicz[93] has pointed out, overload of a Supreme Court—and thus the success of measures against it—should not only be measured in terms of case numbers, average time of proceedings and the extent of backlog, but also according to how well a court fulfils its specific function.

3.3.1 Transformation of the Court's Function

In this context, it is important to point out that the function—or at least general expectations in regard to that function—of the Austrian Supreme Court has undergone a fundamental change since the 1980s. Previously, the opinion prevailed that the main function of the *OGH* was to ensure that justice be done in individual cases and that an effect on the unity and development of the law was merely a—positive—side-effect.[94] This view was also clearly reflected in the provisions of the *Zivilprozessordnung*. As I have mentioned above, the two main filtering criteria were the value in dispute and, hence, the economic importance of the case, and whether the second instance had agreed with the court of first instance, which was clearly seen as an indicator of whether or not review by a third instance court was necessary.

On the one hand, the reforms of 1983 and 1989 were undoubtedly a product of an ongoing change of mind in that regard. At the same time, they accelerated the process towards the 'new' role of the *OGH* and triggered a new perception of the function of this court. They introduced the new postulate into the Code of Civil Procedure that the Supreme Court was primarily there to hear cases when it could contribute to the uniform application of the law and its development.

In some way it even seems that the limitation of access to the *OGH* was not so much the product of a paradigm change with respect to the proper role of a Supreme Court, but rather that the change of role was caused by the insight that restricting the jurisdiction of the *OGH* to the review of particularly important cases would be a fair way out of the overload problem.[95]

This might be one of the reasons why the guiding function never actually became the sole purpose of the *OGH*.[96] As in other German-speaking jurisdictions, the prevailing opinion today attributes to the Supreme Court a 'hybrid' function,

---

[93]Jolowicz (2000), p. 300.

[94]For an overview see, e.g., Lovrek and Musger (2019), marginal numbers 29ff.

[95]Zechner (2005), marginal numbers 7, 9, seems to draw a different conclusion.

[96]According to Rechberger and Simotta (2017), marginal number 1108, this is not even the most important function of the *OGH*.

including both the public-interest purpose of adding to the uniform application and development of the law on the one hand while on the other hand—at least to some extent—ensuring that individual cases are decided correctly.[97] This understanding is also reflected in the *OGH*'s case law on the admissibility of appeals. The court allows applications quite generously on grounds of severe errors by the second instance, even when the legal questions at hand are not relevant for other future cases. The *OGH* bases this approach—which is significantly more generous than that of the German *Bundesgerichtshof*, which operates under similar statutory provisions—on its duty to safeguard legal certainty.[98]

3.3.2 Fulfilment of the Respective Functions

Having set out that today the *OGH* is attributed a 'hybrid' function, the question remains as to how well the court can fulfil its respective functions in light of its current caseload.

3.3.3 Guiding Function

With regard to the guiding function of the *OGH*—which, according to most, is its primary function today—one must say that about 3000 applications and 1000 decisions on the merits seem too much to ensure that the Supreme Court is always able to pay adequate attention to those questions that are really crucial for the development of the law and the protection of its unity. As a result, the decisions of those important cases sometimes do not provide suitable guidance to litigants and lower courts in future cases. There is not only the practical problem that hardly anybody can keep track of this many cases and determine which of them are of general importance for the development of the law.[99] It sometimes seems as though the *OGH* itself does not adequately distinguish between the two categories and frequently treats cases in which really important questions of law are decided in the same way as routine matters.[100] This development is probably also enhanced by the rules that lower the formal standard for the reasoning of *OGH* decisions,[101] because their frequent use makes it harder to understand the reasoning of the court and to extract general guidelines from it.[102]

---

[97]Domej (2017), p. 136. See also, e.g., Kodek and Mayr (2018), marginal number 1088; Rechberger and Simotta (2017), marginal number 1108; Pimmer (2010), p. 280.

[98]Domej (2014), p. 283. See also Zechner (2005), marginal number 44.

[99]All *OGH* decisions are published on the internet in full text at https://www.ris.bka.gv.at/Jus/ (Accessed 25 May 2020), regardless of their importance; see also Oberhammer (2014), p. 171ff.

[100]Oberhammer (2014), p. 171.

[101]See Sect. 2.4 above.

[102]See Rebhahn (2011), p. 1547.

Despite these critical remarks, it must be stated that, generally, the *OGH* indeed adds to the development of the law and often does so by giving well-reasoned decisions and by entering into a lively dialogue with academia.

3.3.4 Safeguarding Individual Interests

When it comes to ensuring that correct decisions are reached in individual cases, I think the framework seems quite appropriate (even though advocates of broad Supreme Court review would, of course, argue that the *OGH* should provide its services to litigants in even more cases). About 3000 cases a year is a reasonable number to guarantee a well-founded and thorough review of the decisions of lower courts if one considers that only about 1000 of these cases result in a decision on the merits.

4 Openness to Transplants

When the Austrian legislator started to establish and later extend a system that allowed *Revision* only in important cases and made it conditional on leave granted by a court,[103] this system was—obviously—not invented from scratch; instead, the drafters could draw on examples from other countries. Nevertheless, the preparatory materials and also academic contributions from the late 1970s and early 1980s only make relatively vague references to such 'foreign examples' without giving further details.

Only one foreign system is explicitly cited as an example on a regular basis. As in many other areas of Austrian lawmaking, a closer look was taken at the German system. In lower value cases, access to the German *Bundesgerichtshof* was already subject to leave to appeal granted by the second instance court; in cases of higher value the *Bundesgerichtshof* itself could refuse to accept *Revision* on the grounds that the case did not raise an important question of law.[104] However, while the German example can be seen as the starting point for the Austrian deliberations, the system that the Austrian legislator established in 1983 differed in many details from the German model and hence was called a 'specifically Austrian solution' at the time.[105] This tendency continued in the following reforms of 1989 and 1997.

Of several points in which the legislator deliberately deviated from the German system as it used to be back then, I just want to focus on one detail. In the former German system, leave to appeal had to be granted by the court of second instance in

[103] See Sect. 2.3 above.

[104] For an overview of the former German system see, e.g., Nassall (2012), p. 114.

[105] cf. Petrasch (1983), who states that at first a 'substantial harmonization' with the German system was considered, but finally a 'specifically Austrian system' was developed.

cases where the value in dispute did not exceed a certain limit, which was DM 40,000 at the time of the first two reforms in Austria and raised to DM 60,000 in 1990.[106] The German *Bundesgerichtshof* was bound by the decision of the second instance on whether to grant appeal. For Austria, this solution was strongly opposed by members of the *OGH* who argued that it would be inadequate (and even unconstitutional) for the court of second instance to decide on the appealability of its own decision.[107] In addition, some argued that it would lead to intolerable discrepancies in the case law if the last word on the criteria for admissibility did not belong to a centralised institution such as the Supreme Court.[108] In this context, it is worth mentioning that in 1997 the last word on the *inadmissibility* of appeal was eventually transferred to the courts of second instance in cases where the relevant value did not exceed a certain amount, which was quite similar to the German DM 40,000 limit. Hence, second instance courts have from that time on been in the position to prohibit further control of their decisions by the *OGH* when they believe that the case does not raise a question of significant importance.[109] The *OGH* still can—and regularly does—reject appeals that have been allowed by the court of second instance, and it is still argued today that the legislator should not take away this power from the *OGH*, because the positive ruling of the second instance on the admissibility of the appeal should not bind the Supreme Court, since their practice is allegedly not as thoughtful as that of their German counterparts.[110]

5 Conclusion

The sections that follow contain a summary of some specific features of the Austrian reform discussion and the statutory provisions on the access to and the organisation of the *OGH* that seem important in the context of the general topic of this volume.

5.1 Absence of Real Crisis and Extent of Reforms

One remarkable feature of the Austrian discussion is that there never actually was a situation that could be referred to as a real 'crisis.' As mentioned earlier, the *OGH* had to handle a sizeable caseload almost from the beginning and judges, as well as other stakeholders, regularly pointed out (and still stress) that the caseload is too high. Nevertheless, there was never an actual threat to the functioning of the

[106] *Rechtspflege-Vereinfachungsgesetz* of November 17, 1990, (German) *BGBl* I 1990, p. 2847.

[107] See, e.g., Petrasch (1983), p. 171.

[108] See, e.g., Wurzinger (1984), p. 179; see also Fasching (1980), p. 67.

[109] See Sect. 1.4.2 above.

[110] See, e.g., Zechner (2005), marginal number 43.

Supreme Court as such. This might be one of the reasons why reforms were always taken in rather small steps instead of one fundamental change at a particular point in time.

5.2 Complexity, Definition of Role and Efficiency of Reforms

The Austrian system of access to the Supreme Court is certainly too complicated. It is the product of decades of reforms carried out by adding exceptions and counter-exceptions to the existing provisions. The main reason for this problematic situation seems to be that the legislator permanently tries to find a compromise between access to the Supreme Court for parties who wish to have their case reviewed by the highest instance and a reasonable control of the caseload that enables the *OGH* to fulfil its function as a guiding court. This compromise is also reflected by the fact that the value in dispute still is a very important filtering criterion in the Austrian system. From a modern point of view this appears to be an anachronism, since the importance of a case for the development of the law and its uniform application does not usually correlate to the sum in dispute. From all of this, one can draw the conclusion that an unclear understanding of the function of a Supreme Court can be a major impediment along the way to an effective and efficient reform concept and its implementation. *Thus, in an ideal situation, a clear definition of the role of the Supreme Court should precede any reform discussion.*

5.3 Size of the Supreme Court and Internal Organisation

With more than 40 civil judges, sitting in ten different senates, the Austrian *OGH* ranks among the bigger Supreme Courts in an international context. Nevertheless, the court is rather successful in keeping a high level of unity and consistency in its case law. This is mainly achieved through a system of specialisation among the senates. This system also helps to organise the work of the *OGH* more efficiently by reducing the time it takes for the respective judges to familiarise themselves with rarely encountered or particularly complicated matters of law, since such matters are always dealt with by the same group of judges.

5.4 Overall Conclusion/Summary

Altogether, today's rules on access to the *OGH* are a compromise in a number of ways. They show a high level of complexity and a lack of consistency. Nevertheless, the court has found a way to operate under these rules that—for the most part—seems satisfactory.

References

Arnold W-D (1989) Gerichtsgebührenrechtliche Überlegungen zur Erweiterten Wertgrenzen-Novelle 1989. Anwalts Blatt:523–530

Bajons E-M (1999) Austria. In: Jolowicz JA, Van Rhee CH (eds) Recourse against judgments in the European Union. Kluwer Law International, The Hague, pp 25–47

Ballon OJ (1987) Die Gerichtsorganisation der Arbeits- und Sozialgerichtsbarkeit. Juristische Blätter:349–357

Danzl KH (2001) Die Anrufbarkeit des OGH in streitigen Zivilsachen – von Franz Klein bis zur Gegenwart: Analyse – Rückblick – Ausblick. In: König B (ed) Festschrift für Rainer Sprung zum 65. Geburtstag. MANZ'sche Verlags- und Universitätsbuchhandlung, Vienna, pp 39–108

Domej T (2014) What is an important case? Admissibility of appeals to the supreme courts in the German-speaking jurisdictions. In: Uzelac A, Van Rhee CH (eds) Nobody's perfect. Comparative essays on appeals and other means of recourse against judicial decisions in civil matters. Intersentia, Cambridge, pp 277–287

Domej T (2017) Squaring the circle: individual rights and the general interest before the Supreme Courts in the German-speaking countries. In: Van Rhee CH, Fu Y (eds) Supreme Courts in transition in China and the West: adjudication at the service of public goals. Springer, Cham, pp 131–148

Fasching HW (1980) Prozeßprinzipien und Reform des Zivilprozesses. In: Haller H et al (eds) Verfahrensgrundsätze – Verfahrensreform im österreichischen Recht. CF Müller Juristischer Verlag, Heidelberg, pp 53–73

Fasching HW (1990) Lehrbuch des österreichischen Zivilprozeßrechts, 2nd edn. MANZ'sche Verlags- und Universitätsbuchhandlung, Vienna

Fasching HW (1998) 100 Jahre österreichische Zivilprozeßgesetze. In: Mayr PG (ed) 100 Jahre österreichische Zivilprozeßgesetze. Verlag Österreich, Vienna, pp 17–31

Felzmann E, Danzl KH, Hopf H (2009) Oberster Gerichtshof, 2nd edn. Neuer Wissenschafltlicher Verlag, Vienna

Fichtenbauer P (1989) Zum Entwurf einer erweiterten Wertgrenzen-Novelle 1989 – WGN 1989. Anwalts Blatt:333–337

Forgó-Feldner B (2012) Der OGH und der Zugang zu seinen Entscheidungen in historischer Perspektive. In: Kodek GE (ed) Zugang zum OGH. MANZ'sche Verlags- und Universitätsbuchhandlung, Vienna, pp 1–42

Fuchs W (2019) Warum gibt es immer weniger streitige Zivilverfahren? Rechtssoziologische Thesen zum Klagerückgang in Österreich und Deutschland. In: Ganner M, Voithofer C (eds) Rechtstatsachenforschung Tagungsband 2018. Innsbruck University Press, Innsbruck, pp 113–144

Geroldinger A (2012) Der Zugang zum OGH in Zivilsachen. In: Kodek GE (ed) Zugang zum OGH. MANZ'sche Verlags- und Universitätsbuchhandlung, Vienna, pp 65–81

Grabenwarter C, Musger G (2015) Praxisfragen der Gesetzesbeschwerde im Zivilverfahren. Österreichische Juristenzeitung 75(12):551–563

Jolowicz JA (2000) Managing overload in appellate courts: 'Western' countries. In: Jolowicz JA (ed) On civil procedure. Cambridge University Press, Cambridge, pp 328–351

Kodek GE (2008) Die Wahrung von Grundrechten durch die Gerichtsbarkeit. Österreichische Juristenzeitung 25(6):216–224

Kodek GE (2012) Funktion und Arbeitsweise des OGH – Die Binnensicht. In: Kodek GE (ed) Zugang zum OGH. MANZ'sche Verlags- und Universitätsbuchhandlung, Vienna, pp 99–118

Kodek GE, Mayr PG (2018) Zivilprozessrecht, 4th edn. Facultas, Vienna

Leonhard O (1950) Aus der Geschichte des Obersten Gerichtshofs. In: Festschrift zur Hunderjahrfeier des Österreichischen Obersten Gerichtshofes. MANZ'sche Verlags- und Universitätsbuchhandlung, Vienna, pp 163–211

Lovrek E (2019) § 510 ZPO. In: Fasching WH, Konecny A (eds) Kommentar zu den Zivilprozessgesetzen, Volume IV/1, 3rd edn. MANZ'sche Verlags- und Universitätsbuchhandlung, Vienna

Lovrek E, Musger G (2019) Vor §§ 502ff. ZPO. In: Fasching WH, Konecny A (eds) Kommentar zu den Zivilprozessgesetzen, Volume IV/1, 3rd edn. MANZ'sche Verlags- und Universitätsbuchhandlung, Vienna

Mayer H, Muzak G (2015) Das österreichische Bundes-Verfassungsrecht, 4th edn. MANZ'sche Verlags- und Universitätsbuchhandlung, Vienna

Mayer H, Kucsko-Stadlmayer G, Stöger K (2015) Grundriss des österreichischen Bundesverfassungsrecht, 11th edn. MANZ'sche Verlags- und Universitätsbuchhandlung, Vienna

Mayr PG (2009) Zivilverfahrensrechtliche Neuerungen des Budgetbegleitgesetzes 2009. Ecolex – Fachzeitschrift für Wirtschaftsrecht 7:562–566

Nassall W (2012) Zehn Jahre ZPO-Reform vor dem BGH. Neue Juristische Wochenschrift:113–119

Nogratnig G, Zeiringer M (2019) Rückgang der Zivilverfahren – eine Suche nach Ursachen. Anwalts Blatt 192(7–8):440–450

Oberhammer P (2014) Kleine Differenzen – Vergleichende Beobachtungen zur zivilistischen Methode in Deutschland, Österreich und der Schweiz. Archiv für civilistische Praxis 214:155–182

Oberhammer P (2015) Civil procedure. In: Grabenwarter C, Schauer M (eds) Introduction to the law of Austria. Wolters Kluwer, Alphen aan den Rijn, pp 251–260

Oberhammer P, Domej T (2010) Delay in Austrian civil procedure and the legislator's response. In: Van Rhee CH (ed) Within a reasonable time: the history of due and undue delay in civil litigation. Duncker & Humblot, Berlin, pp 255–277

Oberhammer P, Koller C (2012) Schiedsrecht im Wettbewerb der Rechtsordnungen – Zum österreichischen Schiedsrechts-Änderungsgesetz 2013. Zeitschrift für Zivilprozessrecht International 17:75–87

Petrasch F (1983) Das neue Revisions-(Rekurs-)Recht. Österreichische Juristenzeitung:169–178, 200–206

Petrasch F (1989) Der Weg zum Obersten Gerichtshof nach der Erweiterten Wertgrenzen-Novelle 1989. Österreichische Juristenzeitung:743–754

Pimmer H (2010) Bemerkungen zur Leitfunktion des Obersten Gerichtshofes in Zivilsachen. In: Fucik R et al (eds) Zivilverfahrensrecht, Jahrbuch 2010. Neuer Wissenschaftlicher Verlag, Vienna, pp 275–285

Ratz E (2013) Gesetzesbeschwerde gefährdet funktionierenden Rechtsschutz. Richterzeitung 4:77

Rebhahn R (2011) Der Urteilsstil des OGH im Vergleich mit den Höchstgerichten Deutschlands, Frankreichs und Englands. In: Fischer-Czermak C et al (eds) Festschrift zu 200 Jahre ABGB. MANZ'sche Verlags- und Universitätsbuchhandlung, Vienna, pp 1539–1564

Rechberger WH (2016) Civil procedure in Austria, 2nd edn. Wolters Kluwer, Alphen aan den Rijn

Rechberger WH, Simotta DA (2017) Grundriss des österreichischen Zivilprozessrechts, 9th edn. MANZ'sche Verlags- und Universitätsbuchhandlung, Vienna

Reindl P (1984) Die Gesetzwerdung der Zivilverfahrens-Novelle 1983. In: Bundesministerium für Justiz (ed) Neuerungen im zivilgerichtlichen Verfahrensrecht. Richterwoche 1983. Schriftenreihe des Bundesministeriums für Justiz, Vienna, pp 37–62

Rohrer R, Kuras G (2012) Gesetzesbeschwerde gegen Entscheidungen ordentlicher Gerichte? Österreichische Juristenzeitung 55(12):529–533

Scholz F (2014) Der neue österreichische Parteiantrag auf Normenkontrolle im Zivilverfahrensrecht. Zeitschrift für Zivilprozessrecht International 19:109–150

Wurzinger L (1984) Das neu gestaltete Revisionsverfahren. In: Bundesministerium für Justiz (ed) Neuerungen im zivilgerichtlichen Verfahrensrecht. Richterwoche 1983. Schriftenreihe des Bundesministeriums für Justiz, Vienna, pp 175–200

Zechner A (2005) Vor §§ 502ff. ZPO. In: Fasching WH, Konecny A (eds) Kommentar zu den Zivilprozessgesetzen, Volume IV/1, 2nd edn. MANZ'sche Verlags- und Universitätsbuchhandlung, Vienna

Croatia: Supreme Court Between Individual Justice and System Management

Alan Uzelac and Marko Bratković

Abstract The Supreme Court of the Republic of Croatia is an excellent example of an overburdened Supreme Court. The prevailing opinion on the role of the Supreme Court in Croatia is that its adjudication in the further (second) appeal procedure serves both the individual and the public purpose, i.e. both individual justice and system management. The authors of this contribution are of the opinion that such an approach is unsustainable, and that an unclear definition of the purpose of supreme adjudication is the main cause of the case overload problem. The Croatian experience with two types of second appeal ('ordinary' and 'exceptional') suggests that a combination of different criteria for the admissibility of cases to the Supreme Court (amount in dispute and importance of legal issue for the uniform application of the law) is not yielding the desired results, but rather has the effect of confusing both the judges of the Supreme Court and the attorneys of the parties as to the actual purpose of second appeal.

1 Introduction

The Supreme Court of the Republic of Croatia may look like an excellent example of an overburdened Supreme Court. However, adequate solutions for its case overload problem are yet to be implemented.

As for the role of the Supreme Court, the prevailing opinion reflected in the leading textbook on civil procedure[1] is that the adjudication by the Supreme Court in the second appeal procedure serves both an individual purpose (in terms of a legally and factually correct resolution of each individual case)[2] and a public purpose

[1]Triva and Dika (2004), p. 719.

[2]Lindblom (2000), p. 104.

A. Uzelac (✉) · M. Bratković
University of Zagreb, Faculty of Law, Zagreb, Croatia
e-mail: auzelac@pravo.hr; marko.bratkovic@pravo.hr

P. Bravo-Hurtado, C. H. van Rhee (eds.), *Supreme Courts Under Pressure*, Ius Gentium: Comparative Perspectives on Law and Justice 83,
https://doi.org/10.1007/978-3-030-63731-6_7

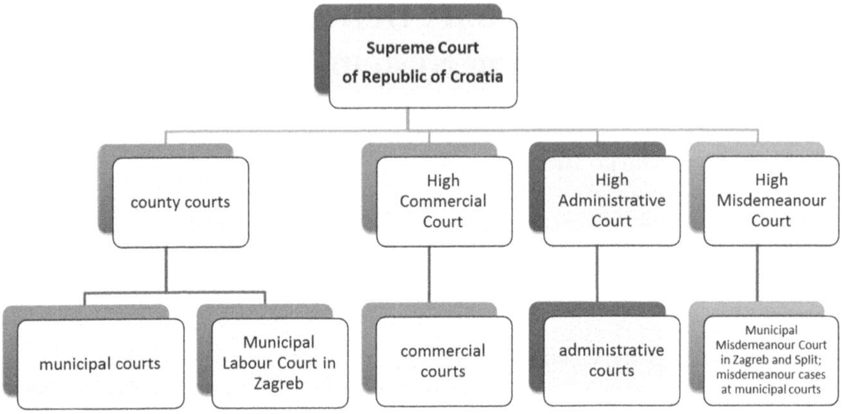

Fig. 1 Court structure in Croatia

(in terms of system management that secures a uniform application of the law and offering guidance to lower courts).[3]

Can the Supreme Court adequately, reasonably and expeditiously fulfil both individual and public purposes?[4] The Croatian experience so far suggests a negative answer. The double role of the Croatian Supreme Court—to ensure individual justice and system management—seems to be unsustainable. At least, it is certainly the main cause of the current case overload problem. Additional explanations for this assertion will be presented later in this contribution. But before embarking on the issue of case overload, we will first give a few introductory remarks about Croatia and its court structure.

The Republic of Croatia gained independence in 1991 and belongs to the circle of successor countries of the former Yugoslavia established after the Homeland War in the 1990s. In 2013, Croatia became a member of the European Union. In terms of both population (about 4.2 million inhabitants)[5] and territory (about 56,500 km^2 of land territory with an additional 31,000 km^2 of sea surface area) it is a relatively small country.[6]

The current structure of the court system in Croatia (see Fig. 1) reveals a relatively simple but dense court network consisting of courts of general jurisdiction (municipal and county courts) and specialised commercial, municipal misdemeanour courts (in Zagreb and Split) and administrative courts, and only one municipal labour court

[3]Galič (2014a), p. 293.

[4]Galič (2014a), p. 292.

[5]Population (mid-year estimate): 4,087,843. The exact figure from the 2011 census was 4,290,612 persons with permanent residence; overall 4,456,096 enumerated persons (Source: *Statistical Reports of the Croatian Bureau of Statistics*. http://www.dzs.hr/. Accessed 24 May 2020).

[6]Uzelac (2014a), p. 229.

located in Croatia's capital city Zagreb.[7] As the result of a reform to rationalise the judicial system, Croatia is indeed gradually reducing the number of courts[8] although the number remains considerably high.

The municipal courts deal with all civil and criminal cases that are not expressly identified as falling within the jurisdiction of other courts. The courts at the second level are essentially courts of appeal, which, in the civil branch, deal almost exclusively with appeals from the lower courts. The relatively high number of courts of second instance (15 appellate courts of general jurisdiction and one in commercial matters) in relation to the size of the population and their, in some aspects, conflicting opinions are two of the causes of the inconsistency in the application of the law in Croatia.

2 The Supreme Court of Croatia

The highest court is the Supreme Court. The Constitution defines the task of the Supreme Court as 'ensuring uniform application of law and equality of all in its application' (Article 119(1)).[9] In civil and commercial cases, the Supreme Court acts as the third and final instance court, deciding on second appeals on points of law (*revizija*) against decisions issued by the courts at the second instance.[10]

Though a large majority of its cases are of a civil and commercial nature, the Supreme Court also plays an important role in criminal cases. For that reason, the court is divided into two divisions, civil and criminal.[11] As the most profound changes in recent times have occurred in respect of the second appeal on points of law in civil and commercial matters, here we will only deal with its Civil Division.[12]

History of the Supreme Court The long history of the Croatian Supreme Court can be roughly divided into three main periods: before 1945, 1945–1990 and from 1991 onwards.

The early stages of the court's history are for our purposes largely irrelevant. In the pre-World War II period the Croatian lands functioned more or less autonomously, first under Austrian and Hungarian rule and later under the royal rule of

---

[7]In all other courts outside Zagreb, labour cases are within the jurisdiction of municipal courts as the courts of general jurisdiction. Outside Zagreb and Split, misdemeanour cases are also dealt with by the municipal courts of general jurisdiction.

[8]Uzelac (2014a), p. 229.

[9]*Ustav Republike Hrvatske* [Constitution of the Republic of Croatia], Official Gazette, 56/90, 135/97, 8/98, 113/00, 124/00, 28/01, 41/01, 55/01, 76/10, 85/10, 05/14.

[10]In rare civil cases where the county courts (or, potentially, the High Commercial Court) decide at first instance, the Supreme Court also acts as the regular appellate body.

[11]Uzelac and Galič (2017), p. 208.

[12]Uzelac and Galič (2017), p. 208; Uzelac (2014a), p. 231.

Serbian Kings.[13] But the lack of national independence affected the status of the judicial institutions. The highest court in the country was therefore relatively weak, unable to be recognised as an independent judicial institution.[14] Furthermore, the judiciary as a whole did not manage to reach the same degree of independence as the judiciaries in other European countries with a well-developed legal tradition.[15]

The genesis of the Supreme Court in Croatia as we know it today was more affected by the developments in the period of socialist Yugoslavia after World War II, when Croatia was a constituent republic of a federal Yugoslavia.[16] In that period, however, the liberal democratic doctrine of separation of powers was rejected, and the judiciary was not conceived as an independent branch of government, but as another layer of executive bodies under the supremacy of the representative bodies (assemblies). In accordance with the doctrine of unity of powers, the judges of all courts were appointed for a limited term of office by assemblies at various levels to which they were accountable for their work and actions.[17] As a response to the lack of independence and the potential danger of political reprimand and sanctions, the socialist courts developed hyper-formal, slow and repetitive court procedures and a complex network of means of recourse, which allowed judges to avoid responsibility for final decision-making.[18] However, in the period between 1945 and 1990 the grip of political control on the judiciary fluctuated. In the final decade of socialist rule this grip was seen to gradually loosen, but it did not disappear.

In dealing with second appeals (*revizije*) the Supreme Court mostly focused on the review of the correctness of decisions in individual cases. Despite doctrinal views on the need to focus on only some categories of cases and only a few limited grounds for appeal which may have a broad relevance, for individual litigants the Supreme Court was *de facto* viewed as just another opportunity for appeal. The low monetary thresholds as filters for access to the Supreme Court and the extensive interpretation of grounds for appeal turned this means of recourse predominantly into a means of providing another chance for the applicants in individual cases to secure a favourable outcome (or delay in execution) after the appellate court's

[13]Uzelac and Galič (2017), p. 209. For more on the organisation of the Yugoslav judiciary see Čulinović (1946), pp. 95–96.

[14]Uzelac and Galič (2017), p. 210.

[15]Čepulo (2006), p. 381.

[16]In Yugoslavia, the apex of the judicial pyramid was in most cases the Supreme Court in each of the constituent federal units, among others the Supreme Court in Zagreb, and not the Federal Supreme Court (which after 1974 was renamed Federal Court), which had limited powers and did not function as a further court of appeal against the decisions of the republic's Supreme Courts. See Galič (2014a), p. 291; Uzelac and Galič (2017), p. 211.

[17]Uzelac and Galič (2017), p. 210. Though formally appointments and extensions of terms of office were made by the assemblies, an important (and often decisive) role in the decision-making was in the hands of the Communist Party.

[18]Uzelac (2010), pp. 377–396. For similar features in Poland and other post-socialist Central European Countries see Mańko (2013).

decision not to quash or overturn the original unfavourable outcome in the lower court.

While individual appeals largely focused on an individual (private) function, the systemic role of ensuring the uniformity of the law was mainly left to another instrument that the court had at its disposal. This was the power to issue 'interpretational statements' on legal issues by the court divisions or its plenary. Such opinions could be issued in an abstract manner upon initiative of the court presidents at the divisional or plenary sessions. The sessions of the Civil Division of the Supreme Court, or even a plenary session, could consider general issues of interpretation of the law if it was established (mainly by means of internal consistency checks) that different panels intended to pass decisions based on conflicting interpretations of the same legal issues. In such cases, the whole section or plenary would consider these issues *in abstracto*. Finally, the majority of judges (irrespective of whether they had ruled in cases where such issues were raised) could form a single 'interpretational statement.' Such a statement (i.e. interpretation of the law) was, at the level of the Supreme Court, binding on all judges of the court.[19]

After declaring independence in 1991, Croatia embraced the doctrine of separation of powers, according to which judicial power forms a separate branch of government, headed by the Supreme Court.[20] In the new Croatian Constitution the Supreme Court was now clearly defined as the 'highest court' and entrusted with an apparently public function and purpose: to ensure the uniform application of the law and legal equality. Still, real changes in the approach to the court's role were slow and procedures and organisational design inherited from the previous socialist period remained largely unchanged, with a number of open issues still to be resolved.[21]

Structure of the Supreme Court The judicial activities of the Supreme Court are carried out by its civil and criminal divisions, while its administrative work is conducted by the Office of the President of the Court. Each division is headed by a president, appointed by the President of the Court according to his annual plan of activities. Each division includes a special service tasked with the monitoring, recording and analysis of case law, all of which is posted on the court's frequently updated website.

In 2020, there is a total of 48 judges of the Supreme Court, of which 25 are in the Civil Division, plus the president.[22] The number of panels, panel presidents and members is determined by the President of the Court in his annual plan of activities, which he prepares at the end of each year for the upcoming year. The Civil Division

[19]See Uzelac and Galič (2017), p. 212. A similar method for the resolution of inconsistencies in the interpretation of the law also existed at the lower courts. Only at first instance were the majoritarian interpretational statements not binding on the judges of the court and had only persuasive power. In Croatia, more or less the same options for the issuance of interpretational statements have survived to the present day. See Bratković (2017), p. 441.

[20]Galič (2014a), p. 291; Uzelac and Galič (2017), p. 213.

[21]Uzelac and Galič (2017), p. 213.

[22]See http://www.vsrh.hr/EasyWeb.asp?pcpid=42. Accessed 25 May 2020.

of the court has five panels of five Supreme Court judges. The work of the panels is carried out in panel sessions, chaired by the panel president, while the cases are presented by a judge rapporteur. The judge rapporteur's role is very important because he or she generally reports the case in the Supreme Court's session and prepares the text of the final judgment.[23]

The Supreme Court also employs additional staff that contributes to the judicial work of the court, especially in preparing and drafting decisions. The lawyers employed at the court are called 'judicial advisers' (*sudski savjetnici*). Each judge of the Civil Division of the Supreme Court has at least one such adviser. Some of them are recruited from among the ranks of the lower court judges; they are invited to temporarily serve as advisers at the Supreme Court.

3 *Revizija* as a Second Appeal on Points of Law

After 2003, when Croatia abandoned the option of the State Attorney intervening in civil proceedings,[24] *revizija* as a second appeal on points of law remained the only means of recourse before the Supreme Court in civil proceedings. Only the parties can bring an appeal to the Supreme Court in civil cases.

The notion of *revizija* in the Croatian language is difficult to translate. It refers to a second appeal on points of law, similar to the remedy of *Revision* in, for example, German or Austrian law, but it can also be compared to cassation in, for example, French or Italian law. In our contribution, the expressions *revizija* and a (second) appeal (on points of law) before the Supreme Court will be used interchangeably.

Since *revizija* before the Supreme Court can only be requested against second instance decisions, not against first instance judgments, there is no possibility of leapfrog appeals (*Sprungrevision*) to the Supreme Court that avoid the regular appeal before a second instance court. For this reason, considerable time is sometimes

[23]Uzelac and Galič (2017), p. 224.

[24]See Article 239 of the Code of Civil Procedure (*Zakon o parničnom postupku*) Amendments (Official Gazette, 117/03). Until this time, the State Attorney could file an independent recourse against most final judgments and some other decisions in civil proceedings if it was suspected that substantive or procedural law was wrongly applied. Such a 'request for the protection of legality' originally seems to be related to the procedure of *nadzor* that existed in the Soviet Union and remnants of which can still be found in the Russian Federation and some former Eastern Bloc states. In Yugoslav law, it was introduced after World War II, motivated by the protection of state interests in private law disputes (Zuglia 1957, p. 573). However, as early as the 1980s and 1990s the practical relevance of such a legal remedy in Croatia was only minor. Unlike in certain European procedural models where the *procureur public* can also submit a special remedy in civil proceedings (e.g. France, Italy, the Netherlands), the judgment of the Supreme Court following the 'request for the protection of legality' might lead to the quashing or altering of the impugned decision, hence affecting the civil rights of the individual parties in the case at hand (which seems to be problematic for the European Court of Human Rights (ECtHR) in terms of violation of the principle of *res iudicata*). See more in Uzelac (2004), p. 29; Galič (2014a), pp. 312–313.

needed for a decision to be reached at the highest level, as the case has to 'travel' through all three instances.[25]

In addition, *revizija* before the Supreme Court (if available) is regarded as a part of the domestic remedies that have to be exhausted for an application before the Constitutional Court of the Republic of Croatia or the European Court of Human Rights in Strasbourg to be admissible.[26]

In Croatian law, three stages of development of second appeal can be distinguished: (a) before 2003, (b) from 2003 to 2019, and (c) from 2019 onwards. For the topic of overburdened supreme courts, the most interesting period is certainly the second one, as the increased overload of the Croatian Supreme Court in the period from 2008 onwards significantly contributed to the adoption of the CCP Amendments in September 2019. As its effects are yet to be seen, the largest part of this contribution, unless otherwise specified, deals with the second appeal as regulated in the period between 2003 and 2019.

Originally transplanted from Franz Klein's Austrian Code of Civil Procedure to Yugoslav civil procedure, *revizija* was in the Yugoslav legal system conceived as a second appeal on points of law, available to the parties against most decisions of the courts of appeal.[27] Since 1976, *revizija* has been considered to be an 'extraordinary' legal remedy because it challenges decisions that have already become final and binding (*res iudicatae*).[28] In principle, submission of a second appeal does not suspend the enforceability of the appealed judgment (Article 384(1) Croatian Code of Civil Procedure (CCP))[29] nor does it prevent the judgment from becoming *res iudicata*.[30]

Representation of the Parties Before the Supreme Court In the civil branch of adjudication, since 2008 the parties generally have not been able to appear before the Supreme Court unrepresented. Unless the party himself is a practising lawyer, or has passed the state judicial exam, the second appeal must be filed by an attorney-at-law.[31] If this requirement is not met, a second appeal is rejected as inadmissible.

---

[25]Uzelac (2014a), pp. 246–247.

[26]See Article 59(3) of the Act on the Constitutional Court (Official Gazette, 99/99, 29/02, 49/02); see also the admissibility criteria in Article 35(1) of the European Convention on Human Rights. Uzelac (2014a), p. 233.

[27]Uzelac and Galič (2017), p. 211.

[28]The CCP was originally enacted in 1976 as a Yugoslav federal law. It continued to be in force as a Croatian law, but was later subject to many amendments. See n. 65 below.

[29]However, the enforcement court may postpone the enforcement in the enforcement proceedings upon a proposal by the respondent if he proves that enforcement would cause irreparable damage or violence. See *Ovršni zakon* [Enforcement Act], Official Gazette, 112/12, 25/13, 93/14, 55/16, 73/17, Article 65(1).

[30]Galič (2008), § 305. For a brief overview of the theory of legal remedies and their classification in Croatian legal theory in English see Uzelac (2014a), p. 236 and, in Croatian, Dika (2010), pp. 13–14.

[31]Alongside several other categories of persons who have passed the state judicial exam. Article 91a CCP as amended in 2008 (Official Gazette, 84/08).

However, compared to some other European countries (e.g. France or Germany), the limitations on the pleadings and representation before the Supreme Court are still relatively modest. All attorneys-at-law can file for a second appeal on behalf of their clients. There are no restrictions nor is special permission required. Nevertheless, the rules on representation have not decisively affected access to the Supreme Court.[32] Moreover, these rules have not caused any tangible improvement in terms of either the efficiency of the proceedings or the stricter selection of incoming cases.[33]

Grounds for an Appeal at the Supreme Court Only a party that raised its claims and defences in the earlier stages of the proceedings, but did not succeed with them before the lower courts, has a legitimate interest in launching a second appeal.[34] The time limit for filing an appeal before the Supreme Court is 30 days.[35] Otherwise, a second appeal is rejected as inadmissible.

As for the grounds for an appeal before the Supreme Court, *revizija* is admissible only on points of law; it cannot be motivated by errors of fact. It can be launched only to correct legal errors (*errores iuris*) and the gravest procedural errors (*errores in procedendo*; so-called 'absolute violations of procedure').[36] Most 'absolute violations of procedure'[37] may be invoked and also those 'relative violations'[38] which were committed in the proceedings in the appellate court.[39] Factual issues generally cannot be appealed before the Supreme Court. However, the differentiation between questions of fact and questions of law is, in certain aspects, difficult. Errors of fact, although *ex lege* inadmissible as grounds for filing a second appeal,

[32]The Constitutional Court rejected the arguments submitted by over 25 applicants questioning the constitutionality of stricter representation rules before the Supreme Court. See Constitutional Court decision U-I-4365/08 of 26 March 2013. However, it seems that even such a modest requirement for representation was interpreted by the Supreme Court in an overly formalistic manner. Thus, in its judgment in *Omerović v Croatia* (No. 2), 22980/09, §§ 42–43, 5 December 2013, the ECtHR found that the Croatian Supreme Court's rejection of the appeal launched by an applicant (who was a lawyer by profession) due to the fact that he did not attach a copy of his judicial exam certificate in the process before the Supreme Court violated his right of access to that court since 'simple skimming through the case file would suffice to detect that the first applicant was admitted to the Bar in 2003' (the applicant had submitted proof thereof in the earlier proceedings). See Article 91a (3) CCP as amended in 2019 (Official Gazette, 70/19).

[33]Uzelac and Galič (2017), p. 215.

[34]Uzelac (2014a), p. 240.

[35]The service of judgments often poses problems. Postal delivery is the most commonly used means of service, but often unsuccessful. Sometimes several months (or, in some cases, even longer) can pass before the judgment is successfully served on the party. Uzelac (2014a), p. 242.

[36]'Absolute violations of procedure,' unlike 'relative violations of procedure' (see n. 38 below), automatically lead to the nullity of the judgment.

[37]Minor errors related to territorial or *in rem* jurisdiction or double litispendence prevent a second appeal before the Supreme Court to be launched although these errors are among the 'absolute violations of procedure.'

[38]For such 'relative violations of procedure' the applicant has to prove that the error has actually had an impact on the correctness and legality of the judgment.

[39]Uzelac (2014a), p. 243; Uzelac and Galič (2017), p. 218.

can sometimes still be discussed before the Supreme Court through alleged 'inconsistencies in the grounds of the judgment,' which fall within an 'absolute violation of procedure' that could be raised as grounds for a second appeal (and in practice are quite commonly invoked by appellants). Another back-door strategy to introduce findings of fact for the consideration of the Supreme Court is through the concept of legal standards (general clauses), which are considered to raise questions of law.[40]

Revisionary and Cassational Powers of the Supreme Court The principle of party disposition commands that the Supreme Court deal only with the appealed part of the judgment. The Supreme Court therefore examines the judgment only in respect of the impugned parts and only within the limits of the reasons stated in the appeal. In proceedings before the Supreme Court, no oral hearings are held, and the entire proceedings are limited to the examination of the case file in so-called closed sessions of court panels.

Doctrine argues that the Croatian system of appeals is a mixed system[41] that has two options—to alter the appealed judgment (the system of revisionary powers) as well as to quash the impugned decision (the system of cassational powers).[42] This is also true for the appeals at the Supreme Court. If a second appeal is well founded, the Supreme Court is empowered not only to quash but also to replace the impugned decision with its own.[43]

The chart (Fig. 2) shows data regarding the outcomes of the second appeal proceedings before the Supreme Court in the period between 2006 and 2019.

In cases in which the Supreme Court rules on the merits of the impugned lower courts' decisions, only about 12% of the submitted second appeals are considered to be well founded. In approximately 36% of the cases the Supreme Court affirms the decisions of the lower courts. However, most of the second appeals filed with the Supreme Court are found to be inadmissible (according to recent statistics, 60% of second appeals filed with the Supreme Court).[44]

Filtering Access to the Supreme Court To ensure that its Supreme Court is able to function, every legislature has to create rules to restrict access to the court.[45] In Croatia, in the period from 2003 to September 2019 there were two filters for access to the Supreme Court. Accordingly, *revizija* before the Supreme Court was

---

[40]Uzelac and Galič (2017), p. 218.

[41]It should be noted that a similar system in Austria cited as an inspiration for the current Croatian law of civil procedure is considered to be revisionary; Uzelac (2014a), p. 247. On the decreasing importance of the distinction between cassation, revision and the appeal model of the Supreme Court see Jolowicz (1999), pp. 2–3; Merryman and Pérez-Perdomo (2007), p. 122; Bravo-Hurtado (2014), p. 321.

[42]Triva and Dika (2004), p. 671; Uzelac (2014a), p. 247.

[43]Galič (2014a), p. 291.

[44]More on that below (Sect. 4).

[45]Domej (2014), p. 277.

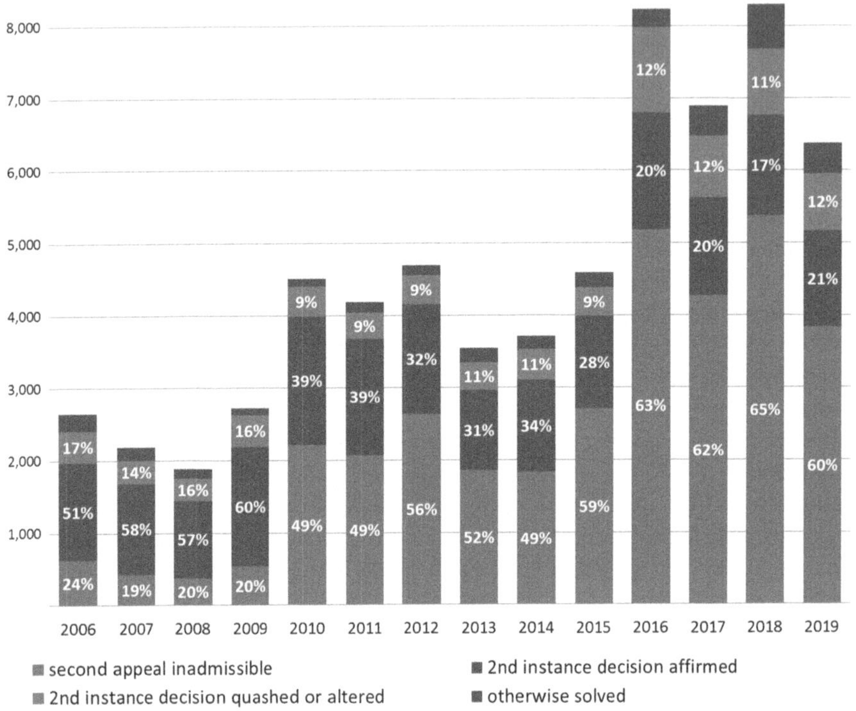

Fig. 2 Outcomes of Second Appeals againsst the Decisions of the Lower Courts before the Supreme Court of the Republic of Croatia. (Data extracted from VSRH Reports 2016 and 2017 and gathered by the authors) [VSRH Report 2016: *Izvješće predsjednika Vrhovnog suda o stanju sudbene vlasti za 2016. godinu*, p. 122, http://www.vsrh.hr/CustomPages/Static/HRV/Files/2018dok/izvjesce_predsjednika_VSRH_o_stanju_sudbene_vlasti_2016.pdf and VSRH Report 2017: *Izvješće predsjednika Vrhovnog suda o stanju sudbene vlasti za 2017. godinu*, p. 64, http://www.vsrh.hr/CustomPages/Static/HRV/Files/2018dok/izvjesce_predsjednikaVSRH_o_stanju_sudbene_vlasti_2017.pdf. Accessed 28 May 2020]

admissible both in the 'ordinary' form (which was the only form of that recourse up to 2003) and in the 'exceptional' form.

In the 'ordinary' form (in German, *Wertrevision*) the filter for access to the Supreme Court was the value of the claim (more precisely, the value of the challenged part of the decision). *Revizija* was admissible if that value is above approximately €25,000 in civil cases and €66,000 in commercial cases (200,000 and 500,000 Croatian kunas, respectively). Apart from the value of the dispute, for certain types of cases (e.g. paternity claims and disputes regarding illegal termination of an employment contract) *revizija* was admissible without exception. Accordingly, if a set of conditions provided by the law were met and *revizija* had been launched, the Supreme Court could neither admit cases not covered by those conditions nor refuse to hear a case if it was admissible under the express rules of the law.[46]

It is clear that such an 'ordinary' *revizija* served primarily for checking whether the law had been applied correctly in the lower courts;[47] in other words, it primarily served the individual interests of the litigants in the case at hand. Conversely, the 'exceptional' appeal (*izvanredna revizija*; in German, *Zulassungsrevision*) intended to be mainly in the service of the Supreme Court's system management. Its primary purpose was to facilitate the uniform application and development of the law, i.e. to help the Supreme Court carry out its public function.[48]

From 2003 to 2019, in Croatia the 'exceptional' appeal before the Supreme Court was available in parallel with the above-described 'ordinary' appeal before the Supreme Court. The 'exceptional' appeal could be launched against a court decision based on the finding that 'the decision raises an important issue of substantive or procedural law that is relevant for securing uniform application of the law and equality of all people in its application' (Article 382(2) CCP).[49] This form of appeal was based on the constitutional function of the Supreme Court. The law contained (and still contains) several typical examples of legal issues that are important for the uniformity of case law, e.g. contradictory case law in different courts of appeal; departure of the courts of appeal from the well-settled case law of the Supreme Court; as well as the need to develop the case law (in particular if this is necessary to bring it into line with international standards or decisions of the Constitutional Court or the European tribunals).

Who decides whether the question at stake is important enough to be discussed before the Supreme Court? Initially, permission to appeal had to be given by the court of second instance. Its decision on the admissibility of such 'exceptional' appeal against its own judgment had to be contained in its appellate judgment, with a full statement explaining the reasons for its decision. Since the CCP 2008 Amendments, permission to appeal has been taken out of the hands of the courts of appeal and transferred directly to the jurisdiction of the Supreme Court.

However, the filtering of cases by the Supreme Court has not been without difficulties either. The continuing increase in the number of 'exceptional' appeals demanded some changes in the law and practice. In the period between 2008 and 2011 a panel of three judges of the Supreme Court had to evaluate whether a second appeal raised an important issue. The panel could reject a second appeal as

---

[46]Uzelac (2004), p. 30.

[47]Bobek (2009), pp. 40ff.; Dika (2010), § 36; Galič (2014a), p. 292.

[48]Bratković (2016), p. 323.

[49]A similar provision can be found in Austrian law. According to § 502 of the Austrian *Zivilprozessordnung*, an appeal to the *Oberster Gerichtshof* is only admissible if the decision depends on the answer to a question of law which is of significant importance for ensuring the uniformity of the law, legal security or the development of the law. See more in Geroldinger (2012), pp. 68ff.

inadmissible by a decision that had to contain a full statement of the reasons for the rejection.[50]

In 2011, new rules in that regard were introduced. The power to reject a second appeal as inadmissible was now given to a panel of five judges of the Supreme Court. However, they were allowed to reject a second appeal without stating the reasons for deciding that the issues raised in the case are not of importance for the uniform application of the law and the equality of all in its application (former Article 392b CCP).

The lack of a full statement of the reasons for the rejection of a second appeal seemed to be an efficient filtering mechanism. However, very soon after its introduction it was impugned before the Constitutional Court, which ultimately declared the provision unconstitutional.[51] The Constitutional Court found 'no valid reasons' for avoiding a reasoned decision, and stated that such a regime deprives not only the parties, but also the general public, including the whole system of lower courts, from obtaining any insight into the reasoning of the Supreme Court on the importance of particular legal issues to the national legal system. However, the Constitutional Court added that the reasons for rejection stated in the decision to reject an application for a second appeal finding the issue of 'little relevance' 'might be of varying lengths' and that they may even be 'compressed into a single sentence, if such a sentence clearly sets out relevant arguments.'[52]

Nevertheless, in its later rulings the Constitutional Court did not find the appellants' right to a fair trial to be violated where the Supreme Court merely listed in its decision to reject the required statutory elements for second appeal, without further providing an actual statement explaining its reasoning.[53]

All in all, despite the access filters (or, conversely, precisely because of them), the Supreme Court is generally regarded as a regular third instance court that is widely available to the parties as a matter of their individual rights. It is thus hardly surprising that the Supreme Court of the Republic of Croatia belongs to the group of overburdened Supreme Courts. This situation renders the Supreme Court unable to fulfil its constitutionally determined role of supreme judicial authority responsible for the unification of case law in a timely and accurate manner.

[50] Uzelac and Galič (2017), p. 220.

[51] See Constitutional Court decision U-I-885/2013 of 11 July 2014.

[52] Ibid., § 12. Uzelac and Galič (2017), p. 221.

[53] For instance, Constitutional Court decisions U-III-3859/12 of 4 November 2014, U-III-380/13 of 19 March 2015, U-III-3204/13 of 9 June 2015, U-III-870/15 of 7 October 2015 and many others. Bratković (2016), pp. 338–339.

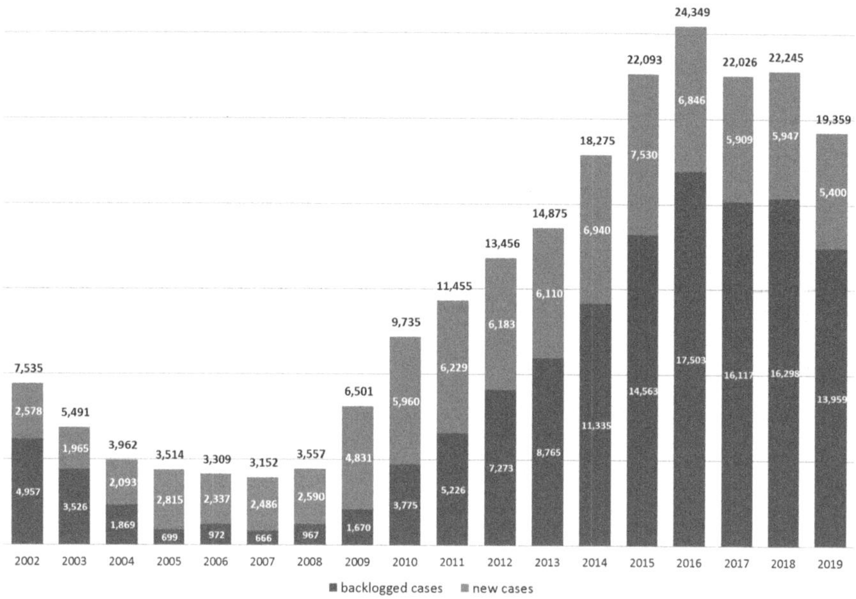

Fig. 3 New and Backlogged Second Appeal Cases (*revizija*) before the Supreme Court of the Republic of Croatia (2002–2019). (Data extracted from VSRH Reports 2016 and 2017 and gathered by the authors) [VSRH Report 2016: *Izvješće predsjednika Vrhovnog suda o stanju sudbene vlasti za 2016. godinu*, p. 122, http://www.vsrh.hr/CustomPages/Static/HRV/Files/2018dok/izvjesce_predsjednika_VSRH_o_stanju_sudbene_vlasti_2016.pdf and VSRH Report 2017: *Izvješće predsjednika Vrhovnog suda o stanju sudbene vlasti za 2017. godinu*, p. 64, http://www.vsrh.hr/CustomPages/Static/HRV/Files/2018dok/izvjesce_predsjednikaVSRH_o_stanju_sudbene_vlasti_2017.pdf. Accessed 28 May 2020]

4 Symptoms of Case Overload

Backlog Backlog is the most obvious symptom of the case overload of the Supreme Court. The Supreme Court, plagued with a large number of cases even before 2008, after the introduction of the so-called 'exceptional' second appeal (*izvanredna revizija*), became overwhelmed by its caseload, and started to produce and further increase significant backlog (see Fig. 3).[54]

It should be noted that data pertaining to the numbers of 'ordinary' and 'exceptional' second appeals were not processed separately. It is clear, however, that the increase in the total number of second appeals was for the most part caused by the increase in the number of 'exceptional' second appeals. Paradoxically, even though the introduction of the 'exceptional' second appeal was supposed to facilitate case filtering and allow only such cases as are relevant for the uniform application of the law and

[54]Uzelac and Galič (2017), p. 216.

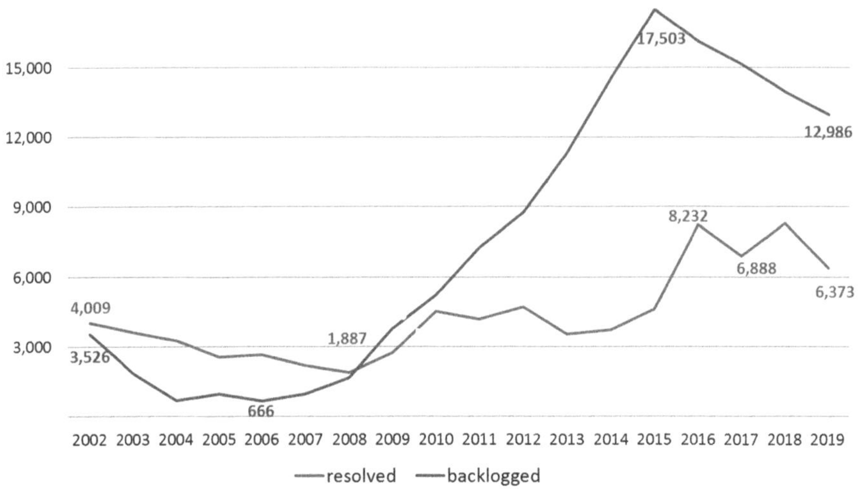

Fig. 4 Resolved and Backlogged Second Appeal (*revizija*) Cases before the Supreme Court of the Republic of Croatia (2002–2019). (Data extracted from VSRH Reports 2016 and 2017 and gathered by the authors) [VSRH Report 2016: *Izvješće predsjednika Vrhovnog suda o stanju sudbene vlasti za 2016. godinu*, p. 122, http://www.vsrh.hr/CustomPages/Static/HRV/Files/2018dok/izvjesce_predsjednika_VSRH_o_stanju_sudbene_vlasti_2016.pdf and VSRH Report 2017: *Izvješće predsjednika Vrhovnog suda o stanju sudbene vlasti za 2017. godinu*, p. 64, http://www.vsrh.hr/CustomPages/Static/HRV/Files/2018dok/izvjesce_predsjednikaVSRH_o_stanju_sudbene_vlasti_2017.pdf. Accessed 28 May 2020]

the equality of all people in its application to reach the Supreme Court, it led to a flood of cases inundating the Supreme Court.

The case backlog at the Supreme Court rapidly grew in the period 2008 to 2015 (Fig. 4). In the period between 2006 and 2015, the number of second appeals filed with the Supreme Court increased threefold (from about 2500 to 7500 cases), while the backlog increased almost 15 times (from about 1000 to almost 15,000 cases). In 2016, the Supreme Court had a workload of over 24,000 cases, of which approximately 72% were unresolved cases from the previous period. At the end of 2017 the number of backlogged cases was slightly reduced, probably due to second appeal cases being assigned to judicial advisers. An interpretational statement of the Supreme Court adopted at the end of 2015 finding all second appeals against costs orders inadmissible also contributed to the reduction of the backlogged cases.

The Volume, Quality and Consistency of the Supreme Court's Case Law The huge volume of case law of the Supreme Court is another symptom of its overload. In the modern era of computerisation, electronic databases have made the court's case law widely available.[55] This is undoubtedly a positive trend. However, the lower courts, the parties and their attorneys still seem to be having difficulty finding

[55]Uzelac and Galič (2017), p. 216. See https://sudskapraksa.csp.vsrh.hr/search. Accessed 29 May 2020.

the relevant decisions. The volume of the Supreme Court's case law is simply too great to be properly studied, analysed and monitored.[56]

By the end of 2015 a total of 166,985 decisions of the Supreme Court had been published on the court's website.[57] More than 17,000 decisions were published just in 2015. These numbers, however, do not pertain only to the decisions of the Civil Division, but to all of the court's decisions; nevertheless they are still illustrative. Considering the enormous number of cases the court is handling, it would not be realistic to expect the court's case law to be coherent, well reasoned and comprehensible.[58] The overwhelming number of decisions, albeit publicly available, does not really contribute much to legal certainty and predictability in the decision-making of the lower courts.[59] What is more, the unpredictability attracts more litigation and generates a vicious circle with an ever-increasing number of cases.

Consequently, Supreme Court judges, often overburdened with routine matters, cannot devote enough time and attention to important cases that raise complex legal questions. For this reason their decisions, drafted in a copy-paste manner, repeat the court's already well-established positions, without much added value that may guide future litigants.[60] On the other hand, due to its heavy caseload and its 'short-term memory' the Supreme Court is not even able to keep track of its own case law.[61]

The case overload problem thus threatens not only the proper exercise of the public function of the Supreme Court, but also any individual interests of the parties. Due to the heavy caseload, a decision in a second appeal procedure takes on average more than 2 years.[62] Moreover, the Supreme Court decides in about 1000 cases per year in which the original lawsuit has been pending for 10 or more years.[63]

To sum up, the legal regulation of 'ordinary' and 'exceptional' appeal on points of law facilitates the carrying out of the Supreme Court's private and public

---

[56]Similar Galič (2014b), p. 6 for Slovenia (and other post-socialistic countries). Bobek (2009), p. 44.

[57]VSRH Report 2015: *Izvješće predsjednika Vrhovnog suda o stanju sudbene vlasti za 2015. godinu* (Supreme Court President Report on the State of the Judiciary in 2015), p. 113, http://www.vsrh.hr/CustomPages/Static/HRV/Files/2016dok/izvjesce_predsjednika_o_stanju_sudbene_vlasti_2015.pdf. Accessed 28 May 2020. Incidentally, the total number published by the end of 2014 was 149,688.

[58]Jolowicz (1999), pp. 332 and 348.

[59]Bobek (2009), pp. 33–34; Galič (2014a), p. 293.

[60]Similar Galič (2014b), p. 6 for Slovenia and Bobek (2009), pp. 33–34 for the Czech Republic.

[61]For example, the decisions of the Supreme Court concerning the calculation of costs in the event of partial success of a party in a civil lawsuit have been very inconsistent.

[62]According to a lecture by the President of the Supreme Court delivered on 23 October 2013, the average duration of unresolved *Rev* (second appeal) cases was 845.12 days (or 28 months). Due to the increasing number of received and delayed cases, the average duration of an unresolved case before the Supreme Court is currently even longer, about 3 years.

[63]See e.g. VSRH Report 2017, *Izvješće predsjednika Vrhovnog suda o stanju sudbene vlasti za 2017. godinu*, p. 61, http://www.vsrh.hr/CustomPages/Static/HRV/Files/2018dok/izvjesce_predsjednikaVSRH_o_stanju_sudbene_vlasti_2017.pdf. Accessed 28 May 2020. Such cases carry a special signature: *Rev-x*.

functions, but this only works well on paper. In reality, as supported by the statistics presented above, the Supreme Court was failing to fulfil either of its primary functions. In our opinion, it is precisely the ambition for the court to simultaneously carry out a private function (individual justice) and a public one (system management) that was (and still is) the principal cause of its overload.[64]

It is generally agreed that the Supreme Court is not functioning as it should. The problem of case overload affects the judges, the parties and their lawyers alike. However, opinions vary as to the appropriate measures which would relieve the court's burden. It appears that some legal actors are motivated by the protection of their own (particular) interests, which renders a general consensus about such measures next to impossible.

5 Case Overload Solutions and Their Effectiveness

The Supreme Court was overburdened with a high volume of cases even before 2008, when the number of cases started to grow beyond control. For this reason, from the 1990s onwards frequent legal amendments have been made in order to keep the number of incoming second appeal cases under control.[65] The Croatian people traditionally seem to think that it is only by legislative changes (and not by changes to the construction of existing provisions) that reforms can take place. Amendments to the law of procedure are so frequent that they look more like panic-driven and messy crisis-management measures than well-thought-out reforms. Such urgently passed measures often have unwanted and undesirable effects, which, in turn, call for new amendments, ensuring a vicious circle of changes devoid of a clear direction.

Raising the Minimum Amount of the Claim for a Second Appeal In contemplating measures for reducing the caseload of the Supreme Court, the easiest choice initially seemed to be to raise the statutory minimum amount of the claim for second appeals to the Supreme Court. The minimum amount set for a second appeal in the 1990s was rather low, as the prescribed nominal sums, owing to an extremely high inflation rate of about 1000% annually, soon amounted to the equivalent of only a few euros. Raising the minimum amount in accordance with the comparable Austrian model seemed to be in order. After 1999, the threshold for a second appeal was set at about €13,000. In 2011, it was doubled and set at the level, which is the equivalent of about €26,000 (in commercial cases: about €66,000).[66]

The tinkering with the monetary threshold for a second appeal can certainly help to reduce the number of cases arriving at a Supreme Court, but not without creating a

[64]Galič (2014a), p. 293.

[65]Amendments to the CCP pertaining to a second appeal are marked in bold. *Official Gazette SFRY*, **4/77**, 36/77, 36/80, **69/82**, 58/84, **74/87**, **57/89**, **20/90**, **27/90**, 26/91, 34/91, 35/91; *Official Gazette RC*, **53/91**, **91/92**, **112/99**, **117/03**, **02/07**, **84/08**, 96/08, 123/08, **57/11**, 148/11, 25/13, **89/14**, **70/19**.

[66]Uzelac and Galič (2017), p. 218.

new set of problems. Firstly, it is questionable whether the cases involving high amounts of claim are necessarily cases that raise important issues of law. Some comparable legislatures (e.g. Germany) eliminated the value in dispute as a criterion for the admissibility of appeals to the Supreme Court, as it was considered to be unfair to use economic criteria for measuring the importance of legal cases. Rather, important issues of law may arise in cases of small value,[67] while 'big' value litigations may contain only routine legal issues and questions that were settled in case law long ago.[68]

Furthermore, as cases in Croatian courts often take years to be resolved, and the rules regarding the amount in dispute are not always fully transparent (and the courts tend to apply them in an overly formalistic manner),[69] satellite litigation and violations of due process may occur while deciding on the value-related admissibility of the second appeal. Some cases have even led to human rights violations as established in proceedings before the European Court of Human Rights in Strasbourg.[70]

Increasing Capacity of the Supreme Court Parallel to raising the minimum amount of claim for a second appeal, the problem of case overload has also been addressed by increasing the number of judges of the Civil Division. The number of judges in the Civil Division of the Supreme Court rose from 19 in 2008 to 28 in 2014 (see Table 1). The number of judicial advisers grew simultaneously.

However, this measure was equally unsuccessful in achieving the desired results. Moreover, it made the tracking and harmonisation of the case law of the highest tribunal even more difficult.[71] In addition, it does not seem realistic that a country of only 4.2 million people can produce a sufficient number of judges who will meet the highest professional and ethical requirements expected of judges at the highest court of the judicial network.[72] The relatively large number of Supreme Court judges has likely negatively affected the esteem afforded them.[73] On top of that, Croatia is already among those countries with the largest number of Supreme Court judges per capita in Europe.[74]

Both measures described above (the raising of the minimum amount of claim for a second appeal and the appointment of additional judges to the Supreme Court)

---

[67]See, for instance, the Christmas bonus case discussed below.

[68]Uzelac and Galič (2017), p. 219; Domej (2014), p. 279.

[69]For an excessively formalistic and restrictive approach to the calculation of the value of the claim see, e.g., the decision of the Croatian Constitutional Court U-III-2646/07 of 18 June 2008. Galič (2014a), p. 296.

[70]See *Egić v Croatia*, 32806/09, 5 June 2014 and *Vusić v Croatia*, 48101/07, 1 July 2010.

[71]Bobek (2009), p. 37; Uzelac (2014b), p. 11.

[72]Bratković (2016), p. 331.

[73]Galič (2014a), p. 294.

[74]One Supreme Court judge is appointed in Croatia per 50,000 to 100,000 inhabitants. In most European countries, one Supreme Court judge serves between 200,000 and 500,000 inhabitants. Uzelac (2014b), p. 9.

Table 1 Number of judges and second appeal cases per judge of the Civil Division of the Supreme Court of the Republic of Croatia (2006–2019)[a]

	2006	2007	2008	2009	2010	2011	2012	2013	2014	2015	2016	2017	2018	2019
Number of judges	21	21	19	22	21	23	23	25	28	25	24	23	24	24
Number of cases per judge	158	150	187	296	464	498	585	595	653	884	1015	958	927	807

[a]Data extracted from VSRH Report 2016, *Izvješće predsjednika Vrhovnog suda o stanju sudbene vlasti za 2016. godinu*, p. 121, http://www.vsrh.hr/CustomPages/Static/HRV/Files/2018dok/izvjesce_predsjednika_VSRH_o_stanju_sudbene_vlasti_2016.pdf (Accessed June 2020), and gathered by the authors

focus on the preservation of the private function of the Supreme Court. Its public function, although guaranteed by the Constitution, only came to prominence in 2003. However, the events from 2003 to the present day have shown that the mere introduction of the new form of second appeal, based on the partially new understanding of the role of the Supreme Court, is not in itself sufficient to change day-to-day practice. This was largely a result of the attitude inherited from the former period, which had its ideological roots in socialist legal theory, in particular the adherence to the principle of material truth[75] and the perception that there should be as many levels of 'control' as possible.[76]

Introduction of Special Permission to Appeal After the minimum amount of claim for a second appeal was set relatively high in the early 2000s, it was thought necessary to create the possibility for the parties to cases which did not meet this criterion to have recourse to the highest judicial instance. The Austrian model of 'exceptional' second appeal was used as a source of inspiration by the Croatian legislator.

The new form of second appeal (*izvanredna revizija*) was supposed to serve as an instrument for the harmonisation and unification of case law at the national level. However, in the Croatian environment major flaws came to the surface in the practical application of this instrument. Initially, as already explained, Croatian law introduced the system that made the admissibility of a second appeal dependent on the special permission of the court of appeal.[77] In general, the courts of appeal were very reserved about allowing appeals against 'their' judgments (inter alia, also due to performance measurement systems that penalised judges who had a high number of judgments quashed or altered).[78] Moreover, some categories of cases could not come within the reach of the Supreme Court because they were expressly excluded by law, such as small claims cases.

So, for example, when the Croatian government ceased to apply the collective labour agreement in force in 2000, and refused to execute the payment of special annual wage supplements to state employees (the so-called Christmas bonus, equalling approximately €150 per person), no appeal to the Supreme Court was available despite the fact that the courts of appeal had developed conflicting case law in those cases. This led several thousand petitioners to turn to the Constitutional Court.[79] Not surprisingly, on petition that questioned the constitutionality of the new rules on

[75]This was an expression of judicial paternalism, but also of the ideological view that courts (that is: the State) are omnipotent and should be able to find the truth in order to provide for substantive justice and to affirm the 'socialist legality' without any hindrances (Uzelac 2004, p. 300).

[76]Uzelac (2010), p. 390.

[77]Unlike the Austrian legal model, Croatian law did not provide for the possibility of reviewing the decision of a second instance court concerning granting or rejecting permission to appeal.

[78]Uzelac and Galič (2017), p. 220.

[79]As the Constitutional Court sometimes exercises a liberal approach to the notion of 'constitutional rights,' in practice, the Constitutional Court is often seen as a court of fourth instance. Uzelac (2014a), p. 234.

second appeal, the Constitutional Court found that the new legal regulation of second appeal did not enable the Supreme Court to fulfil its constitutional role efficiently and effectively.[80]

In response to the critique by the Constitutional Court, in 2008 the access to 'exceptional' second appeal was significantly reshaped. The impossibility to grant leave to file a second appeal before the Supreme Court in small claims cases and other excluded matters was removed.[81] At the same time, permission to appeal was taken out of the hands of the courts of appeal, and put into the hands of the Supreme Court.[82]

Most of the second appeals filed with the Supreme Court after 2008 (decided on by the court since 2010) are found to be inadmissible (see Fig. 1). What is the cause of this situation? Opinions vary widely, and the real answer probably lies somewhere in the middle. The Supreme Court puts at least part of the blame on the quality of the petitions filed by lawyers, arguing that the attorneys who represent the parties are generally only repeating the arguments from their previous appeals, repackaging them to fit the conditions of admissibility.[83] On the other hand, the parties and their lawyers believe that the high number of rejected applications for second appeal due to inadmissibility is nothing more than an excuse created by the Supreme Court for excluding cases in order to get rid of its backlog.

Effectiveness of Case Overload Solutions In any event, the reduction of the backlog, although a desirable objective, should not be the focus, but rather a by-product of a higher goal. The problem lies in the fact that the goal of the measures introduced remains unclear. It is for this reason that none of the applied solutions managed to improve the position of the Supreme Court in the fulfilment of its duties—neither private nor public. Different measures would be appropriate for each of these functions, but a combination thereof rarely yields good results. On the contrary, a hybrid system, with two separate tracks and functions within the, basically, same means of recourse, does not enable all the actors—judges, parties and their lawyers—to recognise what is actually required and expected of them.[84] A 'hybrid' system can thus easily become a 'confused' system.[85]

---

[80]Decision of the Constitutional Court of the Republic of Croatia U-I-1569/2004 of 20 December 2006 (Official Gazette, 2/07). Uzelac and Galič (2017), p. 221.

[81]Supporting the claim that the Croatian legislator is devoid of a clear vision, in 2011 (Official Gazette, 57/11) the system that makes the admissibility of the second appeal dependent on the special permission of the court of appeal was reintroduced for small claims cases.

[82]Uzelac and Galič (2017), p. 221.

[83]See also Dika (2010), p. 839. The same conclusion can be drawn from a number of the reasonings of the Supreme Court justifying their rejection of a second appeal because the applicant only invoked the erroneous application of substantive law, failing to specify the legal issue which constitutes the grounds for the second appeal (Rev-x-228/09-2 of 8 July 2009. See, by analogy, Rev-r-183/2009-2 of 29 April 2009).

[84]Uzelac and Galič (2017), p. 225.

[85]Ibid.

If we accept the line of reasoning (supported by the statistical data presented) that the Supreme Court cannot at the same time carry out both its public and its private functions to a satisfactory degree, and if we argue that its public function, which is, inter alia, provided for in the Constitution, should have precedence, it remains only to find a model which will enable the Supreme Court to carry out its constitutional task by resolving second appeals. The constitutional role of the Supreme Court, as we have demonstrated, may be frustrated not only in the event that access to the Supreme Court is totally closed, but also if the law leaves the doors to the Supreme Court open too wide.[86]

We can conclude that the Supreme Court needs a real and openly recognised paradigm shift[87] towards due fulfilment of its public function of ensuring the uniform application and development of the law, which sees a reasonable number of carefully selected cases of second appeal as a means to an end, and not an end in itself.

6 An Embrace of the Public Function of the Supreme Court?

The reasons just outlined motivated a new legislative project which, for the first time, emphasised the public function of the Supreme Court.[88] The provisions contained in the new regulation are mostly inspired by the Slovenian regulation of second appeals of 2008, the main difference being that, unlike the Slovenian law, the minimum amount of the claim as a criterion for access to the Croatian Supreme Court is absent.[89]

According to the new model, permission to appeal is subject to separate proceedings in which admissibility is examined, followed by another set of proceedings on the merits if leave is granted. In the first phase, the applicant has to seek permission to appeal from the Supreme Court and raise only the issues that are relevant for that purpose.[90] If the Supreme Court grants permission to appeal, then in the second phase the party must, within another time limit, submit a fully and extensively reasoned second appeal on points of law.[91]

---

[86]Galič (2014a), pp. 297–298.

[87]See Lindblom (2000), pp. 105 and 136.

[88]The CCP Amendments entered into force in September 2019.

[89]The removal of monetary thresholds was, however, an element of the later amendments to the Slovenian CCP of 2017.

[90]For certain types of cases (e.g. paternity claims and disputes regarding illegal termination of an employment contract) second appeal is admissible *ex lege*, without permission of the Supreme Court, which is an undesirable remnant from the former regulation of second appeal.

[91]Galič (2014a), pp. 301ff.

In certain circles of legal professionals and academics, such a two-stage process has been met with considerable criticism, not only in Croatia, but in Slovenia as well. Some scholars argued that it was impossible to know whether a certain legal question was important unless it was established that the lower court had decided on it incorrectly, neglecting the fact that the qualification of a particular issue of law as important from a public perspective is quite different from the question of whether the lower courts have decided it incorrectly.

Opponents of the new model were even more critical of the provision according to which the Supreme Court is authorised to reject a second appeal without the need to give the full reasoning for its decision. Few have noted that the aim of this provision was to enable the court to rationally organise its work and dedicate the majority of its time to important legal issues in cases in which a second appeal was granted. Conversely, it was argued that new rules on admissibility 'would lead to arbitrariness which opens the gates for inevitable violations of fundamental rights of the parties.' Such statements are based on the fear of abuse of power by the Supreme Court, and the belief that the court would dismiss most applications without proper justification merely for the purpose of reducing its workload, and regardless of the actual relevance of the issues at stake in second appeal cases.[92] All these criticisms reflect the low degree of trust the general public (but also the legal profession)[93] has in the judiciary, with no exception made for the highest judicial instance.[94]

Regardless of any sociological and political causes of this state of affairs,[95] it should be noted that the proper functioning of the Rule of Law is not possible without trust in the (highest) courts, which should be composed of experienced legal experts who observe the highest ethical standards.[96] Yet trust needs to be deserved (and maintained), which can be best achieved by the consistency of case law and the

[92]Bratković (2016), p. 335. It should be noted that on numerous occasions the ECtHR has confirmed that a mere summary reasoning (or even the absence thereof) of a decision finding an application for an appeal with a Supreme Court inadmissible does not constitute a violation of the Convention (*Nerva* v *UK*, 42295/98, 11 July 2000, *Øvlisen v Denmark*, 16469/05, 30 August 2006, *Persson v Sweden*, 27098/04, 27 March 2008, *Kukkonen v Finland*, Nr. 2, 47628/06, 13 January 2009, *Wnuk v Poland*, 38308/05, 1 September 2009, *Nersesyan v Armenia*, 15371/07, 19 January 2010). However, in *Nersesyan* and *Wnuk* the ECtHR approved the decisions of the Armenian and Polish Constitutional Courts' rulings that their respective Supreme Courts must provide the reasoning for their decisions finding applications inadmissible, considering it a higher standard of protection of human rights. Galič (2014a), p. 311.

[93]Some data indicate that the level of trust in the judiciary in Croatia is among the lowest in Europe. In 2016, as many as 68% of Croatian citizens had a generally negative view of the functioning of the judiciary, 59% of them said they did not trust the courts and 40% considered corruption to be widespread in the judiciary. Bratković (2019), p. 162.

[94]See Bratković (2018), pp. 339 and 344.

[95]See *amplius* Uzelac (2010), pp. 377–396; Mańko (2013), pp. 207–233 (for Poland); Bobek (2009), pp. 50, 55–57 (for the Czech Republic); Zobec (2015), pp. 932ff. (for Slovenia).

[96]Bratković (2016), pp. 335 and 338. It was evidently a lack of trust in their Supreme Courts, i.e. a fear of arbitrariness in their work, that led the constitutional courts in Armenia, Poland, the Czech Republic (for more detail see Bobek 2009, pp. 55ff.), Hungary, but also Croatia to conclude that the legal provisions permitting the Supreme Courts not to provide the reasoning for their decisions

force of arguments in judicial decisions, and by a careful selection of judges who are appointed to the Supreme Court.[97] Retaining the status quo ante of the second appeal and producing several thousand decisions every year will certainly do little to enhance the reputation of the court.

In searching for better legislative models, one should seize the rare opportunity to take into consideration the successes of a comparable reform in a comparable system. The Croatian and Slovenian legal systems are comparable in their essential features, both in terms of their legal culture and traditions and in terms of their legal and political environments. In such a situation, there is little chance that legal transplants from one system would become legal irritants in the other. Indeed, it goes without saying that the operation should be carried out in an appropriate manner, what, unfortunately, is not the case with the CCP Amendments of 2019.

Despite all indicators that prove the success of Slovenian second appeal reforms,[98] a significant part of the Croatian legal community—mainly consisting of practising lawyers, but also of some academics—still has difficulty in accepting the shift in the Supreme Court's role. It seems that it is hard to detach oneself from the accustomed perception under which access to a Supreme Court is a matter of right, even a constitutionally protected right.[99] Some encouragement can be seen in the positive attitude of the majority of the Supreme Court judges, and their general support for the introduction of the new model of second appeal. However, it also remains to be seen whether this will be sufficient for a decisive 'paradigm shift' and full acceptance of the model that underscores the public function of the Supreme Court.

7 Conclusion

In a perfect world, Supreme Courts would be exactly what their 'supreme' designation implies: almighty and omnipotent. They would provide protection to the individual rights of every litigant, and they would diligently and swiftly control the accuracy and legality of adjudication of all the lower courts in each case. At the same time, they would give clear and well-reasoned judgments in all cases of public interest, wisely and profoundly developing the law. They would eliminate all inconsistencies in legal interpretation and ensure uniform application of the law in each individual case.

---

finding a case inadmissible are not constitutional. Galič (2014c), pp. 165ff.; Zobec (2015), pp. 932–933; Galič (2014b), p. 17.

[97]Zobec (2015), p. 937.

[98]Bratković (2016), pp. 329ff.

[99]Galič (2014a), p. 298; Bobek (2009), p. 48. In Croatia, however, the constitutional right to appeal only relates to second instance proceedings, not to third instance proceedings.

So far, however, no Supreme Court has ever come close to this ideal. Every success story has been based on a trade-off, and in most cases the trade-off was based on the prevalence of the Supreme Court's public purpose. Most of the systems that desired to preserve both the public and the private functions of the Supreme Court produced disappointing results, often leading to a situation in which neither of the two functions were able to be exercised in a satisfactory manner.

The Croatian experience with the two types of second appeal ('ordinary' and 'exceptional') suggests that a combination of different criteria for the admissibility of cases to the Supreme Court does not yield the desired results, but rather has the effect of confusing both the judges of the Supreme Court and the attorneys of the parties as to the actual purpose of each of the two types of second appeal.

In order to facilitate a system of second appeal which would allow the Croatian Supreme Court to rule only in cases which are relevant for the uniform application of the law and the equality of all in its application, the number of decisions delivered should be relatively small, but well-publicised and available. A reduction in the number of cases admitted by the Supreme Court should not, however, be an end in itself, but a necessary prerequisite for carrying out the court's public role. If the Supreme Court duly fulfils its public duty, the resulting higher degree of consistency and clarity of its case law will provide a higher level of protection for the individual rights of the parties to the proceedings before the lower courts.

The power of the Supreme Court to summarily dismiss applications for second appeal should by no means be used solely as an instrument for a reduction of its caseload, but rather as a means for the court to rationally organise its work and dedicate the majority of its time to important legal issues arising from the cases in which second appeal has been granted. But, a caveat is also in order. An indispensable condition for a successful implementation of the new model (and of the Rule of Law in general) is public trust in the judiciary and particularly in the Supreme Court. The Supreme Court should be duly and deservedly recognised as the centre of legal knowledge, wisdom and integrity. At present, this remains an unfinished project in Croatia.

References

Bobek M (2009) Quantity or quality? Reassessing the role of supreme jurisdictions in Central Europe. Am J Comp Law 57(1):33–58

Bratković M (2016) Revizija po dopuštenju: hrvatske dvojbe i slovenska iskustva (Admitting further appeals to the Supreme Court: Croatian uncertainties and Slovenian experience). In: Rijavec V et al (eds) Zbornik radova s II. međunarodnog savjetovanja Aktualnosti građanskog procesnog prava – nacionalna i usporedna pravnoteorijska i praktična dostignuća. Pravni fakultet Sveučilišta u Splitu, Split, pp 319–351

Bratković M (2017) De expensis non curat praetor supremus? In: Šago D et al (eds) Zbornik radova s III. međunarodnog savjetovanja Aktualnosti građanskog procesnog prava – nacionalna i usporedna pravnoteorijska i praktična dostignuća. Pravni fakultet Sveučilišta u Splitu, Split, pp 427–448

Bratković M (2018) Roots of the resistance to the change in the Supreme Court's role. In: Uzelac A, Van Rhee CH (eds) Transformation of civil justice. Unity and diversity, Springer, Cham, pp 333–349
Bratković M (2019) Građansko pravosuđe u službi građana (Civil justice as a public service). In: Barbić J (ed) Europska budućnost hrvatskoga građanskog pravosuđa. Hrvatska akademija znanosti i umjetnosti, Zagreb, pp 161–183
Bravo-Hurtado P (2014) Two ways to uniformity: recourse to the Supreme Court in the civil law and the common law world. In: Uzelac A, Van Rhee CH (eds) Nobody's perfect. Comparative essays on appeals and other means of recourse against judicial decisions in civil matters. Intersentia, Cambridge, pp 319–335
Čepulo D (2006) Izgradnja modernog hrvatskog sudstva 1848–1918 (Building up the modern Croatian judiciary). Zbornik Pravnog fakulteta u Zagrebu 56(2–3):325–383
Čulinović F (1946) Pravosuđe u Jugoslaviji (Yugoslav judiciary). Nakladni zavod Hrvatske, Zagreb
Dika M (2010) Građansko procesno pravo. Pravni lijekovi (Civil procedure. Legal remedies). Narodne novine, Zagreb
Domej T (2014) What is an important case? Admissibility of appeals to the Supreme Courts in the German-speaking jurisdictions. In: Uzelac A, Van Rhee CH (eds) Nobody's perfect. Comparative essays on appeals and other means of recourse against judicial decisions in civil matters. Intersentia, Cambridge, pp 277–289
Galič A (2008) Civil procedure. Slovenia. In: Blanpain R (ed) International encyclopaedia of laws. Civil procedure, vol 49. Kluwer Law International, Alphen aan den Rijn, pp 1–222
Galič A (2014a) Reshaping the role of Supreme Courts in the countries of the former Yugoslavia. In: Uzelac A, Van Rhee CH (eds) Nobody's perfect. Comparative essays on appeals and other means of recourse against judicial decisions in civil matters. Intersentia, Cambridge, pp 291–317
Galič A (2014b) A civil law perspective on the Supreme Court and its functions. Paper presented at the conference on the functions of the Supreme Court – issues of process and administration of justice, Warsaw University, Warsaw, 11–14 June 2014. http://colloquium2014.uw.edu.pl/wp-content/uploads/sites/21/2014/01/Ales-Galic.pdf. Accessed 28 May 2020
Galič A (2014c) Does a decision of the Supreme Court denying leave to appeal need to contain reasons? In: Adolphsen J et al (eds) Festschrift für Peter Gottwald zum 70. Geburtstag. CH Beck, Munich, pp 159–173
Geroldinger A (2012) Der Zugang zum OGH in Zivilsachen. In: Kodek G (ed) Zugang zum OGH. Manz, Vienna, pp 65–81
Jolowicz JA (1999) Introduction. Recourse against civil judgements in the European Union: a comparative survey. In: Jolowicz JA, Van Rhee CH (eds) Recourse against judgments in the European Union. Kluwer Law International, The Hague, pp 1–23
Lindblom PH (2000) The role of the Supreme Courts in Scandinavia. In: Lindblom PH (ed) Progressiv process – Spridda uppsatser om domstollsprocessen och samhällsutvecklingen. Iustus Förlag, Uppsala, pp 87–149
Mańko R (2013) Survival of the socialist legal tradition? A polish perspective. Comp Law Rev 4 (2):1–28. https://papers.ssrn.com/sol3/papers.cfm?abstract_id=2332219. Accessed 28 May 2020
Merryman JH, Pérez-Perdomo R (2007) The civil law tradition: an introduction to the legal systems of Europe and Latin America, 3rd edn. Stanford University Press, Stanford
Triva S, Dika M (2004) Građansko parnično procesno pravo (The law of civil procedure). Narodne novine, Zagreb
Uzelac A (2004) Accelerating civil proceedings in Croatia – a history of attempts to improve the efficiency of civil litigation. In: Van Rhee CH (ed) The law's delay. Essays on undue delay in civil litigation. Intersentia, Cambridge, pp 283–313
Uzelac A (2010) Survival of the third legal tradition? Supreme Court Law Rev 49(2):377–396
Uzelac A (2014a) Features and shortcomings of appellate review in civil and administrative cases in Croatia. In: Uzelac A, Van Rhee CH (eds) Nobody's perfect. Comparative essays on appeals

and other means of recourse against judicial decisions in civil matters. Intersentia, Cambridge, pp 229–258
Uzelac A (2014b) Supreme courts in the 21st century: should organization follow the function? Paper presented at the conference on the functions of the Supreme Court – issues of process and administration of justice, Warsaw University, Warsaw, 11–14 June 2014. http://colloquium2014.uw.edu.pl/wpcontent/uploads/sites/21/¬2014/01/UZELAC_Supreme-Courts-in-the-21st-Century.pdf. Accessed 28 May 2020
Uzelac A, Galič A (2017) Changing faces of post-socialist Supreme Courts: Croatia and Slovenia compared. In: Van Rhee CH, Fu Y (eds) Supreme Courts in transition in China and the West. Adjudication at the service of public goals. Springer, Cham, pp 207–228
Zobec J (2015) Od individualnega do javnega (precedenčnega) namena Vrhovnega sodišča: ustavnopravni vidik (From an individual to a public (precedent-setting) goal of the Supreme Court – a constitutional perspective). Podjetje in delo 6–7:919–937
Zuglia S (1957) Građanski parnični postupak Federativne Narodne Republike Jugoslavije (Civil procedural law of the Federal People's Republic of Yugoslavia). Školska knjiga, Zagreb

Part IV
Anglo-American Legal Tradition

The Supreme Court of the United Kingdom and the Court of Appeal in England and Wales: Sharing the Appellate Load

John Sorabji

Abstract The civil justice system in England and Wales is hierarchical in terms of both its first instance jurisdiction and its appellate jurisdiction. Appeals lie from first instance decisions to either the next judicial tier within a court or to a superior court. Second appeals cannot but be brought in the Court of Appeal. The House of Lords, which exercised judicial appellate jurisdiction from the middle ages, and its statutory successor the UK Supreme Court, only hear appeals from inferior territorial appellate courts within the United Kingdom. This hierarchical structure has, historically, ensured that neither the House of Lords nor the UK Supreme Court have suffered from a surfeit of appeals. Furthermore, the fact that appeals to the House of Lords and the UK Supreme Court (*a*) are limited to appeals on questions of law, and only those which raise issues of general public importance, and (*b*) are only permitted if permission to appeal is granted has ensured that the number of appeals they hear has remained relatively static historically. By way of contrast, the appellate jurisdiction of the Court of Appeal in England and Wales has undergone periods of severe increases in its caseload; it recently underwent such an increase, and reforms were introduced to reduce its burgeoning caseload. This increase came despite appeals to the Court of Appeal being subject to a permission to appeal requirement, albeit one that is not as restrictive as that to the UK Supreme Court. This contribution describes those issues, and particularly the reforms introduced in October 2016 aimed at reducing the Court of Appeal's workload.

1 Introduction

The United Kingdom is a unitary state within which there are three separate legal jurisdictions: England and Wales; Scotland; and Northern Ireland. Each jurisdiction has its own courts and judiciaries, procedural rules, both criminal and procedural,

J. Sorabji (✉)
UCL Judicial Institute, London, UK
e-mail: j.sorabji@ucl.ac.uk

P. Bravo-Hurtado, C. H. van Rhee (eds.), *Supreme Courts Under Pressure*, Ius Gentium: Comparative Perspectives on Law and Justice 83,
https://doi.org/10.1007/978-3-030-63731-6_8

including appellate processes, and legal professions. Additionally, the United Kingdom has a single Supreme Court, the United Kingdom Supreme Court (UKSC), the statutory successor to the judicial appellate jurisdiction exercised by the House of Lords from the fourteenth century.[1] Appeals from each of the legal jurisdictions lie to the UKSC in civil proceedings.[2] Appeals in criminal proceedings, however, only lie to the UKSC from the courts of England and Wales, and of Northern Ireland.[3] Furthermore, the UKSC has an a priori constitutional review jurisdiction, whereby it may, on the application of one of the Law Officers to the Crown, consider the constitutionality of devolved legislation, i.e. legislation proposed by the devolved legislatures in Scotland, Wales and Northern Ireland.[4] No court in the United Kingdom, including the UKSC, may however engage in the constitutional review of legislation enacted by the United Kingdom Parliament with a view to determining that it is unlawful or unconstitutional, except as was provided for by the European Communities Act 1972[5] and, the limited review power, provided by the Human Rights Act 1998.[6]

This contribution considers the appellate process before the UKSC and before the Civil Division of the Court of Appeal in England and Wales (the Court of Appeal). It does so in order to examine the caseload of each of these appellate courts. In particular, it seeks to draw a contrast between the two appellate courts in terms of the number of appeals in civil proceedings each determines. Finally, it looks at recent reform to the appellate process in the Court of Appeal, the aim of which was to reduce its caseload. Before presenting a short introduction to the appellate process in the United Kingdom, the relationship between the UKSC and the Court of Appeal is set out.

---

[1]Bevan (1901a), p. 155; idem (1901b), p. 357. Appellate Jurisdiction Act 1876, s. 4; Constitutional Reform Act 2005, s. 40; Supreme Court Practice Direction 1 at 1.1.6, 'The jurisdiction of the Supreme Court corresponds to that of the House of Lords in its judicial capacity together with devolution matters . . .' For a detailed account of the UKSC's jurisdiction see Sorabji (2016), p. 393.

[2]Constitutional Reform Act 2005, s. 40; Administration of Justice Act 1969, ss.12–16; Court of Session Act 1988, ss. 40–43, 24, 27(5), 32(5), and 52(3); Judicature (Northern Ireland) Act 1978, ss. 42–44, and 45.

[3]*Bywater v Lord Advocate* (1781) 2 Pat. 563; Criminal Appeal Act 1968, ss. 33–34; Administration of Justice Act 1960, ss. 1–2; Criminal Appeal (Northern Ireland) Act 1980, ss. 3–32; Judicature (Northern Ireland) Act 1978, s. 41 and schedule 1.

[4]Under which the UKSC may hold that the proposed legislation is *ultra vires* the devolved Parliament's powers and thereby preclude its enactment: see Scotland Act 1998, ss. 33 and 36(5); Government of Wales Act 2006, ss. 96, 99, 112 and 111(7); Northern Ireland Act 1998, ss. 11 and 13(6); *Attorney-General for England and Wales v National Assembly for Wales Commission* [2012] UKSC 53, [2013] 1 AC 792; *Re Agricultural Sector (Wales) Bill, Attorney General for England and Wales v Counsel General for Wales* [2014] UKSC 43, [2014] 1 WLR 2622; *Re Recovery of Medical Costs for Asbestos Diseases (Wales) Bill* [2015] UKSC 3, [2015] AC 1016.

[5]See *Factortame (No. 2)* [1991] 1 AC 603. Following a national referendum held on 23 June 2016, the United Kingdom withdrew from the European Union on 31 January 2020. As a consequence this power will be repealed consistently with the provisions of the European Union (Withdrawal) Act 2018 and the European Union (Withdrawal Agreement) Act 2020.

[6]Human Rights Act 1998, ss. 4 and 10; Kavanagh (2009).

2 Structure and Practice of the Appellate Courts

In order to gain a proper understanding of the UKSC's and Court of Appeal's respective caseloads it is necessary to give some detail as to their constitution, personnel, and respective appellate processes and roles. This section provides that detail.

2.1 The United Kingdom Supreme Court

2.1.1 The Court and Its Personnel

The UKSC has only been in existence since 2009, when upon completion of its court building it commenced operation as the statutory successor to the House of Lords in its judicial capacity, i.e. the Judicial Committee of the House of Lords (the Judicial Committee). Its creation was the product of a desire on the part of the, then, government to introduce reforms that would secure greater separation of powers between the judiciary and the other branches of the State.[7] The court was not created in order to establish a Supreme Court in the sense of a constitutional court with jurisdiction to engage in the constitutional review of legislation. It is constituted of 12 judges, including its President and deputy President.[8] In addition, a small further number of judges who had previously held high judicial office in the United Kingdom may also sit in the UKSC, as acting justices of the court, at the request of its President.[9] The court does not, except in exceptional circumstances, sit *en banc*.[10]

---

[7]*The Governance of Britain*, Green Paper (CM 7170, July 2007) at 60.

[8]Constitutional Reform Act 2005, s. 23(2). At the time of writing, the UKSC judiciary is: Lord Reed, President; Lord Hodge, Deputy President; Lord Kerr; Lady Black; Lord Lloyd-Jones; Lord Briggs; Lady Arden; Lord Kitchin; Lord Sales; Lord Hamblen; Lord Leggatt. By way of constitutional tradition, two justices are appointed from Scotland and one is appointed from Northern Ireland. See https://www.supremecourt.uk/about/biographies-of-the-justices.html. Accessed 24 May 2020.

[9]Constitutional Reform Act 2005, ss. 38–39. The current acting justices are: Lord Neuberger of Abbotsbury; Lord Thomas of Cwmgiedd; Lord Hughes of Ombersley; Lord Sumption, https://www.supremecourt.uk/about/supplementary-panel.html. Accessed 24 May 2020.

[10]The UKSC sat *en banc* as a panel of all 11 currently serving justices (the 12th seat being vacant at the time) to hear the appeal from the High Court concerning whether the government could rely on the royal prerogative to give notice of withdrawal from the European Union (Brexit) in *R (Miller & Anor) v Secretary of State for Exiting the European Union (Rev 3)* [2017] UKSC 5; [2017] 2 W.L.R. 583. This was the first time the court has sat *en banc*. It also sat *en banc* in *R (Miller & Ors) v Ministry of Justice* (Rev 1) [2019] UKSC 60, which considered the government's power to prorogue (suspend) Parliament. Again, 11 justices heard the appeal. The 12th justice was not permitted to sit in order to ensure that there was an uneven number of justices to hear and determine the appeal.

Ordinarily, five justices will hear an appeal before the court,[11] although since 2000 and particularly since 2009 it has become more common (albeit it remains rare) for the Judicial Committee and now the UKSC to sit in panels of seven and nine justices,[12] where the issue before the court is one which raises particularly significant issues of public importance.[13]

The court's judiciary is supported by a small administrative staff and a small number of judicial assistants, the latter being highly qualified lawyers at the start of their legal careers who serve for a 12-month period.[14] The judicial assistants' main responsibility is to draft synopses of permission to appeal applications, known as bench memoranda, to assist the judges dealing with such matters to familiarise themselves with them easily. They play no role in preparing first or other drafts of appeal judgments.[15] Finally, the court's procedures are governed by the Supreme Court Rules 2009 and Practice Directions,[16] and by the House of Lords' Practice

---

[11]The UKSC applies specific criteria to determine whether its panel size should depart from the usual five-justice rule:

> 'Criteria to be used when considering whether more than five Justices should sit on a panel.
> If the Court is being asked to depart, or may decide to depart from a previous decision.
> A case of high constitutional importance.
> A case of great public importance.
> A case where a conflict between decisions in the House of Lords, Judicial Committee of the Privy Council and/or the Supreme Court has to be reconciled.
> A case raising an important point in relation to the European Convention on Human Rights.'

See *Panel Numbers Criteria*, https://www.supremecourt.uk/procedures/panel-numbers-criteria.html. Accessed 24 May 2020.

[12]Examples being: *R v Bow Street Metropolitan Stipendiary Magistrate, ex parte Pinochet Ugarte* (No. 3) [2000] 1 A.C. 147; [1999] 2 W.L.R. 827; *A v Secretary of State for the Home Department* [2005] UKHL 71; [2006] 2 A.C. 221; *A v Secretary of State for the Home Department* [2004] UKHL 56; [2005] 2 A.C. 68; *R (Jackson) v Attorney-General* [2005] UKHL 56; [2006] 1 A.C. 262; *R (E) v Governing Body of JFS & Ors* [2009] UKSC 15; [2010] 2 A.C. 728. In 2000 the Human Rights Act 1998, which incorporated the European Convention on Human Rights into domestic law, came into force. As such, the potential number of appeals which could raise issues of particular importance increased; a point reflected by the specific criterion acknowledged by the UKSC that cases raising important issues concerning the European Convention on Human Rights may require more justices than five to hear an appeal.

[13]For a discussion see Tomlinson et al. (2016); Burrows (2013), p. 305.

[14]Further details are provided by the United Kingdom Supreme Court Annual Review 2015 (HC 32), https://www.supremecourt.uk/docs/annual-report-2015-16.pdf. Accessed 28 May 2019.

[15]Paterson (2013), pp. 248ff.

[16]The Supreme Court Rules 2009 (SI 1603/2009) and Supreme Court Practice Directions 1–14, https://www.supremecourt.uk/procedures/rules-of-the-court.html. Accessed 28 May 2019.

Statement (Judicial Precedent) of 1966[17] which provides that the UKSC is not bound by its own previous decisions.[18]

2.1.2 Appellate Jurisdiction

As the statutory successor to the Judicial Committee the UKSC is the apex appellate court in the United Kingdom and has jurisdiction to hear appeals from all three of the United Kingdom's legal jurisdictions.[19] As an appellate court it has no trial jurisdiction;[20] apart from its review jurisdiction of devolved legislation, it only has jurisdiction to hear appeals from lower courts. In respect of civil proceedings in England and Wales,[21] as a general rule appeals lie to the UKSC from the Court of Appeal. In exceptional circumstances, an appeal may lie direct to the UKSC from the High Court, i.e. the appeal would 'leapfrog' over the Court of Appeal. The UKSC's jurisdiction to hear appeal cases is however limited in a number of ways.

First, and most substantively, not all decisions of lower courts may be appealed to the UKSC. Its jurisdiction,[22] as noted by Burton, is 'restricted and exceptional.'[23] The limitation arises as the UKSC only hears appeals that meet a threshold criterion, that the issue in the appeal: first, raises a legal question. Appeals on issues of fact cannot be brought; and secondly, the legal question must raise an issue of general public importance. As Lord Bingham described in the House of Lords' decision in 2000 in *R v Secretary of State for Trade & Industry, ex parte Eastaway*:

> In its role as a Supreme Court the House must necessarily concentrate its attention on a relatively small number of cases recognised as raising legal questions of general public

---

[17][1966] 1 WLR 1234; *Austin v Southwark LBC* [2011] AC 355 at [24]; and see Burton (2013), pp. 249ff.

[18]As a consequence, the UKSC is, unlike all other courts within the United Kingdom, not subject to the doctrine of precedent. In 2016, the UKSC identified a further basis, i.e. further to the 1966 Practice Direction, on which it is not subject to the doctrine of precedent; see *Willers v Joyce & Or (Re: Gubay (deceased) No. 2)* [2016] UKSC 44; [2016] 3 WLR 534.

[19]Andrews (2014), pp. 2, 4.

[20]Constitutional Reform Act 2005, s. 40 only provides it with an appellate jurisdiction, and see Appellate Jurisdiction Act 1876, s. 3.

[21]For further information on appeals to the UKSC from criminal courts in England and Wales and Northern Ireland, and civil courts in Scotland and Northern Ireland see: *A Guide to bringing a case to the Supreme Court*, https://www.supremecourt.uk/docs/a-guide-to-bringing-a-case-to-the-supreme-court.pdf. Accessed 28 May 2019; and, The Jurisdiction of the Supreme Court of the United Kingdom in Scottish Appeals: Human rights, the Scotland Act 2012 and the Courts Reform (Scotland) Act 2014, https://www.supremecourt.uk/docs/jurisdiction-of-the-supreme-court-in-scottish-appeals-human-rights-the-scotland-act-2012-and-the-courts-reform-scotland-act-2014.pdf. Accessed 28 May 2019.

[22]Unless otherwise stated, references to the UKSC include reference to the Judicial Committee of the House of Lords.

[23]Burton (2013), p. 1.

importance. It cannot seek to correct errors in the application of settled law, even where such are shown to exist.[24]

Examples of such questions of general public importance are, for instance: the juridical basis of the law of restitution of unjust enrichment;[25] the nature of the duty of care in the tort of negligence.[26] As its decisions bind all lower courts within the United Kingdom legal jurisdiction from which the appeal originated and are highly persuasive throughout the other United Kingdom legal jurisdictions, they are the ultimate means by which the courts clarify and, where appropriate and subject to Parliamentary intervention through a subsequent Act of Parliament, develop, clarify or correct the law through what is known as the doctrine of precedent.[27] As such, the primary function of the Judicial Committee and now the UKSC can properly be described as focusing on that aspect of the public function of the appellate process, which as Zuckerman put it 'responds to the need for authoritative interpretation of the law, for an effective machinery to develop it in response to socio-economic changes.'[28] It is a function that does not have as its aim the provision of corrective justice, i.e. correcting judicial error arising in lower courts. Its focus is on the public function of the creation and correct and consistent interpretation of the law.[29]

Secondly, on its own it is not sufficient that the legal issue arising from a High Court or Court of Appeal decision is one of general public importance. Such questions must, as a general rule, arise in the context of litigation where there is a live dispute between parties. The UKSC does not hear academic or hypothetical appeals, ones that, for instance, arise in circumstances where the parties have settled their substantive dispute.[30] As Zuckerman notes, this approach may pose substantial problems for the proper conduct of litigation, as a refusal by the UKSC to clarify a

[24]*R v Secretary of State for Trade & Industry, ex parte Eastaway* [2000] 1 W.L.R. 2222 at 2228.

[25]*Lipkin Gorman v Karpnale Ltd* [1991] 2 AC 548.

[26]*Donoghue v Stevenson* [1932] AC 562. For a discussion see Stevens (2011).

[27]Constitutional Reform Act 2005, s. 41(2); see Cross and Harris (1991).

[28]Zuckerman (2013), p. 1112. See also Bowman (1997), p. 2.

[29]See Andrews (2013). This function has been described, for instance, by Blake and Drewry, as a supervisory function. It is suggested that the UKSC has a supervision role in that it provides new precedent, updates others and thereby gives authoritative guidance to lower courts on the law and its application: see Blake and Drewry (2004), pp. 266ff. Use of the term 'supervisory' is a little strained in this context, as creation of new law via the doctrine of precedent is difficult to conceive of as supervision.

[30]See Zuckerman (2013), pp. 1171ff. Exceptions may arise to this general rule where, for instance, the proposed appeal involves a public authority and raises a question of public law: *R v Secretary of State for the Home Department, ex parte Salem* [1999] 1 A.C. 450 per Lord Slynn, 'My Lords, I accept, as both counsel agree, that in a cause where there is an issue involving a public authority as to a question of public law, your Lordships have a discretion to hear the appeal, even if by the time the appeal reaches the House there is no longer a lis to be decided which will directly affect the rights and obligations of the parties inter se.' Such appeals may also in future arise from appeals from decisions made under the High Court's Market Test Case procedure, which permits claims to be brought where there is no active dispute between the parties in order to clarify an issue of law of importance to the financial markets; see CPR PD51M.

legal issue of general public importance may result in otherwise unnecessary litigation by other individuals or businesses, thus unnecessarily increasing litigation before the courts and causing an avoidable drain on the court's resources as well as on the resources of the parties. It also poses a wider societal problem, as in the case of *Ainsbury v Millington*,[31] where the House of Lords refused to hear an academic appeal that would otherwise have determined which of two opposing lines of authority were correct in respect of whether the court had power to remove tenants from local authority tenancies. By refusing to hear the appeal, legal uncertainty was maintained, posing a problem for both courts, local authorities and local authority tenants to be able to make court orders, order their affairs, etc. based on a reasonably certain and predicable legal base.[32]

Finally, there are a number of areas where appeal to the UKSC is prohibited. It is not, for instance, permissible to appeal to the UKSC from a Court of Appeal decision which itself refused permission to appeal to it, i.e. the Court of Appeal.[33] Appeals cannot be brought to challenge either incidental or preliminary decisions made by the Court of Appeal in respect of which permission to appeal to that court was not granted.[34] Furthermore, certain appeals from County Court, and High Court and Court of Appeal, decisions concerning probate and electoral claims, respectively, cannot be brought before the UKSC. [35]

2.1.3 Permission to Appeal Requirements

In order to ensure that only those proposed appeals that do in fact raise a legal issue of general public importance are brought before the UKSC, a filter mechanism is in operation. No appeal, whether an appeal from the Court of Appeal or a leapfrog appeal from the High Court, may be brought unless permission to bring the appeal has been granted either by the UKSC or by the court whose decision is to be appealed.[36] In the case of leapfrog appeals, permission to appeal can only be granted by the UKSC, and then only if the High Court has issued a certificate stating that the 'case is suitable for appeal direct to the Supreme Court.'[37] Such a certification will only be granted if, as noted in *Burton on Civil Appeals*,[38]

---

[31] [1987] 1 WLR 397.

[32] See Zuckerman (2013), p. 1172.

[33] Prohibited by Access to Justice Act 1999, s. 54(4). See Supreme Court Practice Direction 1 para 1.2.7 for full details.

[34] Senior Courts Act 1981, s. 58; *Lane v Esdaile* [1891] AC 210.

[35] County Courts Act 1981, s. 82; Representation of the People Act 1983, Pt III.

[36] Constitutional Reform Act 2005, s. 40.2.

[37] Burton (2013), p. 236. See Administration of Justice Act 1969, ss. 12–15.

[38] Burton (2013), p. 236.

- the appeal involves a point of law of general public importance;
- the point of law relates either to the construction of an act of Parliament (or statutory instrument) or is a point on which the Judge is bound by a decision of the Court of Appeal or Supreme Court;
- that a sufficient case has been made out to justify an application for permission to appeal to the Supreme Court; and
- that all parties consent.

The requirement to obtain permission to appeal has been in place since 1934, prior to which there was an unfettered right to appeal to the House of Lords, i.e. there was no public importance test nor any corresponding implementation mechanism. As noted by Drewry, Blom-Cooper and Blake, the right of appeal was made subject to control, as a consequence of recommendations by the Hanworth Committee[39] and Section 1 of the Administration of Justice (Appeals) Act 1934, for two reasons: first, a concern that impecunious and relatively impecunious litigants would, absent control of the right to appeal, be subject to the fear of further cost and delay which may then make them improperly susceptible to settlement at the instigation of a wealthier party; and, second, due to concerns that Law Lords[40] (the judges who sat in the Judicial Committee) were subject to too great a workload.[41] It should be stressed, however, that the second issue was not concerned with the Judicial Committee's workload. The concern arose from additional work that the Law Lords were required to carry out in a separate appellate court, the Judicial Committee of the Privy Council (JCPC), which at that time heard appeals from courts based in Britain's overseas territories.[42]

The permission to appeal process is ordinarily carried out on the papers, i.e. without an oral hearing either before the Court of Appeal or the UKSC. Permission applications before the former may be made at the time when judgment is handed down, i.e. issued in writing, by the Court of Appeal in open court. The normal practice, though, is for such applications to be made to the Court of Appeal on paper following the hand down. As noted by Paterson,[43] it is rare for the Court of Appeal to grant permission save where the proposed appeal concerns an issue that is causing acute concern or where it relates to the possible over-ruling of very long-established common law precedent. While the practice in the House of Lords was originally for such applications to it to be made orally before a panel of Law Lords,

[39]Royal Commission on the Business of the Courts Committee (Cmd 4471, 1933); for a discussion see, Drewry et al. (2007), pp. 34ff., 148.

[40]The 'Law Lords' were properly called either Lords of Appeal in Ordinary, who were members of the House of Lords appointed to it under the Appellate Jurisdiction Act 1876, and Lords of Appeal, who were other members of the House of Lords who had held or held high judicial office in the United Kingdom, e.g. the Lord Chief Justice of England and Wales, the, then, current and former Lord Chancellors.

[41]For a discussion see Drewry et al. (2007), pp. 148ff.

[42]Drewry et al. (2007), pp. 148–149.

[43]Paterson (2013), p. 69.

since the 1970s the predominant position has been for permission applications to be dealt with on the papers.[44] Only in exceptional circumstances will there be an oral permission application before a panel of, usually, three Justices of the Supreme Court.

2.1.4 Permission to Appeal and Appeal Statistics

Since the UKSC's creation, figures have been published in respect of both the number of permission to appeal applications and the number of appeals heard by the court. The figures are issued on an annual basis. Access to comparable figures prior to its creation is more difficult to obtain, although what data is available points clearly to the Judicial Committee dealing with a limited number of permission to appeal applications and appeals annually. Drewry, Blom-Cooper and Blake note, for instance, that between 1952 and 1968 the Judicial Committee dealt with a total of 366 civil appeals (without differentiating which of the UK's legal jurisdictions they arose from); an average of 23 per year.[45] Carmichael and Dickson provide comparable figures from 1967 until 1994. In 1967 they record that there was a total of 62 permission to appeal applications, whereas this had grown to 196 in 1994. The number of appeals in 1967 was 39, whereas this had grown to 58 in 1994.[46] The picture is continued by Paterson, who states that from 1999 to 2009, i.e. the final year the Judicial Committee sat prior to the transfer of its jurisdiction to the UKSC, the Judicial Committee dealt with on average 220 permission to appeal applications and on average 55 appeals annually.[47] The permission to appeal statistics are particularly in stark contrast, as Paterson notes rightly, with the 10,000 petitions for leave or certiorari petitions which the United States Supreme Court deals with annually.[48]

The figures for both permission to appeal applications and appeals since the UKSC commenced dealing with such matters from all of the United Kingdom's legal jurisdictions are as shown in Table 1.

The figures for permission to appeal applications received from each of the United Kingdom's legal jurisdictions was as shown in Table 2.

The figures for permission to appeal applications granted from each of the United Kingdom's legal jurisdictions was as shown in Table 3.

It is not possible to give figures for applications for permission from England and Wales that were granted in each of the years, as the published figures do not permit of an accurate calculation of that figure. They do not, because unlike for Scotland and Northern Ireland, figures are not published. Nor is it possible due to the manner

[44]As noted by Drewry et al. (2007), pp. 150ff.

[45]Drewry et al. note (2007), p. 146.

[46]Carmichael and Dickson (1999), p. 139, setting out the figures from 1967 to 1994 at three yearly intervals.

[47]Paterson (2013), pp. 17, 67.

[48]Paterson (2013), pp. 67, 249.

Table 1 Permission to appeal applications and appeals—judicial committee & UKSC[a]

Year	Permission to appeal applications received	Permission to appeal applications granted	Appeals heard
1994[b]	209	64	44
1995	206	37	47
1996	184	35	41
1997	222	59	57
1998	253	63	52
1999	220	68	52
2000	161	56	69
2001	250	69	70
2002	267	99	50
2003	212	67	69
2004	262	94	56
2005	218	77	74
2006	173	45	57
2007	172	55	58
2008	Not available	Not available	Not available
2009–2010[c]	135	44	43
2010–2011[d]	228	67	76
2011–2012[e]	249	64	69
2012–2013[f]	259	86	83
2013–2014[g]	229	81	120
2014–2015[h]	231	88	89
2015–2016[i]	230	84	92
2016–2017[j]	209	67	91
2017–2018[k]	228	65	85
2018–2019[l]	Not Available	59	91

[a]Figures pre-2009 for the tables following Table 1 are not readily available
[b]All figures for 1994–2007 drawn from Shah and Poole (2009), pp. 10–11
[c]United Kingdom Supreme Court, *Annual Report 2009-2010*, at 22–25, https://www.supremecourt.uk/docs/ar_2009_10.pdf. Accessed 24 May 2020
[d]United Kingdom Supreme Court, *Annual Report 2010-2011*, at 20–22, https://www.supremecourt.uk/docs/ar_2010_11.pdf. Accessed 24 May 2020
[e]United Kingdom Supreme Court, *Annual Report 2011-2012*, at 22–25, https://www.supremecourt.uk/docs/annual_report_2011_12.pdf. Accessed 24 May 2020
[f]United Kingdom Supreme Court, *Annual Report 2012-2013*, at 20–25, https://www.supremecourt.uk/docs/annual-report-2012-13.pdf. Accessed 24 May 2020
[g]United Kingdom Supreme Court, *Annual Report 2013-2014*, at 24–28, https://www.supremecourt.uk/docs/annual-report-2013-14.pdf. Accessed 24 May 2020
[h]United Kingdom Supreme Court, *Annual Report 2014-2015*, at 26–30, https://www.supremecourt.uk/docs/annual-report-2014-15.pdf. Accessed 24 May 2020
[i]United Kingdom Supreme Court, *Annual Report 2015-2016*, at 20–24, https://www.supremecourt.uk/docs/annual-report-2015-16.pdf. Accessed 24 May 2020
[j]United Kingdom Supreme Court, *Annual Report 2016-2017*, at 22–26, https://www.supremecourt.uk/docs/annual-report-2016-17.pdf. Accessed 24 May 2020
[k]United Kingdom Supreme Court, *Annual Report 2017-2018*, at 25–30, https://www.supremecourt.uk/docs/annual-report-2017-18.pdf. Accessed 24 May 2020
[l]United Kingdom Supreme Court, *Annual Report 2018-2019*, at 39–41, https://www.supremecourt.uk/docs/annual-report-2018-19.pdf. Accessed 24 May 2020

Table 2 Permission to Appeal Applications from the UK Legal Jurisdictions

Year	England and Wales Applications received	Scotland Applications received	Northern Ireland Applications received
2009–2010[a]	104	22	9
2010–2011[b]	209	10	9
2011–2012[c]	226	6	17
2012–2013[d]	237	6	16
2013–2014[e]	207	3	19
2014–2015[f]	205	5	21
2015–2016[g]	218	4	8
2016-2017[h]	177	21	11
2017-2018[i]	196	21	11
2018-2019[j]	Not available	18	10

[a]United Kingdom Supreme Court, *Annual Report 2009–2010* at 24
[b]United Kingdom Supreme Court, *Annual Report 2010–2011* at 22
[c]United Kingdom Supreme Court, *Annual Report 2011–2012* at 24
[d]United Kingdom Supreme Court, *Annual Report 2012–2013* at 22
[e]United Kingdom Supreme Court, *Annual Report 2013–2014* at 26
[f]United Kingdom Supreme Court, *Annual Report 2014–2015* at 28
[g]United Kingdom Supreme Court, *Annual Report 2015–2016* at 22
[h]United Kingdom Supreme Court, *Annual Report 2016–2017*, at 24
[i]United Kingdom Supreme Court, *Annual Report 2017–2018*, at 26
[j]United Kingdom Supreme Court, *Annual Report 2018–2019*, at 40

in which the figures for the United Kingdom as a whole are published, to determine what were the figures for England and Wales.

Finally, the number of criminal and civil appeals disposed of, i.e. heard or otherwise resolved, during this period was as shown in Table 4:

What can be properly concluded from the figures available is the following:

1. The total number of applications for permission issued have been broadly comparable for each year after 2009–2019 and within a range of 177–237 per year for England and Wales, within a range of 3–21 for Scotland, and 8–21 for Northern Ireland;
2. The total number of applications for permission granted has risen from 44 in 2009–2010 to a maximum of 88 in 2014, before dropping back to 59 in 2019, with permission granted for applications from Scotland and Northern Ireland being within a range of 2–22 during that period;
3. The total number of appeals heard was within a range of 43 to 120, with an average per year of 84;
4. The total number of appeals heard was within a range of 42 to 120, with an average per year of 82;
5. Criminal appeals constituted a fraction of the total number of appeals, with the total number of such appeals ranging from 2.5% to 10% of the total number of appeals.

Table 3 Applications for Permission to Appeal Granted—Scotland and Northern Ireland

Year	Scotland[a] Applications granted	Northern Ireland[b] Applications granted
2009–2010[c]	0	2
2010–2011[d]	2	3
2011–2012[e]	16	3
2012–2013[f]	17	5
2013–2014[g]	13	4
2014–2015[h]	11	4
2015–2016[i]	12	7
2016–2017[j]	13	7
2017–2018[k]	12	9
2018–2019[l]	6	3

[a]These figures include appeals from Scotland which do not need a grant of permission to appeal, i.e. they can be heard as of right. The figures also include applications heard that were filed during a previous year
[b]These figures include appeals from Northern Ireland which do not need a grant of permission to appeal, i.e. they can be heard as of right
[c]United Kingdom Supreme Court, *Annual Report 2009–2010* at 24
[d]United Kingdom Supreme Court, *Annual Report 2010–2011* at 22
[e]United Kingdom Supreme Court, *Annual Report 2011–2012* at 24
[f]United Kingdom Supreme Court, *Annual Report 2012–2013* at 22
[g]United Kingdom Supreme Court, *Annual Report 2013–2014* at 26
[h]United Kingdom Supreme Court, *Annual Report 2014–2015* at 28
[i]United Kingdom Supreme Court, *Annual Report 2015–2016* at 22
[j]United Kingdom Supreme Court, *Annual Report 2016–2017*, at 24
[k]United Kingdom Supreme Court, *Annual Report 2017–2018*, at 26
[l]United Kingdom Supreme Court, *Annual Report 2018–2019*, at 40

While exact figures are not available, the UKSC has a published target of ensuring that permission to appeal applications are determined within 8 weeks of issue and that appeals are determined within 9 months of a grant of permission to appeal.[49]

2.2 *The Court of Appeal*

2.2.1 The Court and Its Personnel

Appellate jurisdiction within England and Wales is exercised by each of its civil courts: County Court; High Court; and Court of Appeal. The first two courts are, however, primarily first instance, trial courts, whereas the last has no originating

[49]See for instance United Kingdom Supreme Court, *Annual Report 2015-2016* at 20–21. https://www.supremecourt.uk/docs/annual-report-2015-16.pdf.

Table 4 Criminal and civil appeals—UKSC

Year	Criminal appeals	Civil appeals
2009–2010	Figures not available	Figures not available
2010–2011	Figures not available	Figures not available
2011–2012	Figures not available	Figures not available
2012–2013[a]	5	72
2013–2014[b]	12	103
2014–2015[c]	2	79
2015–2016[d]	5	76
2016–2017[e]	4	72
2017–2018[f]	6	72
2018–2019	Not available	Not available

[a]United Kingdom Supreme Court, *Annual Report 2012-2013* at 24
[b]United Kingdom Supreme Court, *Annual Report 2013-2014* at 28
[c]United Kingdom Supreme Court, *Annual Report 2014-2015* at 30
[d]United Kingdom Supreme Court, *Annual Report 2015-2016* at 24
[e]United Kingdom Supreme Court, *Annual Report 2016-2017*, at 26
[f]United Kingdom Supreme Court, *Annual Report 2017-2018*, at 29

jurisdiction[50] and is the senior appellate court.[51] The Court of Appeal is a relatively small court, which, like the UKSC, is based in London. Unlike the UKSC, it does on occasion sit in major regional centres such as Birmingham, Manchester and Cardiff to hear cases.[52] Unlike the High Court, which has 110 full-time, puisne judges and four *ex officio* judges, and the County Court which has approximately 680 circuit judges and 450 district judges,[53] the Court of Appeal has 44 full-time judges. Additionally, Supreme Court justices who held or could hold judicial office in England and Wales are also, *ex officio*, judges of the Court of Appeal and, furthermore, High Court judges and retired Court of Appeal and High Court judges can be specially authorised to act as judges of the Court of Appeal.[54] When hearing appeals, the Court of Appeal has historically sat in panels of three judges, although panels may sit with two judges. By way of contrast, appeals in the County Court and High Court are heard by a single judge.[55] The court's administration is provided by Her

[50]The High Court and the Court of Appeal also have a supervisory jurisdiction. For a discussion in respect of the Court of Appeal see Burton (2013), pp. 389ff.

[51]Supreme Court of Judicature Act 1873, s. 4; Senior Courts Act 1981, ss. 2–3, 15–18. The Court of Appeal, in addition to its appellate jurisdiction, has a supervisory jurisdiction in common with the High Court. For a detailed discussion see Jackson (2016), commentary to Pt 52.

[52]This may change in future. The UKSC sat, for the first time, outside London in 2017, when it sat in Edinburgh. It sat in Belfast for the first time in 2018 and then in Cardiff, for the first time in 2019.

[53]Up-to-date details can be found at https://www.judiciary.gov.uk/about-the-judiciary/. Accessed 24 May 2020.

[54]Senior Courts Act 1981, ss. 2, 9.

[55]Appeals in a Divisional Court of the High Court, by way of exception to the general rule, must sit in panels of two judges, one of whom is ordinarily a Court of Appeal judge sitting in the High Court: see Senior Courts Act 1981, s. 66(3).

Majesty's Courts and Tribunals Service. As with the UKSC, support is also provided to the Court of Appeal by a number of judicial assistants who perform a similar role akin to that carried out in the UKSC; the latter's judicial assistant scheme being based on the Court of Appeal's scheme.[56] The court's procedure, in respect of civil proceedings, is contained within Part 52 of the Civil Procedure Rules 1998.[57]

2.2.2 Appellate Jurisdiction

The appeal process before the Court of Appeal, and lower appeal courts, serves two distinct functions: private and public.[58] In this it differs therefore from the UKSC. The private function is the correction of judicial error.[59] As such, it promotes accuracy in decision-making in lower courts through providing a means to correct errors in individual decisions[60] and, due to the possibility of appellate accountability that this secures, incentivising first instance judges to approach their role properly.[61] Its public function has a number of facets: as with the UKSC, it can develop, clarify or correct the law and it can promote confidence in the administration of justice and the Rule of Law, through correcting error in judicial decision-making (the concomitant of the private function of correcting judicial error).[62]

Appellate jurisdiction is, as a general rule, strictly hierarchical and based on both the judge who made the decision subject to appeal and the court within which the decision was made.[63] As such, not all appeals may, or do, lie to the Court of Appeal. Broadly speaking, the position is as follows:

[56] Historically, the number of judicial assistants has ranged from eight to ten at any one time, with individual judicial assistants acting as such for three months to a year. In October 2016, the number of judicial assistants was increased to 25 as part of reforms to improve the court's efficiency: see below.

[57] Civil Procedure Rules 1998 (SI 3132/1998). For a detailed commentary on CPR Pt 52 see Jackson (2016). For a history of the Court of Appeal see Drewry et al. (2007).

[58] *Bowman Report* (1997) as cited by Zuckerman (2013), p. 1112.

[59] *Colley v Council of Licensed Conveyancers* [2001] EWCA Civ 1137, [2002] 1 W.L.R. 160 at [31].

[60] In terms used by Blake and Drewry this is a 'review' function: see Blake and Drewry (2004), pp. 226ff.

[61] Andrews (2013), p. 419.

[62] Andrews (2013), pp. 418–419.

[63] A process for leapfrog appeals within England and Wales also exists. A first appeal that ought to lie to a court other than the Court of Appeal may be transferred directly to the Court of Appeal, under either Access to Justice Act 1999, s. 57 or CPR r.52.23. Such transfers will only be made, however, where there is a compelling reason justifying the Court of Appeal hearing the appeal. NB: unless otherwise stated references to the provisions within CPR Pt 52 are to the rules in force from 3 October 2016: see http://www.justice.gov.uk/courts/procedure-rules/civil/rules/part52. Accessed 24 May 2020.

1. Appeals from district judges sitting in the County Court lie to a circuit judge sitting in the County Court;
2. Appeals from a circuit judge sitting in a County Court lie to the High Court;
3. Appeals from a High Court judge sitting in the High Court lie to the Court of Appeal.[64]

In other words, an appeal always lies to either a superior judge in the judicial hierarchy from the one whose decision is subject to appeal or to the Court of Appeal, which sits as a panel of either two or three judges. From this, a distinction can be drawn. In respect of appeals to the Court of Appeal, the greater number of judges hearing the appeal arguably increases that court's ability to, as Andrews puts it,[65] work as a team. This better enables them to develop the law, i.e. perform the public function of the appeal process. Equally, it could be said to increase the prospect that the Court of Appeal will be able to correct any judicial error in the decision which is subject to appeal where the suggested error is one of law. In questions of appeals on matters of fact, the Court of Appeal has recognised that it is in no better a position to reach a correct factual decision than that of the trial court.[66] In terms of appeals in the County Court and High Court, the focus is on the correction of judicial error by a judge, albeit a single judge hearing the appeal, who is more experienced and more highly qualified than the judge whose decision is subject to appeal: the hierarchical nature of the appeal process mirroring the nature of the judicial appointment process, which requires increasingly greater experience and qualifications the further up the judicial hierarchy the judicial office is.[67]

Any appeal which is made from a decision that was itself made on an appeal, i.e. a second appeal, lies to the Court of Appeal and only to the Court of Appeal.[68] Appeals from the Court of Appeal, as noted above, lie to the UKSC. Additionally, appeals from the United Kingdom's tribunals, the Upper Tribunal, the Employment Appeals Tribunal and certain statutory bodies, follow a similar approach as above, with appeals being heard in the Court of Appeal.[69] The rationale behind this hierarchical approach is the need to ensure that court resources are targeted properly, so that appeals from the lowest value claims, i.e. ones before district judges in the County Court, are allocated a proportionate amount of the civil justice system's resources through appeals lying to a senior judge within the County Court. Conversely, this ensures that the Court of Appeal's resources are rationed such that they

---

[64]The Access to Justice Act 1999 (Destination of Appeals) Order 2016 (SI 917/2016), which replaced The Access to Justice Act 1999 (Destination of Appeals) Order 2000 (SI 1071/2000).

[65]Andrews (2013), p. 419.

[66]Zuckerman (2013), p. 1184. See *Assicurazioni Generali Spa v Arab Insurance Group* [2002] EWCA Civ 1642; [2003] 1 W.L.R. 577.

[67]See the Judicial Appointments Commission for differences in the statutory and other appointment criteria for different judicial office-holders at https://jac.judiciary.gov.uk. Accessed 24 May 2020.

[68]Access to Justice Act 1999, s. 55.

[69]The Appeals from the Upper Tribunal to the Court of Appeal Order 2008 (SI 2834/2008). Also see the provisions on permission to appeal from these various tribunals at: CPR rr.52.9–52.11.

are only expended on the most significant, complex and high-value claims, as well as most significantly on second appeals.[70]

2.2.3 Permission to Appeal Requirements

Appeals in England and Wales cannot, except in a small category of cases,[71] be brought as of right. As with appeals to the UKSC, permission to appeal must be granted by either the court whose decision is to be subject to appeal or by the appeal court. Where a party wishes to bring a second appeal permission may, however, only be granted by the Court of Appeal.[72] There are two different tests for permission to appeal in respect of civil proceedings depending on whether the permission application relates to a first or a second appeal. The current test for permission to bring a first appeal is contained in CPR r.52.6:

52.6

(1) Except where rule 52.7 applies, permission to appeal may be given only where—

(a) the court considers that the appeal would have a real prospect of success; or

(b) there is some other compelling reason for the appeal to be heard.[73]

The current test for permission to bring a second appeal is contained in CPR r.52.7, and is derived from Section 54(4) of the Access to Justice Act 1999:[74]

52.7

(1) Permission is required from the Court of Appeal for any appeal to that court from a decision of the County Court, the family court or the High Court which was itself made on appeal, or a decision of the Upper Tribunal which was made on appeal from a decision of the First-tier Tribunal on a point of law where the Upper Tribunal has refused permission to appeal to the Court of Appeal.

(a) The Court of Appeal will not give permission unless it considers that:

(2) the appeal would:

(i) have a real prospect of success; and

---

[70] *Tanfern v Cameron-MacDonald (Practice Note)* [2000] 1 W.L.R. 1311.

[71] For instance, appeals from decisions to commit to prison an individual who has been found to be in contempt of court; see Administration of Justice Act 1960 s. 13 or a refusal of habeas corpus: see Jackson (ed 2016: 52.3.2); and CPR r.52.3(1)(a).

[72] CPR r.52.7(1).

[73] Prior to 3 October 2016 this rule in identical form was set out in CPR r.52.3(1).

[74] Access to Justice Act 1999 s. 55 provides that, '(1) Where an appeal is made to a county court or the High Court in relation to any matter, and on hearing the appeal the court makes a decision in relation to that matter, no appeal may be made to the Court of Appeal from that decision unless the Court of Appeal considers that:

(a) the appeal would raise an important point of principle or practice, or
(b) there is some other compelling reason for the Court of Appeal to hear it.'

(ii) raise an important point of principle or practice; or

(b) there is some other compelling reason for the Court of Appeal to hear it.[75]

Permission to appeal applications were, until 3 October 2016, carried out through a three-stage process. An initial application could, but did not have to be, made orally before the judge whose decision was to be subject to appeal. If that application were unsuccessful, a fresh application could be made in the appeal court. That application would, initially, be determined on the papers by a single judge. If that application was unsuccessful, the putative appellant could renew the application, which would then be argued in a 20-minute oral hearing in the appeal court. Ordinarily, the oral hearing would be heard by the appeal judge who had determined the matter on paper.[76] The respondent to the appeal would not normally have a role to play at this stage and would take no part in the application for permission process. This process was revised in October 2016, such that there is now no right for an oral application hearing. Applications will be determined on the papers in the first instance. Where the application is made in either the County Court or the High Court, subject to a limited number of exceptions, the putative appellant may request that the matter be reconsidered at an oral hearing. Where the application is made in the Court of Appeal there is no right to seek an oral rehearing, however the judge deciding the matter on the papers retains the discretion to direct that the matter be determined not on the papers but at an oral hearing. Thus, in the County Court and High Court the three-stage process remains broadly in place, whereas in the Court of Appeal there is now only a two-stage process, including both instances the stage where a putative appellant may seek permission from the judge whose decision is to be appealed.[77]

2.2.4 Permission to Appeal and Appeal Statistics

The Court of Appeal's appellate jurisdiction has, historically, been subject to a number of changes. Most notably there have been numerous changes, not least in 1993, 1995 and 2000 to the permission to appeal requirement, its scope and application and the process by which it is carried.[78] Historically, there is also a lack of generally available statistics concerning the number of permission to appeal applications and appeals heard. As such, it would be difficult to present an account of

[75]The additional requirement, of needed to demonstrate 'a real prospect of success' was made under power provided by Access to Justice Act 1999 s. 54.3(d). Prior to 3 October 2016, the second appeal test was contained in CPR r.52.13 and did not contain the 'real prospect of success' criterion.

[76]The process was set out in the pre-3 October 2016 CPR rr.52.3. For a discussion see Jackson (2016), pp. 52.3.1ff.

[77]The permission process is now contained in CPR rr.52.4–52.5.

[78]For an account of the various changes see Bowman (1997), pp. 29–30; Drewry et al. (2007), pp. 58ff.

appeals and applications for permission to appeal comparable to that provided for the House of Lords and UKSC.

The Court of Appeal has, however, been the subject of a number of reform reports, most significantly the *Bowman Report* in 1997,[79] which formed the basis of substantial reform to the appeal process that was implemented in 2000, and most recently in 2016 a review which formed the basis of a formal consultation issued by Lord Dyson MR, the President of the Court of Appeal (Civil Division) (the *Dyson Consultation*). Both the *Bowman Report* and the *Dyson Consultation* contain statistical data concerning the operation of the Court of Appeal. Further information is also available via statistics published by the government. These various sources provide the data given in Tables 5 and 6 concerning permission to appeal applications and appeals heard by the Court of Appeal.

Care needs to be taken with the figures, as it is not apparent from the sources that they review the same types of appeal. It is not apparent, for instance, whether the statistics from the three sources refer to final appeals and interlocutory appeals, or whether they only refer to final appeals. Moreover, the figures pre-2000 will refer to appeals that arose under a different procedural regime concerning the scope of the permission to appeal requirement than that in place post-2000. The one reliable conclusion that can be drawn from each of the three sets of statistics is that in each of the three periods the number of appeals disposed of remained within a broadly comparable annual range.

3 Caseload Problems and Reform Attempts

The available statistics tend to support differing caseload trends in the UKSC and the Court of Appeal. In the former, they suggest that despite some growth since the early 1990s caseloads in terms of permission to appeal applications have remained relatively stable. In terms of appeals there has been some growth since the early 1990s, albeit only from an average of 55 per year from 1999–2009 to an average of 84 per year during 2009–2019. In the latter, in respect of permission to appeal applications during a period when the same approach and test to such applications was in force, i.e. 2000–2015, two distinct phases can be discerned. In the first, from 2000–2004, the annual number of permission applications remained broadly similar. Starting from 2006, however, there has been an annual increase in such numbers, the consequence of which is that by 2015 more than twice as many such applications were being disposed of each year than had been the case in 2000. This growth has not been matched by any comparable increase in judicial numbers to deal with the applications. Figures for the Court of Appeal for 2016–2019 are not available.[80]

[79] Bowman (1997), pp. 29–30.

[80] Her Majesty's Courts and Tribunals Service does produce annual statistics for the Court of Appeal. They only, however, deal with the number of applications for permission filed. See, for

Table 5 Permission to Appeal Applications Disposed of—Court of Appeal

Year	Applications for permission to appeal disposed of
2000[a]	2437
2001	2433
2002	2448
2003	2402
2004	2415
2005	No figures available
2006[b]	2998
2007	3458
2008	3561
2009	3349
2010	3677
2011	4132
2012	4286
2013	4871
2014	5182
2015	5206

[a]Figures for 1987–1996 are available from Bowman (1997), pp. 214ff. Due to the significant differences in the scope of application of the requirement prior to the implementation of the *Bowman Report's* recommendations in 2000 and the requirements post-2000 only the latter figures are set out here. Figures post-2000 from Drewry et al. (2007), p. 84

[b]Figures for 2006–2015 from Civil Procedure Rule Committee, *Appeals to the Court of Appeal: Proposed amendments to the Civil Procedure Rules and Practice Direction*, (19 May 2016) Appendix 1 (*Dyson Consultation*), https://www.judiciary.gov.uk/publications/moj-consultation-appeals-to-the-court-of-appeal-proposed-amendments-to-civil-procedure-rules-and-practice-direction/. Accessed 24 May 2020

3.1 *No Overload in the UKSC*

The two sets of statistics for the two courts might lead to the conclusion that for the UKSC there was no real caseload pressure, whereas for the Court of Appeal the opposite may well be the case. To a certain extent such conclusions are borne out. However, in respect of the UKSC and its predecessor there was a period during the 1990s when the Judicial Committee was unable to dispose of claims in a properly timely fashion. As Le Sueur and Cornes noted in 2001, the Judicial Committee was 'a court under considerable pressure.' This was evidenced by an increasing backlog of appeals awaiting determination, which were noted to have been 66 in 1996, 53 in

instance, HMCTS, *Civil Justice Statistics Quarterly, England and Wales*, January to March 2019 (provisional), https://assets.publishing.service.gov.uk/government/uploads/system/uploads/attachment_data/file/806896/civil-justice-statistics-quarterly-Jan-Mar-2019.pdf. Accessed 24 May 2020.

Table 6 Appeals Heard—Court of Appeal

Year	Appeals Heard
1987[a]	1647
1988	1572
1989	1578
1990	1600
1991	1553
1992	1521
1993	1645
1994	1513
1995	1764
1996	1643
1997	No figures available
1998	No figures available
1999[b]	1127
2000	1065
2001	1020
2002	1088
2003	1075
2004	1059
2005	No figures available
2006[c]	1220
2007	1254
2008	1297
2009	1258
2010	1269
2011	1275
2012	1178
2013	1208
2014	1287
2015	1222

[a]Figures for 1987–1996 from Bowman (1997), pp. 214ff
[b]Figures from 1999–2004 from Drewry et al. (2007), p. 84
[c]Figures for 2006–2015 from Civil Procedure Rule Committee, *Appeals to the Court of Appeal: Proposed amendments to the Civil Procedure Rules and Practice Direction*, (19 May 2016) Appendix 1 (*Dyson Consultation*), https://www.judiciary.gov.uk/publications/moj-consultation-appeals-to-the-court-of-appeal-proposed-amendments-to-civil-procedure-rules-and-practice-direction/. Accessed 28 May 2019

1997, 66 in 1998 and 94 in 1999.[81] It was further anticipated at the time that the coming into force of, amongst other statutory reforms, the Human Rights Act 1998 would cause a substantial increase in proceedings before the Judicial Committee,

[81]Le Sueur and Cornes (2001), p. 143.

and lower courts, and this would increase the number of permission to appeal applications, appeals and backlog of appeals awaiting decision.[82] It was expected that the reforms would double the Judicial Committee's workload without any commensurate increase in judicial or other resources.[83]

The increase in workload did not materialise as anticipated. While there was a gradual increase in caseload, as noted above, it did not reach a doubling of the workload either in terms of permission to appeal applications or in terms of appeals. While human rights cases did increase from pre-1998 levels of 7% of total appeals before the Judicial Committee during the period 1990–1993, to 9% from 2000–2002, 16% during 2003–2005, 19% during 2006–2008, and then back down to 14% in 2009–2013, the increase was not as much as anticipated. Moreover, the increase in such cases was offset by decreases in the number of other types of appeals coming before the Judicial Committee, i.e. there was a steady reduction in criminal appeals and tax appeals coming before it.[84] As Shah and Poole put it, the post-Human Rights Act position was one that saw the Judicial Committee from 2000–2007 being only 'slightly busier' than it was prior to the Act's enactment;[85] as was the case also post-2009. That it was slightly busier did not however translate into increasing backlogs or delays in dealing with permission applications or appeals. That this is the case can most clearly be seen by the number of days each year that the UKSC could sit but does not, i.e. days on which it could be dealing with hearings but due to an absence of need to do so to complete its work it did not have to (Table 7).[86]

A reasonable conclusion from the data is that, notwithstanding the fact that the levels of permission to appeal applications and appeals post-2009 are to a small extent higher than they were historically, they have not overburdened the UKSC. That the court does not have sufficient work to require it to sit on all available sitting days[87] and that it records no data equivalent to that noted by Le Sueur and Cornes concerning backlogs in dealing with permission applications or appeals is clearly suggestive of there being no extant problem concerning the UKSC's workload. On the contrary, the sitting days data suggests that the court has spare capacity; that it

[82]Idem, pp. 143–145.

[83]Per Lord Browne-Wilkinson cited in Le Sueur and Cornes (2001), p. 143.

[84]Paterson (2013), p. 17.

[85]Shah and Poole (2009), p. 14.

[86]NB: this is not to suggest that the justices were not working during these periods when the court was not sitting. Preparation work for hearings and judgment writing will necessarily be taking place during out-of-court time. The point being made is that the UKSC is not sitting during times when it was scheduled to sit because the in-court workload was not sufficient to meet the anticipated demand. There will, of course, be a consequential reduction in judgment-writing time due to this. There may, however, be no significant reduction in pre-hearing preparation work due to appeals that were scheduled to take place being withdrawn prior to a scheduled hearing but after the justices have carried out their pre-reading.

[87]And this is the case notwithstanding the fact that the UKSC now sits more commonly than its predecessor in panels of seven and nine; the Judicial Committee would sit in panels of five.

Table 7 UKSC sittings

Year	Total number of sitting days available	Total number of sitting days used
2009–2010[a]	87.9	65
2010–2011[b]	154	121
2011–2012[c]	138	117
2012–2013[d]	144	118
2013–2014[e]	147	127
2014–2015[f]	144	136
2015–2016[g]	133	104
2016–2017[h]	153	142
2017–2018[i]	Not available	95.5
2018–2019	Not available	Not available

[a]United Kingdom Supreme Court, *Annual Report 2009–2010* at 22. Figures are lower because of the shorter legal year due to the commencement date for the UKSC's jurisdiction upon the transfer of jurisdiction from the Judicial Committee
[b]United Kingdom Supreme Court, *Annual Report 2010–2011* at 21
[c]United Kingdom Supreme Court, *Annual Report 2011–2012* at 23
[d]United Kingdom Supreme Court, *Annual Report 2012–2013* at 21
[e]United Kingdom Supreme Court, *Annual Report 2013–2014* at 25
[f]United Kingdom Supreme Court, *Annual Report 2014–2015* at 27
[g]United Kingdom Supreme Court, *Annual Report 2015–2016* at 22
[h]United Kingdom Supreme Court, *Annual Report 2016–2017*, at 23
[i]United Kingdom Supreme Court, *Annual Report 2017–2018*, at 25

could cope with, at the least, a gradual increase in its workload, with no adverse impact on its ability to deal with it efficiently and in a timely fashion. Rather than a backlog in terms of its workload, as was the case in the late 1990s, there would now appear to be a deficit in workload: the UKSC is not suffering an appellate overload, but an appellate deficit. A number of factors may, reasonably, be understood to underpin this transformation:

- First, during the late 1990s the increase in workload could, partly at least, be attributed to the fact that Lord Saville was unable to sit in Judicial Committee or in the JCPC due to his appointment to chair a full-time public inquiry (the Saville Inquiry) and the consequently increased demand placed on the Law Lords to sit in both the Judicial Committee and the JCPC. The UKSC has generally had a full complement of justices available to it. There have also been reduced demands generally to sit in the JCPC;
- Secondly, the efficacy of the permission to appeal test;
- Thirdly, a decrease in oral permission to appeal hearings with their replacement with permission decisions being taken on the papers only;[88]

[88]Drewry et al. (2007), pp. 150–153.

- Finally, the operation of the doctrine of precedent, which generally reduces the potential number of appeals to the UKSC.[89]

3.2 *Case Overload in the Court of Appeal and Procedural Reform*

Unlike the UKSC, which, notwithstanding a gradual increase in its annual workload, has not been noted to have undergone any adverse consequences as a result of that increase, the Court of Appeal has recently faced serious difficulties in terms of its caseload. This is not the first time that it has found itself in this position. The *Bowman Report* noted a serious backlog in work in the court and significant delays in the processing of proceedings before it.[90] The Review made a number of significant recommendations concerning reform of the court's procedure and administration aimed at eliminating those delays and the backlog of work. Those recommendations were implemented in 2000 through reforms to CPR Pt 52, which specifically introduced the across the board permission to appeal requirements noted above. Although, it should be noted that the permission to appeal test for second appeals did not, as it now does, contain an explicit requirement that the proposed appeal demonstrate a 'real prospect of success.' That explicit requirement was added in October 2016, albeit it was arguably implicit to the test prior to that. The Bowman reforms were underpinned by six principles, which were noted by the Court of Appeal in *Tanfern v Cameron-MacDonald* (2011), the most important of which were that: (*a*) appeals were not to be permitted absent a grant of permission to appeal (subject to limited exceptions where individual liberty was at stake); (*b*) the basic criterion for permission to appeal was that the proposed appeal had a real prospect of success; (*c*) appeals were, as a general rule, to be by review and not by rehearing; (*d*) in all but exceptional circumstances only one appeal would be allowed, the effect of which would be to divert first appeals from the County Court to either a more senior County Court judge or the High Court, and to leave the Court of Appeal as a general rule the first appeal court for the High Court only. The reforms were thus intended to leave the Court of Appeal as predominantly a

[89]The JCPC's workload is detailed in the various UKSC Annual Reports noted earlier. The reduction in its workload from the period prior to 1999, when it was recorded by Lord Browne-Wilkinson as sitting daily (Le Sueur and Cornes 2001, p. 143) can be seen, for instance, as follows: 2011–2012, 65 out of 138 sitting days used; 2012–2013, 50 out of 144 sitting days used; 2013–2014, 49 out of 147 sitting days used; 2014–2015, 56 out of 144 sitting days used; 2015–2016, 48 out of 133 sitting days used. See United Kingdom Supreme Court, *Annual Reports 2011–2012, 2012–2013, 2013–2014, 2014–2015 and 2015–2016* at 31, 34, 36, 37, 33, respectively. The same pattern can be seen in 2016–2017 and 2017–2018; see United Kingdom Supreme Court, *Annual Reports 2016–2017 and 2017–2018*, at 35 and 39 respectively. No figures are available for 2018–2019.

[90]Bowman (1997).

second appeal court, akin to the Judicial Committee, only dealing with cases of public importance.[91] As such, in terms of first appeals the County Court, High Court and Court of Appeal's role focused on both the private and the public functions of the appeal process. In terms of second appeals, with the focus on issues of public importance, the Court of Appeal's role was and is one that focuses more on the public function of the appeal process.

Against this background of the practice and procedure reforms introduced following the *Bowman Report*, the number of appeals the Court of Appeal has disposed of annually has remained, broadly, static since 2006 following an increase in the numbers dealt with annually from 2000–2004. Notwithstanding this there has, however, been a significant increase in applications for permission to appeal from 2437 in 2000 to 5206 in 2015. As noted in the *Dyson Consultation*, the increase in the Court of Appeal's workload through the increase in permission to appeal applications has been highly detrimental. In the words of the *Dyson Consultation*:

> Quite simply, the Court is overwhelmed by the current level of incoming work, it has been steadily rising for over 5 years and the increase shows no sign in ending . . .[92]

The consultation further noted that this increase had however only become particularly acute since 2014. Prior to that date the court had 'managed to absorb the increase in its workload largely by the judges working longer hours.'[93] The court could no longer do so. It had reached the maximum workload that it could deal with effectively and in a timely manner. As a consequence, the consultation further noted, the court had reached the point where it was 'now falling significantly behind in dealing with [its increased workload].'[94] It went on to state that the court was 'currently running at a deficit of 179 full appeals a year . . . which, of course, get added to the Backlog.'[95] The cause of the backlog and increased workload, according to a statistical assessment of the court's workload conducted by Professor Genn, was—as might be expected—the increase in permission to appeal applications. As the consultation put it:

> The main element of the increasing burden in terms of pure numbers is PTA [permission to appeal applications]. The [Court of Appeal] is currently running at a deficit of 47 paper PTA applications and 183 oral PTA hearings a year . . . Again these get added to the Backlog.[96]

In addition to an increased judicial workload, increases in administrative work and extra-curial responsibilities, referred to as 'leadership' work, in respect of running the justice system, conducting formal Public Inquiries, amongst other things, meant the court was becoming less productive at the time when the number

[91] Bowman (1997), 135ff. Also, [2000] 1 W.L.R. 1311 at [15]ff.

[92] *Dyson Consultation* at 35.

[93] Ibid.

[94] Ibid.

[95] Ibid.

[96] Ibid.

of permission to appeal applications and appeals were increasing.[97] Its judiciary was being required to deal with increasing appellate work at a time when it was being given less time to do so.[98] Finally, it was noted that additionally, and this was seen as the most significant source of the problems facing the court, its workload concerning full appeals had increased significantly. While it was correct to say that the number of appeals heard had remained broadly static, with some small increase, the work required for preparing, hearing and judgment writing in connection with full appeals had increased. The conclusion was drawn that this additional work was being caused by the fact that the court was hearing an increasing number of cases where the law in issue was of 'ever increasing complexity.'[99] While the point was not made, it would appear that the increase in appeal-based workload was a result of the Bowman reforms' focusing the court's work on second appeals, i.e. those that raised points of public importance. By concentrating its work on 'the most difficult cases,'[100] the court had created a problem for itself in terms of its own workload. The three main consequences of the increased workload, which was it would appear primarily linked to increases in applications for permission to appeal and appeals in respect of immigration and asylum proceedings,[101] were the following:

1. Waiting times for appeals to be heard, from issue, had increased from 9 months to 19 months. This was expected to continue increasing;
2. Court of Appeal judges were being required to spend increasing time working outside of their required working hours;
3. There would be increasing delays in the provision of written judgments.[102]

Increased delay was thus becoming embedded into the court process both prior to appeals being heard and after appeals were heard. The time required to eliminate the backlog of work this had caused would have required a year's judicial time.[103] Absent reform, this was expected by the end of 2016 to have increased to 2 year's judicial time to clear.[104]

The *Dyson Consultation* concluded that there were three potential options for reform that would cure the problems identified, and if implemented halt the increase in time to clear the backlog: first, increase the number of Court of Appeal judges; second, reduce the court's jurisdiction so that it would hear fewer appeals; and, third, reform the court's working practices and procedures to enable it to deal with its workload more efficiently.[105] The first option was dismissed out of hand: in an age of

---

[97]Ibid. 39.

[98]Ibid. 36.

[99]Ibid.

[100]Ibid. The figures are set out in the Appendices to the *Dyson Consultation*.

[101]*Dyson Consultation*, Appendix 3.

[102]Ibid. 36.

[103]Ibid.

[104]Ibid. 37.

[105]Ibid. 39.

austerity the idea of increasing the number of Court of Appeal judges was one that was unrealistic. It was one that the government rejected prior to the consultation being issued. The second option was already being implemented, through procedural reforms that would ensure that exceptions to the routes of appeal (outlined above) would be removed and that the only first appeals that would come to the Court of Appeal were appeals from the High Court. This reform was however noted to be insufficient a reform to meet the caseload problem the court faced.[106]

The third option, reforming the Court of Appeal's working practices and procedure, was thus the one to be pursued. Two main proposals were put forward to implement it: first, increasing the threshold test for granting permission to appeal from 'real prospect of success' to 'substantial prospect of success'; and, second, removing the right to an oral permission hearing in the Court of Appeal, i.e. removing one of the two permission stages in that court. This was to be replaced with a single paper-based permission stage with the discretion for the court to direct that permission be determined not on the papers but at an oral hearing before the court.[107] The former was intended to reduce the number of permission applications brought before the court, ensuring that its resources were focused in future on second appeals and on only those first appeals where there was a real risk rather than something more than a merely fanciful risk (the real prospect of success test) that the merits-based trial judgment had gone wrong. The latter was intended to streamline the permission to appeal process itself, reducing the amount of work undertaken by the court to determine such applications by eliminating one stage of the process.

Following the consultation, the second of the two proposals (the introduction of a single paper-based permission to appeal process with discretion to direct the application be determined at an oral hearing) was introduced on 3 October 2016.[108] The proposal to introduce a higher permission to appeal test for first appeals to the Court of Appeal was postponed pending further consideration.[109] This was the result of objections to its introduction to the effect that raising the threshold test would: reduce the court's ability to correct judicial error in trial courts; increase uncertainty in the law through, again, reducing the court's ability to correct incorrect interpretations and applications of the law as well as reducing the court's ability to develop

[106]Ibid.

[107]Ibid. 7–10.

[108]Civil Procedure (Amendment No. 3) Rules 2016 (SI 2016/788).

[109]Briggs writes (2016), 9.10: 'The public response to consultation included further opposition to the raising of the threshold test and to the removal of oral renewal of PTA applications, although it was by no means unanimous. The CPRC approved all those parts of the package needing implementation by Rule or Practice Direction change, except the raising of the threshold merits test for permission to appeal. This proposal was adjourned for further review, in the light of a disinclination to have two slightly different merits thresholds for appeals to different courts. There will probably be further consultation as to whether the raise in the threshold from "real" to "substantial" prospect of success should be applied to all appeals, rather than only to appeals to the Court of Appeal.' https://www.judiciary.gov.uk/wp-content/uploads/2016/07/civil-courts-structure-review-final-report-jul-16-final-1.pdf. Accessed 28 May 2019.

the law; and, the proposed increase to substantial prospect of success was not based on any evidence to support the view that the present real prospect of success test was too low a threshold.[110] Further consideration by the Civil Procedure Rule Committee during 2017 brought to light problems with the statistical evidence upon which the proposal had been based. In particular, an error in calculating the success rate of immigration appeals that were granted permission to appeal was seen to be significantly higher than had previously been believed: raising the threshold might then be taken to reduce the number of valid applications being granted permission to appeal. The question of raising the permission threshold was postponed, in February 2017, pending further evidence-gathering and analysis.[111] It has not been considered further, nor has any evidence or analysis been made public. It would either appear that this question has been set aside for the foreseeable future, those reforms that were introduced yielded a positive result, and/or there has been a reduction in the Court of Appeal's caseload for unrelated reasons that has meant further reform is unnecessary at present.

4 Conclusion

The appellate caseload of the UKSC and the Court of Appeal in England and Wales is a tale of two courts. Caseload in the former is and has been relatively stable, and following a degree of overload in the 1990s is such now that the court's work is not such as to require its justices to fulfil its full complement of sitting days per annum. Caseload in the latter due to a number of disparate factors, some court-related and some administrative, has over recent years been such that the court has developed a backlog of outstanding appeals and permission to appeal applications: a workload that was reduced in 2000 through the introduction of a generally applicable permission to appeal test and other reforms aimed at concentrating the court's resources on second appeals. Reforms have been introduced to reduce the Court of Appeal's caseload, albeit partially. It remains to be seen what long-term effect, if any, they will have on the Court of Appeal's workload. Equally, it remains to be seen whether—after the pause for reconsideration—the proposal to increase the threshold test for the grant of permission to appeal to the Court of Appeal will be introduced, although it seems unlikely at the time of writing that it will be reconsidered for the foreseeable

[110]See for instance The Law Society, *Response of the Law Society of England and Wales to the consultation issued by the Ministry of Justice on Appeals to the Court of Appeal: proposed amendments to Civil Procedure Rules and Practice Direction* (June 2016). Other responses welcomed the proposal to raise the threshold test on the basis that it would reduce the number of permission applications that were speculative; see, for instance, Justice, *Consultation on Appeals to the Court of Appeal: proposed amendments to Civil Procedure Rules and Practice Directions – Response* (24 June 2016) at https://justice.org.uk/wp-content/uploads/2016/06/Court-of-Appeal-Consultation_JUSTICE-Response.pdf. Accessed 24 May 2020. Fouzder (2016).

[111]Civil Procedure Rule Committee, *Minutes of the Rule Committee Meeting*, 7 February 2017.

future. If it is introduced however, it then remains to be seen whether it produces a positive benefit in terms of workload and, equally, if it does, in fact, reduce the court's workload, it produces the negative consequences that its critics suggested it would.

References

Andrews N (2013) On civil processes, vol 1. Intersentia, Cambridge

Andrews N (2014) The Supreme Court of the United Kingdom and English judgments. Legal Studies Research Paper Series, paper No. 23/2014, 2, 4

Bevan T (1901a) The appellate jurisdiction of the House of Lords I. Law Q Rev 17:155–170

Bevan T (1901b) The appellate jurisdiction of the House of Lords II. Law Q Rev 17:357–371

Blake C, Drewry G (2004) The role of the Court of Appeal in England and Wales as an intermediate court. In: Le Sueur A (ed) Building the UK's Supreme Court. Oxford University Press, Oxford, pp 221–236

Bowman J (1997) Review of the Court of Appeal (Civil Division): a report to the Lord Chancellor. Lord Chancellor's Department, September 1997

Briggs M (2016) Civil court structure review – final report, July 2016. https://www.judiciary.uk/wp-content/uploads/2016/07/civil-courts-structure-review-final-report-jul-16-final-1.pdf. Accessed 11 Feb 2021

Burrows A (2013) Numbers sitting in the Supreme Court. Law Q Rev 129:305–309

Burton M (2013) Civil appeals. Sweet & Maxwell, London

Carmichael P, Dickson B (1999) The House of Lords: its Parliamentary and Judicial Roles. Hart, Oxford

Cross R, Harris J (1991) Precedent in English law. Clarendon, Oxford

Drewry G, Blom-Cooper L, Blake C (2007) The Court of Appeal. Hart, Oxford

Fouzder M (2016) Court of Appeal threshold to remain unchanged. Law Gazette, 24 August 2016. https://www.lawgazette.co.uk/law/court-of-appeal-threshold-to-remain-unchanged/5057226.article. Accessed 28 May 2019

Jackson R (ed) (2016) Civil Procedure 2016, vol 1. Sweet & Maxwell, London

Kavanagh A (2009) Constitutional review under the UK Human Rights Act. Cambridge University Press, Cambridge

Le Sueur A, Cornes R (2001) The future of the United Kingdom's Highest Courts. Constitution Unit. https://www.ucl.ac.uk/constitution-unit/sites/constitution-unit/files/76.pdf. Accessed 11 Feb 2021

Paterson A (2013) Final Judgment. Hart, London

Shah S, Poole T (2009) The impact of the Human Rights Act on the House of Lords. LSE Working Papers 8/2009, 10–11. https://www.lse.ac.uk/collections/law/wps/WPS2009-08_Shah_Poole.pdf. Accessed 28 May 2019

Sorabji J (2016) Access to the Supreme Court – the English approach. Revista de Processo 41 (257):391–413

Stevens R (2011) Torts. In: Blom-Cooper L et al (eds) The judicial House of Lords 1876–2009. Oxford University Press, Oxford, pp 629–652

Tomlinson J, Rylatt J, Fairgrieve D (2016) And then there were eleven: some context on the Supreme Court sitting en banc in the Article 50 Case. U.K. Const Law Blog, 9th Nov 2016. https://ukconstitutionallaw.org/. Accessed 28 May 2019

Zuckerman A (2013) Zuckerman on Civil Procedure: Principles of Practice. Sweet & Maxwell, London

A Happy-Go-Lucky Story: The American Supreme Court and Overload Problems

Richard Marcus

Abstract Nowadays, the U.S. Supreme Court controls its own docket thanks to the discretion it enjoys to select cases based on the writ of certiorari. As a result, the current court has no serious problems of overload and, in fact, the number of cases has decreased by half compared to previous generations. Furthermore, the reduced caseload has not diminished the prominent role that the Supreme Court plays in American society today. But it was not always so. In its beginnings, the Supreme Court was a 'feeble institution,' with justices riding circuit, with almost no cases and with not enough justices showing up anyway. After the Civil War, the federal courts and the Supreme Court gained more jurisdiction on 'federal questions' and, consequently, more cases to resolve. This increase in powers was not accompanied by changes in the judicial structure—which produced a case overload problem—until 1891. In that year, the U.S. Congress abolished the task of riding circuit for Supreme Court justices and created the intermediate circuit courts of appeals. This reform, however, brought only temporary relief. Litigants kept an automatic right to appeal to the Supreme Court, increasing its caseload pressures again. In the Judiciary Act of 1925, combined with other reforms in a similar direction, Congress redefined the role of the Supreme Court by giving it near-complete control of its docket. This contribution recounts the long journey through which the U.S. Supreme Court became its own master and how case overload problems are now long forgotten.

1 Introduction

Given the gloomy title of this volume, it may seem odd to have such a cheerful title for the American contribution. After all, the U.S. Supreme Court is 'the world's best-known Supreme Court.'[1] But, to get to the bottom line first, the current reality of the

[1]Lord Bingham of Cornhill (2002), p. 10.

R. Marcus (✉)
University of California, Hastings College of the Law, San Francisco, CA, USA
e-mail: marcusr@uchastings.edu

P. Bravo-Hurtado, C. H. van Rhee (eds.), *Supreme Courts Under Pressure*, Ius Gentium: Comparative Perspectives on Law and Justice 83,
https://doi.org/10.1007/978-3-030-63731-6_9

U.S. Supreme Court is that it is its own master, and it does not suffer any significant problems of caseload overload. To the contrary, during the last generation the caseload of the court has fallen by about half without seeming to impair its prominence or fame.

It was not always so. The U.S. Supreme Court is an old institution, and it had beginnings that differ greatly from its current eminence. At key points in its development, as explored later in this paper, it experienced severe caseload pressures. But revisions in the role it plays, and in the judicial apparatus, changed all that. Those developments will be described below.

For the present, it seems appropriate to introduce the original court. The Constitution of the United States provides that, 'The judicial power of the United States, shall be vested in one supreme Court, and in such inferior Courts as Congress may from time to time ordain and establish.'[2] What that court would have done if Congress had not created lower federal courts might be pondered. There was a stark division in drafting the Constitution about whether there should even be lower federal courts. One group preferred that there be only one federal court—the Supreme Court. Another wanted a single federal court system to bind the new nation together. Ultimately, the contending factions agreed to compromise and leave the question of lower federal courts to Congress.

Congress did not tarry long; in 1789 the First Congress adopted the First Judiciary Act,[3] creating lower federal courts organized in judicial districts corresponding to the geographic boundaries of the states, and gave these courts jurisdiction over cases involving litigants from different states (called 'diversity jurisdiction'). The Supreme Court, meanwhile, had a difficult time during its early years. When it first assembled in New York, it could not muster a quorum because two justices were unable to get to New York in time and two others nominated to the court declined the appointments. And the new court had no cases to hear—the extreme opposite of a case overload problem.

The early court was a 'feeble institution.'[4] The first Chief Justice, John Jay, left his post on the court to become governor of New York because he thought that a much more important position.[5] John Rutledge, meanwhile, declined a nomination to serve on the court because he preferred to become the Chief Justice of the South Carolina Court of Common Pleas.[6]

But Chief Justice John Marshall cemented the position of the court in the early nineteenth century by affirming the power of judicial review, and the court became, over time, the ultimate arbiter of a variety of American legal matters. That is the tale we have to tell in this paper, and it may be a useful one for others facing either

[2]U.S. Constitution, Article III, §1.

[3]Judiciary Act of 1789, 1 Stat. 73.

[4]Crowe (2011), p. 1.

[5]Cannon (1974), p. 334.

[6]Greenhouse (2012), pp. 8–9.

overburdened courts or under-appreciated ones. Institutional change is possible and, over time, very important.

2 The Purpose Served by the U.S. Supreme Court

Much can flow from the purpose a Supreme Court is to serve, both in a judicial system and, in a different sense, in the governmental structure. Differences in approach to the court's purpose can affect attitudes toward overload, so it seems a useful place to begin.

There are at least two basic models for appellate review, including review performed by Supreme Courts. As Professor Jolowicz[7] explained, one version—which he calls 'appeal'—involves a court of second instance that regards the decisions of the court of first instance as nothing more than a brief introduction to the case, and undertakes to ensure that the outcome it reaches is the correct one under the law without much regard for the decision of the first instance court. Such a court will not hesitate to consider evidence and arguments not presented to the court of first instance. And it would not be particularly preoccupied about whether the lower court made mistakes in handling the evidence or arguments presented to it. As Professor Jolowicz[8] explains, 'Its business is to decide for itself, as a court of second instance, and its decision replaces the first instance decision for all purposes.'

On the face of it, this approach to appellate review would likely produce caseload pressures because it could prompt many disappointed litigants to 'go it again,' and might require intense consideration of each case to make certain that the outcome was really correct. On the other hand, it could be justified on the ground that first instance proceedings were brief and inexpensive, and that few litigants even wanted a second instance review after learning the first instance outcome. That attitude might explain how an appellate review process could function efficiently—say in Germany—while the opportunity for such full-dress review might not fare well in systems with substantial delays—Italy might be an example of that.

An alternative approach is often referred to as a court of cassation. This court *is* concerned with errors, and limited to the record of the proceedings below, but responsible for ensuring that the outcome reached by the lower court was not seriously incorrect. 'The role of a jurisdiction of cassation is said to be exclusively to examine the legality of the decision under attack ... and the court has only two options: it must either affirm or annul.'[9]

As Professor Jolowicz[10] recognizes, the distinction between appeal and cassation is not as clear as originally stated, but this distinction sets the scene for the evolution

---

[7]Jolowicz (2000), Chapter 15.

[8]Idem, p. 300.

[9]Idem, p. 300.

[10]Idem, pp. 320–321.

of the function of the American Supreme Court. As U.S. Supreme Court Chief Justice Rehnquist recognized in 1987:

> Many would intuitively say that the task of the 'highest court in the land' is to make sure that justice is done to every litigant, or some similarly general and appealing description. The Supreme Court of the United States once played a role in the federal system corresponding fairly closely to that description, but the days when it could do so are long gone.[11]

For Professor Jolowicz's purposes,[12] 'The American appeal is treated as a form of cassation rather than of appeal.'

One could insist that the U.S. Supreme Court at least adhere to its cassation responsibilities despite caseload pressures. Indeed, when in the late nineteenth century the first reform designed to relieve the U.S. Supreme Court of its caseload burden was proposed, a senator protested that such a change would go against the Bible:

> I understand that out of some 115 cases that come here the Supreme Court decided that a mistake was made in appealing eighty-odd cases. I submit that if one man's rights were preserved and safeguarded the Court in that action served a just purpose and it could well afford to consider 100 to 200 cases if necessary, in order to do justice by even one American citizen. The Bible tells us that it were better that 99 guilty persons go free than 1 innocent man should suffer. ... I am not ready to surrender the average citizen's right to appeal and accept in its stead discretionary power given to the judges of the Supreme Court.[13]

But Senator Heflin's colleagues were persuaded that the caseload pressures justified reducing the court's work burden, and the Supreme Court was in 1891 given some discretion to decline to review cases in which the losing litigant claimed error. By the mid-twentieth century, Chief Justice Vinson (1949) was able to declare that, 'The Supreme Court is not, and never has been, primarily concerned with the correction of errors in lower court decisions.'[14] As Professor Provine put it in 1980, 'The belief that the Supreme Court should not function primarily as an appellate court for correcting lower court errors constitutes an important element of the modern Court's conception of itself.'[15]

Instead, as now set forth in a Supreme Court rule, there are only narrow grounds for review by the court—a conflict among the lower federal courts on a legal principle, or a decision of 'an important federal question' by a state court that conflicts with the decision of a lower federal court or the court of another state.

---

[11]Rehnquist (1987), p. 267. See also Study Group on the Case Load of the Supreme Court (1972), p. 1 (asserting that the court is 'not simply another court of errors and appeals').

[12]Idem, p. 299.

[13]Senator Heflin, quoted in Frankfurter and Landis (1927), p. 261, n. 19.

[14]For the same sort of views from Chief Justice Rehnquist, consider Rehnquist (1987), p. 269: 'Occasionally, these [federal] trial judges make mistakes, but the federal courts of appeals sit to correct these mistakes within the federal system, and state appellate courts sit to do the same in every state system. It would be a useless duplication of these functions if the Supreme Court of the United States were to serve simply as an even higher court for the correction of errors in cases involving no generally important principle of law.'

[15]Provine (1980), p. 12.

The rule makes it clear that error is not enough: 'A petition for a writ of certiorari is rarely granted when the asserted error consists of erroneous factual findings or the misapplication of a properly stated rule of law.'[16]

The court's role as supreme arbiter of federal legal issues—constitutional and otherwise—thus is far removed from either version of appellate work outlined by Professor Jolowicz. Instead, it depends on the distinctive—perhaps unique—role this Supreme Court plays in the American legal culture, a topic to which we will return below. As a study group addressing the caseload of the Supreme Court in the 1970s said, the court reflects 'a process at the opposite pole from the "processing" of cases in a high-speed, high-volume enterprise.'[17] But before tracing the evolution of the Supreme Court from the error-correction mode to the current regime, it is first necessary to examine the evolution of the American federal judiciary that produced the present arrangements, and the ways in which that evolution has affected appellate caseload burdens.

3 The Long Path to the Current U.S. Supreme Court Apparatus

As De Tocqueville[18] observed in the early nineteenth century after studying the U.S. Supreme Court's role, 'a more imposing judicial power was never constituted by any people.' By the time he wrote, the stresses of case overload—or at least of function overload—had already begun to be felt by the Supreme Court. Those stresses were to endure until Congress changed the federal court structure in 1891, and again to lead to a change in the Supreme Court's responsibilities in 1925.

The original federal judicial structure was very different from the current setup. The first Congress created lower federal courts of first instance, but no courts of appeals. For a nation with a population of slightly more than four million, that seemed sufficient. Instead of providing an appellate court system, the First Judiciary Act directed that Supreme Court justices were to 'ride circuit,' reviewing district court decisions on a three-judge panel with local federal judges. For the Supreme Court justices, the duty of riding circuit was a logistical nightmare due in large measure to the difficult travel arrangements of the time. As the nation grew dramatically in geographic size and population, some justices had to traverse many hundreds of miles each year at a time when transportation was rudimentary and roads were bad, and to deal with the increased judicial business that resulted from urbanization and industrialization. Supreme Court justices became increasingly upset at this burden.

---

[16]U.S. Supreme Court Rule 10, 'Considerations Governing Review on Writ of Certiorari.'

[17]Study Group on the Case Load of the Supreme Court (1972), p. 1.

[18]De Tocqueville ([1835] 1990), p. 150.

But a different feature of the original setup might cause even more worry. Owing to the small number of federal judges, it could happen that the three-judge panel reviewing a district court decision would include the judge who made the decision. As one lawyer reported, 'Such an appeal is not from Philip drunk to Philip sober, but from Philip sober to Philip intoxicated with the vanity of a matured opinion and doubtless also a published decision.'[19]

Over the course of two centuries, the original arrangement was substantially changed, as detailed in Sect. 4 below. The current focus of the court is as set out in Sect. 2 above—resolving important issues of federal law. Before turning to details about its current operation, it is important to stress that the U.S. Supreme Court is hardly the only Supreme Court in America. To the contrary, all 50 American states have Supreme Courts as well, and under long-established doctrine those courts are the supreme arbiters of the law of their states (with review by the U.S. Supreme Court only on the ground that a state law, as so interpreted, violates federal law). Most of those Supreme Courts are structured like the U.S. Supreme Court, and have discretion to select the cases they decide according to their own criteria. Most of those states also have intermediate courts of appeal that do function as courts of error.

On the contemporary U.S. Supreme Court, there are nine justices, a number that has become somewhat sacrosanct as a result of the 'court-packing' effort of President Roosevelt in 1937 (described in Sect. 5.1 below).[20] Considered in comparison to the American population today of around 320 million, that is a very small number of justices. As Professor Uzelac[21] has noted, that works out to one justice per 34 million inhabitants, a vastly different ratio from that found in most countries.[22] Those nine American justices all sit together as one panel[23] to decide all matters collectively unless one of them is recused from a given case. The Constitution directed that there be 'one supreme Court,' so operating by panels might even be unconstitutional. Indeed, there is not even a process for replacing a recused justice with another judge, and it can happen that due to recusals the court is unable to decide a case because its vote is tied or there are not enough justices eligible to constitute a quorum.

As detailed later in this contribution, the court now has nearly absolute discretion in deciding which cases to add to its plenary docket, so its main functions are to

---

[19]Hill ([1889, pp. 289–290] 1927), p. 87.

[20]See Wright and Kane (2011), p. 14: The court-packing fight of the 1930s was so bitter that it 'has given the notion of a nine-judge Court such sanctity that it is unlikely that the size will again be changed.'

[21]Uzelac (2014).

[22]Putting aside tiny Monaco (with one Supreme Court judge for every 2392 inhabitants), Professor Uzelac shows that the U.S. ratio is nearly 1000 times larger than that of Montenegro (one per 34,446), Bosnia and Herzegovina (one per 40,033) and Greece (one per 41,888). Larger countries also have a much larger supply of Supreme Court judges compared to their populations. For example, France has one per 194,110 inhabitants. The U.S. ratio is about 175 times larger.

[23]See Wright and Kane (2011), p. 15: 'The Supreme Court is not authorized to sit in divisions.'

decide which cases to hear and to decide those cases. It operates under the 'rule of four,' under which it takes four votes (less than a majority of the nine-member court) to accept a case for hearing. Those decisions are made by the court as a whole, in conference, although (as also detailed later) there has been some sharing of the initial review function by Supreme Court law clerks, who now divide up the thousands of petitions seeking Supreme Court review and provide the justices with one memo per petition rather than (as was true in the past) with a separate memo for each justice about each petition.

The ordinary mode of proceeding is nonetheless fairly atomized. With regard to cases selected for plenary review, the justices do not ordinarily confer at all before the oral argument occurs. As a consequence, the oral argument of a case may depend significantly on exchanges between justices as well as interchanges between counsel and the court. After the oral argument, the justices meet in conference again and vote initially on the outcome, after which one of the justices is assigned the responsibility to prepare an opinion for the court. If the Chief Justice is in the majority, the assignment is made by the Chief Justice, but if not, the senior justice in the majority makes the assignment. Other justices in the majority can circulate their own supplemental opinions, and justices who disagree with the majority can (and usually do) circulate dissenting opinions or join in the dissent of another justice. As a consequence, it can happen that decisions come out without an official opinion of the court because no opinion commands five votes. On some issues, this sort of division has produced uncertainty about important issues that has lasted for decades.[24]

The court does not sit to decide fact issues, as noted above, but it may consider materials not submitted by the parties. Indeed, in recent years there has been a proliferation of briefs from *amicus curiae*, whose role seems often to be to offer additional arguments or authorities not presented by the parties. But the American orientation toward appeals does not encourage anything resembling the full reconsideration at second instance mentioned in Sect. 2 above.[25] The court may affirm or

---

[24]One prominent example deals with due process limits on personal jurisdiction. One view was that any entity that could foresee that its products would reach the forum state via the stream of commerce could be subjected to jurisdiction in a suit in that state for injuries occurring there due to alleged defects in its products. In a globalized world, that rule would obviously be very important. But another view emphasized that in a globalized world it may be 'foreseeable' that one's products could end up almost anywhere, so that more than foreseeability should be required. In *Asahi Metal Industry Co. v Superior Court*, 480 U.S. 102 (1987), the court decided a case rejecting jurisdiction over a Japanese manufacturer, but the vote was 4-1-4 on the basic legal question. One justice said it was unnecessary to answer that question, so although four endorsed one answer and four others endorsed another answer, there was no opinion for the court on the question. In 2011, the court returned to what it described as 'decades-old questions left open in Asahi Metal Co. v. Superior Court,' *J. McIntyre Machinery, Ltd. v Nicastro*, 564 U.S. 873 (2011). But again it did not decide the question. A plurality of four took one view, three dissenters took another view, and two justices declined to decide the question. So the basic question has remained unanswered for at least a generation.

[25]For a discussion of the American approach to appellate review, and limitations on it, see Marcus (2014).

reverse, and may send the case back to the lower courts with instructions to proceed in accordance with the legal rules it has announced. On occasion, it announces a new legal rule to apply prospectively only, and even if portions of its opinions can be described as *dictum* because they are unnecessary to the result it reached in the case before it, Supreme Court pronouncements are likely to have a considerable effect on the lower courts.

Any disappointed litigant can petition the Supreme Court for review without a lawyer, and sometimes those *pro se* petitions lead to important precedents.[26] But when it grants such a petition, the court ordinarily appoints a lawyer to present the case. Any lawyer admitted to practice in any state can be admitted to the court's bar. In recent years, however, a coterie of experienced and expert advocates has emerged, and they reportedly are more successful in obtaining Supreme Court review of cases than most lawyers.[27] Further details will emerge as we examine the ways in which caseload pressures have prompted changes in the court's operations over the centuries.

4 Caseload Pressure and Institutional Evolution in the U.S. Supreme Court

As noted at the beginning, the U.S. Supreme Court certainly did not originally have a problem with a heavy caseload. To the contrary, when it first met in 1790 it had no cases, and not enough justices showed up to constitute a quorum. But under the original arrangement of the federal court system it developed considerable responsibilities during the nineteenth century, and the burdens of travelling bad roads made the job of Supreme Court Justice a very difficult one. In the period leading up to the Civil War (1861–1865), the federal court 'machinery was carrying a load beyond its capacity. The existing judicial structure was unequal to the volume and the range of litigation coming to the federal courts.'[28] Shortly after the Civil War, Congress added 'federal question' cases to the jurisdiction of the federal courts (in addition to 'diversity' cases involving citizens of different states), which 'gave the federal courts a vast range of power which had lain dormant in the Constitution since 1789.'[29] But the judicial structure remained unchanged, leaving the Supreme Court 'staggering under a load which made speedy and effective judicial administration impossible.'[30]

[26]See, e.g., *Gideon v Wainwright*, 372 U.S. 335 (1963), in which a petition from an uneducated, imprisoned man led the court to hold that the Constitution requires the government to provide a lawyer for those unable to employ one in all felony cases. The petitioner did not have to brief his own case. Instead, the court appointed Abe Fortas of the Washington D.C. bar (later appointed a justice of the court himself) to represent him. For an informative book about the case see Lewis (1964).

[27]See Lazarus (2008), pp. 1502–1507.

[28]Frankfurter and Landis (1927), p. 52.

[29]Idem, p. 65.

[30]Idem, p. 86.

For decades, the American Congress was deadlocked about whether to change that judicial structure. Many in Congress favored the old circuit-riding activity of justices as a way of keeping them in contact with the country outside the nation's capital. 'The result was a continually growing docket at the Court and increasingly more desperate calls—from lawyers, from the American Bar Association, from attorneys general, from presidents, and from the justices themselves—for Congress to unburden the Court.'[31]

Eventually, in 1891, Congress responded by abolishing the circuit-riding responsibilities of the justices and creating a new intermediate system of circuit courts of appeals. Appeal (after final judgment) would first go to the court of appeals for the area of the country in which the district court judgment was entered. Only after that decision could disappointed litigants seek review in the Supreme Court. 'In terms of unburdening the Supreme Court, the Circuit Courts of Appeals Act was an immediate and unqualified success' in reducing the court's docket and resulting delays in decision.[32]

But the respite was temporary, for litigants still had a right to seek ultimate review in the Supreme Court. Due to 'cumbersome procedures like automatic appeals to the Supreme Court, . . . [by the 1920s] the number of petitions to the Supreme Court for certiorari had nearly doubled (from 270 to 539).'[33] In 1925, Congress responded with legislation that 'drastically redefined the role of the Supreme Court by converting much of its obligatory jurisdiction into certiorari jurisdiction.'[34] 'By limiting the automatic right of appeal to the Supreme Court and expanding the types of cases that could be heard only with the Justices' assent, the Judiciary Act of 1925 gave the Court near-complete control over its docket for the first time in history.'[35] As Frankfurter and Landis noted in 1927, the passage of this act 'marks a new chapter in the history of the federal judiciary.'[36]

Although there have been significant changes to the federal judicial system since 1925—including the creation of two additional federal circuit courts of appeals and elimination of some obligatory Supreme Court jurisdiction that endured after 1925—the basic framework for the current arrangements dates from that Act. Based on nearly a century of experience under the current arrangements, it is possible to examine the effect of the transformation.

---

[31]Crowe (2011), p. 179.

[32]Idem, p. 185. See also Frankfurter and Landis (1927), p. 101: 'The remedy was decisive. The Supreme Court at once felt its benefit. A flood of litigation had indeed been shut off.'

[33]Crowe (2011), p. 199.

[34]Idem, p. 200.

[35]Idem, p. 211.

[36]Frankfurter and Landis (1927), p. 1. This is the first sentence in the book. Frankfurter and Landis (1927), p. 187 added, 'Perhaps the decisive factor in the Supreme Court is its progressive contraction of jurisdiction. This tendency has been particularly significant since the Civil War. In contrast with the vast expansion of the bounds of the inferior federal courts, the scope of review by the Supreme Court has been steadily narrowed.'

5 Caseload Cures and Consequences in the U.S. Supreme Court

The 1925 Act was viewed as a godsend initially, but as time went by some became unhappy with it. Although this story merits telling, it is important to appreciate initially that the structural arrangements for the Supreme Court have remained constant for almost a century. Nonetheless, alarm about caseload pressure has arisen from time to time.

These concerns about caseload pressures have also sometimes had a vaguely 'political' flavor. For example, in 1960 Justice Douglas—a notorious fast worker—announced that 'the idea that the Court is overworked' was a 'myth.'[37] More recently, as detailed below, proposals to revise the federal judicial structure in the 1970s and 1980s were vigorously opposed on the ground that there actually was not a serious overload problem at the Supreme Court.[38]

An eminent panel appointed by the Chief Justice to study the caseload problem opined in 1972 that the 1925 Act's solutions 'have become part of the problem' because 'the task of coping with discretionary jurisdiction on certiorari overhangs all of the Court's work.'[39] As noted, however, no significant actual changes have occurred.[40] So it seems appropriate to focus on possibilities as much as actualities.

5.1 *Expanding the Court*

One response to an expanding workload is to add more workers. Though in the early nineteenth century the U.S. Supreme Court had a varying number of justices, the number stabilized at nine in 1869, and has remained there ever since. If caseload pressures were to prompt thoughts of expanding the number of justices, the fact that the Constitution calls for 'one supreme Court' and therefore that sitting in panels would not be allowed suggests that expanding the cast of justices would not cause the work to diminish. To the contrary, it could even cause the workload to increase, as more justices would have to be persuaded to agree to decisions that might more easily be reached by a smaller group.

Putting aside that reason, there is a political reason why the cast will not likely be increased. Barely a decade after the 1925 Act, President Franklin Roosevelt used

[37]Douglas (1960), p. 401.

[38]See Hellman (1983), p. 29, regarding proposals for 'the most far-reaching change in the structure of the federal judicial system since the creation of intermediate appellate courts nearly a century ago,' which the author regarded as unsupported by the caseload reasons advanced.

[39]Study Group on the Case Load of the Supreme Court (1972), p. 9.

[40]It is true that a considerable portion of the court's obligatory jurisdiction that persisted after the 1925 Act has since been made discretionary, but because that was not a large proportion of the court's work it seems a minor point.

workload as his argument to support expanding the size of the court. During the mid-1930s, several pieces of legislation that were adopted as part of President Roosevelt's New Deal were held unconstitutional by the Supreme Court. After a huge victory in the 1936 election, the president proposed in 1937 that he be allowed to appoint a new justice for each one then over the age of 70. The rationale was that the elderly justices could not get their work done on time. Many saw a naked political motivation rather than a genuine concern with delayed decisions, and the legislation was eventually retracted. The bitterness of this political fight in the 1930s has persuaded very sophisticated commentators to conclude that the current number of justices has 'such sanctity that it is unlikely that the size will again be changed.'[41]

A different possibility might be worth mentioning—setting term limits for justices. Professors Crampton and Carrington have for some time urged that this be done.[42] It seems that no country except the United States has bestowed lifetime tenure on its judges.[43] The argument is that the tenure for justices in the late twentieth century far exceeded the average tenure in the early nineteenth century, and that the resulting stability of the court's membership is a bad thing. That stability results from at least two things—improved medical care and the propensity of presidents to nominate younger candidates to be justices to 'leave their mark on the Supreme Court.' But the United States has adopted lifetime tenure for all federal judges, including Supreme Court justices. Particularly given the intensity of the fight over President Roosevelt's court-packing scheme, it is unlikely that such ideas would be embraced. And if they were, they would almost certainly require an amendment to the Constitution, a very difficult process.

A different problem emerged in February 2016, when Justice Antonin Scalia died. Under the U.S. constitutional structure, all judges with lifetime tenure are nominated by the president and confirmed by the Senate. The president duly nominated a successor in March 2016. Though the judge so nominated was widely applauded as a highly-qualified centrist, the Republican majority in the Senate announced that it would not consider this nomination because the new justice should be selected by the next president. So at least until the election in November 2016, there was an impasse about replacing Justice Scalia. This impasse ended with the confirmation of Judge Neil Gorsuch in April 2017.

While this impasse persisted, the court continued to function with eight justices, raising the prospect of tie votes. But because the court almost always disposes of its entire caseload by the end of its term,[44] a tie vote means the court cannot decide the case, and the decision of the lower court stands. On several occasions in the spring of 2016 that was the result, and the issues presented remained unresolved. Some are

[41]Wright and Kane (2011), p. 14.

[42]Crampton and Carrington (2006). See also Calabresi and Lindgren (2005).

[43]Greenhouse (2012), p. 84.

[44]In rare instances, cases are set for reargument during the next term rather than being decided. In Spring, 2020, due to the coronavirus pandemic, argument and decision of a number of cases was postponed until the following term.

vexed by this situation. The late Justice Ginsburg, for example, told a judicial conference that 'eight ... is not a good number for a multimember court.'[45] But Professor Cass R. Sunstein suggested that the possibility of tie votes might provide a stimulus toward compromise and what he calls judicial 'minimalism'—avoiding sweeping decisions. That could tend to reduce the court's valence as a factor in the country's public life. As *The Economist* recognized, however, 'It is hard to see how a denuded court is appealing in the medium or long term. . . . America's constitutional design is not consonant with confusion about what the law means on controversial questions. . . . [A] Supreme Court with eight judges is not a court that can live up to its name.'[46]

On balance, then, a formal change to the composition of the Supreme Court is unlikely to be adopted, or to have a considerable effect on its caseload.

5.2 Adding Staff

Although the number of justices has remained stable for almost 150 years, the staffing of the Supreme Court has changed a great deal. The area of most pertinence is the position of law clerk, permitting the judge to delegate some decisional tasks to underlings. As Professor Jolowicz notes, 'It is in the United States that the search for this kind of efficiency has been carried the furthest. There, judicial time is saved, or sought to be saved, by the widespread use of assistants to the judges, not only during the preparatory stages of an appeal but also in the formation of decisions.' He asks, 'Is this the way ahead for other systems, or is the provision of extensive assistance to appellate judges something peculiar to the United States?'[47]

The introduction of law clerks at the U.S. Supreme Court did not occur until the late nineteenth century, when Horace Gray, who had been Chief Justice of the Supreme Court in Massachusetts, was appointed to the U.S. Supreme Court. The Massachusetts court had used law clerks to assist its justices, so Justice Gray introduced the idea in Washington. Gradually, the idea took hold, and over time Congress authorized salaries for an increasing number of them, rising to four per justice at present.

Law clerks sift through the mountain of certiorari petitions for a hearing before the court, and thus provide triage for one of the court's functions—selecting the cases for plenary hearing. In addition, they are given roles to play in the drafting of opinions. Different justices give them different roles in the drafting of opinions.

Presumably, until the late nineteenth century the justices did all their own work. At that time, of course, there was no need to review petitions for hearings as there was a right to Supreme Court review until the 1925 Act. Moreover, in the famous

---

[45]Liptak (2016), p. A10.

[46]The Economist (2016b).

[47]Jolowicz (2000), p. 346.

words of Justice Brandeis, the reason that the U.S. Supreme Court received respect was that, 'We do good work because we do our own work here.'[48] The court regarded itself as different from other organs of government in which the drafting work was done by underlings.

Since Brandeis's time, law clerks have had increasingly important roles, and they have often fascinated outsiders. Whole books focus on these staff members. One recent book even called them 'sorcerers' apprentices.'[49] To some extent, that fascination may be due to the fact that a considerable number of American law professors were law clerks for the Supreme Court, and considerably more wish they had been. To some extent that fascination may result from the fact that it seems that law clerks believe that they have broad influence on what the court does.

As Professor Jolowicz noted, Supreme Court law clerks do play a role in drafting the court's opinions. Some justices allow clerks to provide the initial draft, and others permit clerks only to offer comments or supply citations for opinions drafted by the justice. Certainly some clerks think they play a major role in fashioning the content of the court's opinions, but it is far from certain whether their confidence on that score is warranted.[50]

Some observers believe that the growing length of the court's opinions, and the appearance of frequent dissents or concurring opinions, is partly a result of the proliferation of law clerks.[51] Perhaps the role of law clerks contributes to the proliferation of what some call 'judicial gobbledygook' in the court's opinions. One observer recently asserted that 'legal writing at the Court has become more complex and difficult to read in recent decades.'[52] But even if that is true, one could respond that the legal questions that the court addresses have become more uniformly complex and difficult. That could be a result of giving the court discretion to select the cases it hears; in the absence of 'easy' cases, one might expect that the decisions would be more challenging and involve trickier issues.

And it is not clear that—whatever the extent of delegation of tasks to law clerks—this delegation results from the court's workload. Instead, some warn of 'the alluring trap of assuming that increased workload is responsible for the rising amount of delegation to clerks.'[53]

[48]Kester (1982).

[49]See Ward and Weiden (2006).

[50]Writing in 1980, Provine (1980), p. 24 concluded that there was no evidence that Justices were having difficulty maintaining independence from their law clerks.

[51]For discussion see Black and Spriggs (2008).

[52]Whalen (2015), p. 200.

[53]Stras (2007), p. 962.

5.3 *Choosing the Cases: Limiting the Caseload via the Certiorari Decision*

The way in which the U.S. Supreme Court now chooses its cases is to decide whether to grant a writ of certiorari, which puts a case on the court's plenary docket. Each year the court grants a hearing in fewer than 1% of the cases in which it is asked to grant a hearing.[54] Indeed, the screening process has recently been startlingly effective in guarding the Supreme Court against overload. As a commentator wrote in 2007: 'At a time when the lower courts are confronting unprecedented numbers of cases and disposing of more cases summarily, the Supreme Court is deciding, on a relative basis, nearly four times fewer cases than it did in 1986, which is a staggering change in less than twenty years.'[55] A *New York Times* article labelled this development 'the case of the plummeting Supreme Court docket.'[56] But 'the criteria the Court uses to select cases for decision on the merits have always been shrouded in mystery.'[57]

The official view is that the court's denial of certiorari is a matter of no moment to any but the parties to the case; it is not precedent and says nothing about whether the court regarded the decision below to be correct.[58] That is consistent, of course, with the idea that the court does not take cases merely to correct errors. Nonetheless, at least some observers urge that the court should provide reasons (mini-opinions?) to explain its decision to reject certain petitions for certiorari.[59] That is not likely to happen. Justices regard a considerable percentage of the petitions for certiorari as presenting nothing of substance. And, with something like 10,000 petitions presented each year even though fewer than 100 are granted, the additional workload would obviously be severe. In addition, the court might worry that offering something like an opinion or statement of reasons to accompany certiorari denials could prompt more litigants to seek review in hopes at least of getting that sort of statement of reasons—10,000 petitions might become 20,000 petitions. As noted below, the caseload of the courts of appeals has risen dramatically in recent decades, so the volume of the Supreme Court's certiorari docket could as well.

The method of dealing with this certiorari docket has, however, produced changes in the way staff are used. For decades, each justice had his or her own staff

[54]The Supreme Court's own website reports that it receives approximately 10,000 petitions for certiorari per year, and hears oral argument in 75–80 cases.

[55]Stras (2007), p. 967.

[56]Liptak (2009). The article describes an academic conference 'to explore the mystery of the court's shrinking docket.' See also Lazarus (2008), pp. 1507–1520, examining 'the paradox of the Court's shrinking docket.'

[57]Provine (1980), p. 74.

[58]For discussion see Linzer (1979).

[59]For a less aggressive argument see Segall (2014). Professor Segall urges that the votes on all petitions for certiorari be made public, while agreeing that 'requiring the justices to have to agree on reason for more than 7,000 denials annually would not be worth the effort.'

independently review all incoming certiorari petitions. But as Chief Justice Rehnquist[60] explained, by the early 1970s law clerks 'were frequently pressed for time, scrambling between having memos describing the certiorari petitions ready when they should be, and drafts or revisions of Court opinions or dissents ready when they should have been.' The solution, proposed by Justice Lewis Powell, was a 'cert. pool' arrangement under which several justices would 'pool' their clerks for the purpose of reviewing certiorari petitions, and primary responsibility for drafting a memorandum analyzing a petition would rest with a single clerk for the participating justices, instead of having a clerk for each justice independently review each of the petitions. Initially only some of the justices participated, but participation has become universal in recent years. Some attribute the low rate of certiorari grants to this new arrangement, on the notion that law clerks regard it as much easier to recommend denial than say that a given case warrants a hearing.

Though the certiorari mechanism has surely guarded the court against overload in recent decades (given the dramatic decline in the number of cases it has decided on the merits), it also seems to give 'an advantage to sophisticated and experienced petitioners, especially the U.S. government.'[61] But it is likely that any discretionary selection process would favor those more familiar with the process.

5.4 *Limiting the Court's Jurisdiction*

Rather than giving the court authority to pick its cases, one could limit its jurisdiction by excluding categories of cases. Various methods of doing so might be imagined—topical limitations might be preferred, or case value might be employed. For U.S. federal courts, there is already one case-value limitation—cases that are filed in federal courts because the parties come from different states must involve a controversy with a value of at least $75,000.[62] To the extent the Supreme Court reviews decisions of the federal courts, then, this limitation may apply. As a general matter, however, external limitations have not played a significant role with regard to the U.S. Supreme Court's docket.

There is no monetary limitation on the Supreme Court's authority to review a decision of a state court, although the court's authority extends only to cases in which state courts have resolved federal law issues.[63] And when a claim arises under federal law it may be in federal court without regard to the amount in controversy.[64]

From time to time, there have been efforts to limit the topics on which the Supreme Court may pass. For example, during the mid-twentieth century there

[60]Rehnquist (1987), pp. 263–264.

[61]Provine (1980), pp. 175–176.

[62]See 28 U.S.C. § 1332.

[63]28 U.S.C. § 1257(a).

[64]28 U.S.C. § 1331.

was considerable discussion in Congress of legislation preventing the court from taking further actions on topics that had provoked controversy, such as ordering busing to achieve racial integration in schools.[65] Nobody argued for imposing such limitations to enable the court to cope with the burden of its caseload, however. Instead, the political reaction resulted from what the court had done in cases it already *had* decided. Given that the Supreme Court was created by the Constitution and implicitly was intended to provide judicial review of the constitutionality of actions of the other branches of government, there are strong arguments that efforts to prevent it from doing what the Constitution must have intended that it do are themselves invalid.[66]

5.5 The Burden of the Plenary Docket

Besides culling petitions for certiorari, the caseload burden of the Supreme Court consists of deciding the cases it chooses to take for plenary review.[67] In terms of numbers, the recent 'incredible shrinking docket' of the court shows that it is not overwhelmed. In terms of decisional burdens, however, the effort involved can be considerable. The court is regularly rushed to complete the remaining undecided cases on its docket as its annual term comes to a close each June. The 'hard' cases that required the most effort are often announced only then. But it is not really possible to characterize this burden as a result of caseload pressures. It may result in part from divisions about basic legal issues among justices. It may result from the difficulty of fashioning principles to decide the most difficult issues. But it does not result from having too many cases.

5.6 A Real Caseload Crisis in the U.S. Courts of Appeals?

As a contrast to what one might regard as placid caseload circumstances at the Supreme Court, one might turn to the U.S. courts of appeals. They were created by Congress in 1891 to deal with a Supreme Court caseload crisis, and they worked (see Sect. 4 above). But in the last 50 years they have seen a dramatic rise in the volume of appeals. During the 1980s and 1990s, there were repeated warnings of a caseload

[65] See generally Fallon (2010).

[66] For an example of such disputes involving a state court, note that the Kansas Supreme court held that legislation removing its authority over the operation of the lower Kansas state courts was unconstitutional under the Kansas Constitution. The legislature had threatened to defund the entire state court system if the state Supreme Court held the legislation invalid. See Associated Press (2015), p. A10.

[67] As noted in Sect. 6.3 below, the Supreme Court—and particularly the Chief Justice—has additional responsibilities.

crisis in the courts of appeals. For example, in 1990 the Federal Courts Study Committee[68] reported that, 'Few deny that [the] appellate courts are in a "crisis of volume" that has transformed them from the institutions they were even a generation ago.' Moreover, that report asserted, the decline in Supreme Court plenary review of courts of appeals decisions threatened the uniformity of federal law.[69] These circumstances produced a variety of 'solutions' that merit mention here.

Creating a New Tier of Appellate Courts In various forms, proposals surfaced in the 1970s and 1980s for creation of additional appellate capacity to bring order to the interpretation of federal law. Some urged that a new fourth level of the federal court system be created between the current courts of appeals and the Supreme Court. Some urged that a composite appellate body be created to receive assignments from the Supreme Court that it regarded as insufficiently important for plenary decision by the court but needing a uniform legal rule.

Expanding the Size of Courts of Appeals or the Number of Courts of Appeals Rather than create a new layer of the federal court system, another approach was to subdivide some existing courts of appeals. The vision of the appellate courts of a generation ago invoked by the Federal Courts Study Committee might thus be restored, as courts of appeals might again become small and integrated in a way that some sprawling courts were not. The Fifth Circuit, for example, was split in two in 1982, creating a new Eleventh Circuit. But the Ninth Circuit, the behemoth of the current federal court system, has resisted subdivision, in part because the only way to achieve a meaningfully smaller appellate court would be to split the state of California between two circuits, a remedy rightly regarded as extreme and problematical.[70] Nonetheless, pressure to split the Ninth Circuit persists. In January 2016, the governor of Arizona announced that he would support breaking up the circuit 'because of the [Ninth Circuit's] extreme caseload [and] large geographic area.'[71] But increasing the number of circuits likely would increase the number of 'circuit conflicts' in interpretation of federal law, potentially increasing the caseload burden of the Supreme Court, if it were required to resolve those conflicts.

Increasing the Use of Non-precedential Decisions One way of speeding up decisions in the courts of appeals would be 'short cut' decisions. Many courts of appeals adopted a practice of abbreviated opinions or decisions by 'memorandum opinion.' Many forbade citation to these decisions on the ground that they did not articulate new legal principles and should not be relied upon as establishing legal principles.

---

[68]Federal Courts Study Committee (1990), p. 109.

[69]See Federal Courts Study Committee (1990), p. 111, Table 1, showing that between 1945 and 1989 the proportion of court of appeals merits terminations subject to plenary Supreme Court review declined from 7.9% to less than 1%.

[70]To illustrate, assume that a federal judge in northern California orders the state to do something that a judge in southern California orders the state not to do. What should the state do then?

[71]Christie (2016).

Although that may look ordinary to those from the civil law background, where *stare decisis* supposedly does not exist, it did not sit well with American common law judges.[72] In partial recognition of these problems, the Federal Rules of Appellate Procedure were amended to ensure citation was permitted.[73] This rule drew heavy criticism from appellate judges when proposed but it was adopted notwithstanding.

Upshot – The Crisis Seems to Have Abated So one concerned about a caseload crisis in the U.S. federal court system probably should not focus on the Supreme Court, but on the courts of appeals. Nonetheless, 'the doomsday clamor has died away and the sense of urgency has disappeared,'[74] because the courts of appeals 'manage to decide about as many appeals as are filed each year . . . [c]ases are not queuing up on the docket, although disposition times have lengthened appreciably.'[75] But all is not necessarily tranquil; a recent study suggested that divergent caseload burdens in different courts of appeals were actually affecting outcomes—courts 'flooded' with cases involving deportations. Seemingly as a consequence of this flooding, two courts of appeals 'began to reverse district court rulings less often' with the result that 'deference [to the actions of the district judges] increased, tilting the balance of authority toward the district courts.'[76]

6 The Role of National Legal Culture

In comparative law circles, relying on national legal culture may sometimes seem the perennial way to duck issues. But the long history of the U.S. Supreme Court means that it has a place in the American legal and political order that affects the range of reforms one might seriously contemplate. The possibility of increasing the size of the court runs into not only the constitutional directive that there be 'one supreme Court,' but also the historical-political baggage associated with the 'court-packing' effort of President Roosevelt in the 1930s (see Sect. 5.1, second para above). So, other nations might actually have more latitude in revising judicial arrangements than America does. Moreover, as noted above, there is presently no pressing concern with judicial overload on the Supreme Court, even though there is concern about the length of service of justices that has become commonplace in the last few decades, and the consequent reduction in judicial turnover.

---

[72]Indeed, at least one court of appeals held that it was unconstitutional. See *Anastasoff v United States*, 223 F.3d 898 (8th Cir. 2000).

[73]Fed. R. App. P. 32.1: 'A court may not prohibit or restrict the citation of federal judicial opinions, orders, judgments, or other written dispositions.'

[74]Baker (2006), p. 102.

[75]Baker (2006), pp. 113–114.

[76]See Huang (2011), p. 1115.

6.1 *Narrowing Judicial Functions: Advisory Opinions and Political Questions*

Different countries ask their judges to do different things. The tasks that American judges could perform were not entirely clear at the outset. In 1793, for example, President Washington sent a letter to the Chief Justice and associate justices of the Supreme Court asking for the court's opinion on the obligations of the United States with respect to the war between Great Britain and France. The justices declined, concluding in a letter that 'the lines of separation drawn by the Constitution between the three departments of the government' prohibit the federal courts from issuing such advisory opinions.[77] This sort of overture from the other branches has been characterized as an 'advisory opinion,' and is something that American federal courts cannot do because the Constitution's limitation of federal judicial power to 'Cases' and 'Controversies'[78] requires a concrete adversary litigation. But it is not anathema to all American states, some of which permit their courts to provide such advice, and other nations do also. But since 1793, the Court has regarded this prohibition as 'the oldest and most consistent thread in the federal law of justiciability.'[79]

Somewhat connected to the prohibition on advisory opinions is the rule against judges deciding 'political questions.' This doctrine insulates the justices against deciding what could be very contentious issues. For example, in 1979 a U.S. senator sued, challenging the decision by the president, acting without a vote in the U.S. Senate, to terminate the mutual defense treaty the United States had with Taiwan. The court refused to decide the case on the ground that the method of terminating a treaty was a political question because it was not specifically spelled out in the Constitution.[80] By way of contrast, the Philippine Supreme Court recently decided a challenge to an agreement negotiated by the Philippine president on the ground that approval by the Philippine Senate was required.[81]

In caseload terms, these limitations on judicial authority in the United States do not reduce the burden on the Supreme Court. But in terms of workload impact (not to mention adverse publicity) they probably are significant. It is said that the Americans transform social issues into legal issues more frequently than other peoples. Perhaps that also has prompted the caution with which the judiciary ventures into such areas. But its abiding responsibility to enforce the Constitution can nonetheless bring it into the line of fire, as efforts to constrict its jurisdiction have suggested (see Sect. 5.4 above).

---

[77] *Campbell Ewald Co. v Gomez*, 136 S.Ct. 663, 678 (Roberts, C.J., dissenting).

[78] U.S. Constitution, Article III, § 2.

[79] *Flast v Cohen*, 392 U.S. 83, 96 (1968).

[80] *Goldwater v Carter*, 444 U.S. 996 (1979).

[81] See Hernandez and Whaley (2016).

6.2 A Broadened View of Finality

Finality may be inherent in the role of a Supreme Court; as Justice Jackson of the U.S. Supreme Court put it, 'We are not final because we are infallible, but we are infallible because we are final.'[82] But as Justice Cassese of Italy has recently noted, for many national Supreme Courts (even constitutional courts) this sort of finality or infallibility is no longer guaranteed because there are many supranational organs of review.[83] For the U.S. Supreme Court this possibility does not exist, but for other national courts it may loom in the future.

A more pertinent feature of caseload pressures, however, is the question of finality within the national judicial system. One view might be that no decision is ever final; an extremely vigorous commitment to making sure that every decision was right could support such a view. Indeed, Professor Damaška suggested a generation ago that an 'activist' state (probably he had in mind the socialist state of Cold War vintage) would regard stability of judgments as a 'matter of low priority,' with the result that there would be almost no finality for decisions.[84] What he called the 'dispute resolution' model, on the other hand, would result in much more vigorous finality because 'the conflict-solving style of proceeding is averse to changing decisions—even if they rest on legal or factual error.'[85]

For one concerned about limiting burdens on appellate courts, and ultimately Supreme Courts, a stronger view of finality would be a godsend. Yet, although most modern European states adopted a laissez faire attitude toward litigation, leaving the conduct of the case mainly up to the parties,[86] it seems that they have a much more diffident attitude toward making the decisions of first instance courts binding. U.S. courts are not so diffident. To the contrary, most U.S. judicial decisions are never subject to appellate review because they can only be reviewed after the first instance court has entered a 'final judgment,' and most cases are settled before that happens.[87] Not only may no new matter or arguments be raised against the judgment of the first instance court, but the appellate court may not second-guess the initial decision even when the materials on which it is based are equally available to the court of appeals.

In such a system, there is a natural constraint on the number of appeals because they are extraordinary rather than normal, and reversal is very difficult to justify. Many European systems seem to offer a much-enhanced incentive to seek appellate review. (It should be noted, however, that the American rule that ordinarily the winning litigant must pay its own lawyer may encourage some appeals as compared

[82]*Brown v Allen*, 344 U.S. 443, 540 (1953) (Jackson, J., concurring).

[83]See Cassese (2015).

[84]Damaška (1986), pp. 178–180.

[85]Idem, p. 145.

[86]Van Rhee (2005), p. 6.

[87]For background on this discussion of American standards of review see Marcus (2014), pp. 117–121.

with a more conventional loser pays system in place elsewhere.) So one move that might constrain the caseload pressures on Supreme Courts in other systems might be strengthening the binding effect of first instance decisions.

But this remedy might be unpalatable outside the United States because European systems have a fundamentally different attitude toward populating their court systems. In Europe, it seems that junior (and therefore first instance) judges are new initiates fresh from their legal education and committed to a career in the judicial bureaucracy. Advancement in that judicial apparatus is then largely or entirely controlled by higher-level judges. In such a system, the idea that first instance decisions should be final may seem inherently wrong. Better to have them regularly and intensely reviewed by more experienced appellate judges.

The U.S. system is dramatically different in ways that bear on appellate (and thus Supreme Court) caseload. The American institution of jury trial emphasizes the commitment to finality. By constitutional command, the ultimate decision in the case is committed to an ad hoc group of lay participants. It is true that they operate under 'instructions' from the judge about the legal principles they should apply to decide the case. But unless the evidence is so overwhelming in favor of one side or the other,[88] the judge may do no more than 'instruct.' There is a narrow opportunity for the first instance judge to direct a new trial before a different jury when the judge is convinced that the jury's decision was a 'miscarriage of justice' in light of the weight of the evidence.[89] But the decision whether to grant a new trial is within the discretion of the first instance judge; an appellate court may not review it unless the decision is so obviously wrong that the trial judge can be faulted for abusing his or her discretion.

In criminal cases, the constraints on appellate review are potentially even more limiting. After a trial has commenced, there can be no appellate review of a not guilty decision, whether rendered by a judge or a jury. The Double Jeopardy Clause of the Constitution ensures that such a decision is final. And no judge can enter a judgment of conviction against a defendant who has invoked the right to a jury trial no matter how strong the evidence.

So even though one may, as Professor Jolowicz did (see Sect. 2 above), regard the American system as more akin to cassation than full-fledged appeal, it is cassation with very significant limitations. And those limitations carry over to other issues. Juries must base their decisions on evidence presented at the trial, and the United States accordingly has fairly elaborate rules about what is proper or 'admissible' evidence.[90] Technically, appellate courts may review rulings on the admissibility of

[88]See Fed. R. Civ. P. 50(a), permitting the judge to enter 'judgment of a matter of law' against a party only on finding that 'a reasonable jury would not have a legally sufficient evidentiary basis to find for the party.'

[89]For a general discussion of the judge's power to grant a new trial on the ground that the verdict was against the great weight of the evidence see Wright et al. (2012), § 2806. As a leading case said, a judge's grant of a new trial 'effects a denigration of the jury system' and may 'usurp the function of the jury as the trier of facts.' *Lind v Schenley Indus., Inc.*, 278 F.2d 79, 90 (3d Cir. 1960).

[90]See, e.g., the Federal Rules of Evidence.

evidence, but those rulings are normally reviewed only for an 'abuse of discretion.' A completely wrong interpretation of a rule of evidence is a ground for reversal, but so long as the trial judge evinced a correct understanding of the pertinent evidence rule the decision about admissibility can be reversed only if very clearly—almost always aggressively—wrong.

And this deference carries beyond jury trial. If the case is tried before the judge, the judge's findings are subject to revision on appeal only if 'clearly erroneous,' a limitation that applies even if the findings are based entirely on documentary evidence.[91]

In sum, the American attitude toward appellate 'intrusion' into the first instance handling of cases inherently curtails appellate caseload. Of course, that limitation has not entirely prevented what the United States regards as a serious caseload increase for the federal courts of appeals (see Sect. 5.6, para 1 above). But it does underscore the potential reduction in caseload pressures that result from absolving the appellate courts of the most vigorous cassation requirements. It even more surely guards against the caseload burdens that would result from adopting the more vigorous attitude that appellate courts should routinely start from scratch and decide for themselves whether the right party won, including consideration of additional evidence and arguments not presented to the first instance court.

Besides jury trial, the American willingness to permit first instance decisions to stand without withering appellate scrutiny is also a result of other features of the American legal system. U.S. judges are appointed to trial courts only after they have decades of experience as practicing lawyers, often more experience than the appellate judges who review their decisions. The discretion the procedure and evidence rules afford trial court judges relies on this experience. Moreover, many substantive legal standards rely on a 'reasonable person' standard or take account of multiple factors that must be balanced, standards that are peculiarly suited to resolution by on-the-spot deciders (judge or jury) familiar with the entire fabric of a case.

Such an orientation may be incompatible with a vision of the judiciary as engaged in relatively routinized implementation of relatively precise legal standards adopted by the legislature. But this legal culture has a good deal to do with the eventual adoption in the United States of the certiorari system that enables the Supreme Court to limit itself to a manageable number of cases each year; the more one is willing to entrust decisions to lower court judges, the more one can look calmly at a Supreme Court that does not aggressively ride herd on those lower courts.

6.3 *Ancillary Responsibilities*

Caseload may not be the only load a Supreme Court must bear. As the discussion of 'advisory opinions' above suggested, courts may be asked to undertake tasks beyond

[91]Fed. R. Civ. P. 52(a)(6).

deciding cases. Indeed, in some nations the constitutional court reviews proposed legislation before it goes into effect.

The U.S. Supreme Court does not have significant responsibilities of this nature, so its caseload is almost its only official burden. At least one exception should be noted. Since the 1930s, the Supreme Court has been responsible for developing uniform rules of practice and procedure for the American federal courts.[92] But it has not undertaken this task itself. Instead, it has delegated the task to a set of committees that laboriously develop rule proposals that are subject to final review by the court.[93] Some have deplored the distance between the court and the actual nuts and bolts of rulemaking,[94] but the result has unquestionably been that this ancillary responsibility does not weigh heavily on the justices.

Beyond that, the Chief Justice has considerable administrative powers. The Chief Justice chairs a body called the Judicial Conference that sets policy for the federal court system. He selects the judges and others who serve on rules committees and other important bodies, and also plays a prominent role in the operation of the Administrative Office of the U.S. Courts, the national bureaucracy that facilitates and guides the federal courts. Though these are considerable additional responsibilities, there is no indication that any Chief Justice has regarded them as imposing a heavy burden. To the contrary, the principal reaction has been that too much power is concentrated in one person.[95]

6.4 *Receptiveness to Transplants*

As noted at the beginning, the U.S. Supreme Court has been around a long time and has evolved a great deal from its eighteenth-century origins. Several stages in that evolution—particularly the 'court-packing' effort of the 1930s—have involved considerable political controversy. Making further changes is therefore subject to considerable political constraints. Unlike other national courts, its decisions are not subject to review by any supranational tribunal (see Sect. 6.2 above).

Partly as a consequence, the U.S. Supreme Court is probably not receptive to transplants of the sort that might address caseload concerns. For one thing, the American attitude toward the proper role of appellate courts is dependent on both constitutional constraints and long-standing judicial tradition.[96] But beyond that, there is a sometimes fierce resistance in the United States to accepting legal doctrines

[92]For discussion see Burbank (1982).

[93]See 28 U.S.C. §§ 2073 and 2074, describing the procedure for adopting rules.

[94]See Friedenthal (1975) (deploring the fact that the Supreme Court became less involved in rulemaking during the 1960s and 1970s).

[95]See Resnik (2006).

[96]See Sect. 6.2 above relating to the right to jury trial and the reliance on trial court disposition of cases based on decisions by experienced trial court judges.

from abroad. For example, between 1799 and 1810 the legislatures of three states passed statutes forbidding their courts from citing cases from English courts.[97] Much more recently, members of the U.S. Congress have considered directing by legislation that the U.S. Supreme Court could not cite any foreign law or decision when interpreting the U.S. Constitution.[98] (Of course, that legislation itself might be of dubious constitutionality; the court could well consider itself free from congressional meddling with its sources when it is called upon to determine what should be consulted to assist in interpreting the Constitution.)

So the prospects for transplanting non-American legal practices into U.S. judicial systems are not rosy. With regard to Supreme Court caseload, more significantly for present purposes, it seems that there is no urgent reason to consider such transplants. Although other Supreme Courts may labor under backbreaking caseload pressures, that surely is not true of the US Supreme Court, for it has instead experienced in the last generation a 'shrinking docket.'[99] Even were it receptive to borrowing from other systems, then, it would not likely be inclined to do so.

7 Conclusion

Frankly, caseload pressures do not look like the most significant problems for Supreme Courts around the globe right now. Political meddling seems a greater threat. In 2016, the Polish government tried to 'pack more sympathetic judges on the nation's highest court and blunt its ability to overturn new laws,'[100] and it has continued to apply pressure to that court. The year before, in Venezuela, the outgoing majority in the National Assembly approved an additional 13 judges for the Supreme Court,[101] and *The Economist* forecast that, 'In the battle that now looms with parliament, the Supreme Court may become the regime's main weapon.'[102] By 2016, the court had blocked four legislators from taking their seats.[103] In Argentina, as a transition to the new government occurred in 2016, '[a] decision to temporarily appoint Supreme Court judges by decree, bypassing Congress during its summer recess, was criticized as an overreach of executive power.'[104] Even the Chief Justice

[97]Greenhouse (2012), p. 83.

[98]See, e.g., Sepp (2006) and Delahunty and Yoo (2005).

[99]See Lazarus (2008), p. 107.

[100]Lyman (2016). In June 2016, the European Commission issued a formal opinion stating that the Polish government had failed to uphold the Rule of Law by 'efforts to blunt the powers of the constitutional court' (Bilefsky 2016, p. A4).

[101]Torres and Neuman (2015).

[102]The Economist (2016a), p. 29.

[103]San Francisco Chronicle (2016).

[104]Gilbert (2015), p. A8.

of the U.S. Supreme Court has worried publicly that political disputes are damaging public perceptions of the Court's fairness.[105]

Despite that concern, it is still true that this court seems happy-go-lucky. And it is clear that caseload pressures are not the most important challenges after all. The American court's membership has recently been near an all-time high in terms of age,[106] and the justices nonetheless do not seem overwhelmed by their caseload. It's a good life.

References

Associated Press (2015) High court strikes law cutting its power. New York Times, 24 December 2015

Baker TE (2006) Applied freakonomics: explaining the 'crisis of volume'. J Appellate Pract Process 8:101–114

Barnes R (2016) The political wars damage public perception of the Supreme Court, Chief Justice Roberts says. Washington Post, 7 February 2016

Bilefsky D (2016) E.U. delivers rebuke over failure by Poland to uphold rule of law. New York Times, 2 June 2016

Black RC, Spriggs JF II (2008) An empirical analysis of the length of U.S. Supreme Court opinions. Houston Law Rev 45:621–682

Bump P (2016) The average age of the Supreme Court is close to a record high. Washington Post, 10 January 2016

Burbank S (1982) The rules enabling act of 1934. Univ Pa Law Rev 130:1015–1197

Calabresi SG, Lindgren J (2005) Term limits for the Supreme Court: life tenure reconsidered. Harv J Law Public Policy 29:769–877

Cannon MW (1974) Administrative change and the Supreme Court. Judicature 57:334–341

Cassese S (2015) Interactions between national and supranational levels of jurisdiction. Int J Proc Law 5:190–200

Christie B (2016) Arizona governor wants to split 9th Circuit Court of Appeals. Washington Post, 28 January 2016

Crampton RC, Carrington PD (2006) Reforming the court: term limits for Supreme Court justices. Carolina Academic Press, Durham

Crowe J (2011) Building the judiciary: law, courts, and the politics of institutional development. Princeton University Press, Princeton, Oxford

Damaška M (1986) The faces of justice and state authority. Yale University Press, New Haven, London

De Tocqueville A ([1835] 1990) Democracy in America. In: Bradley P (ed) Vintage Books Edition, New York

Delahunty RJ, Yoo J (2005) Against foreign law. Harv J Law Policy 29:291–330

Douglas WO (1960) The Supreme Court and its case load. Cornell Law Q 45:401–414

Fallon RH Jr (2010) Jurisdiction-stripping reconsidered. Va Law Rev 96:1043–1135

Federal Courts Study Committee (1990) Report of the federal courts study committee. Government Printing Office, Washington DC

[105]See Barnes (2016), reporting on a speech by Chief Justice John Roberts that said that 'partisan extremism is damaging the public's perception of the role of the Supreme Court.'

[106]See Bump (2016).

Frankfurter F, Landis JM (1927) The business of the Supreme Court: a study in the federal judicial system. The Macmillan Co, New York
Friedenthal J (1975) The rulemaking power of the Supreme Court: a contemporary crisis. Stanford Law Rev 27:673–686
Gilbert J (2015) Argentina's new president moves swiftly to shake up the economy. New York Times, 28 December 2015
Greenhouse LA (2012) The U.S. Supreme Court. Oxford University Press, Oxford, New York
Hellman AD (1983) Caseload, conflicts, and decisional capacity: does the Supreme Court need help? Judicature 67:28–48
Hernandez JC, Whaley F (2016) Philippine Supreme Court approves agreement on return of U.S. forces. New York Times, 13 January 2016
Hill WB ([1889] 1927) The federal judicial system. Am Bar Assoc Rep 12:289–290
Huang BI (2011) Lightened scrutiny. Harv Law Rev 124:1111–1149
Jolowicz JA (2000) On civil procedure. Cambridge University Press, Cambridge, New York
Kester JG (1982) An un-Supreme Court. New York Times, 30 September 1982
Lazarus RJ (2008) Advocacy matters before and within the Supreme Court: transforming the court by transforming the bar. Georgetown Law J 96:1487–1565
Lewis L (1964) Gideon's trumpet. Random House, New York
Linzer P (1979) The meaning of certiorari denials. Columbia Law Rev 79:1227–1305
Liptak A (2009) The case of the plummeting Supreme Court docket. New York Times, 28 September 2009
Liptak A (2016) Justices divided over 8-member court. New York Times, 31 March 2016
Lord Bingham of Cornhill (2002) A new Supreme Court for the United Kingdom. The Constitutional Unit Spring Lecture 2002 (1 May 2002). https://www.ucl.ac.uk/constitutionunit/sites/constitution-unit/files/90_0.pdf. Accessed 11 Feb 2021
Lyman L (2016) Head of Poland's governing party leads a political shift rightward. New York Times, 12 January 2016
Marcus R (2014) Appellate review in the reactive model: the example of the American federal courts. In: Uzelac A, Van Rhee CH (eds) Nobody's perfect: comparative essays on appeals and other means of recourse against judicial decisions in civil matters. Intersentia, Cambridge, Antwerp, Portland, pp 105–126
Provine DM (1980) Case selection in the United States Supreme Court. University of Chicago Press, Chicago, London
Rehnquist WH (1987) The Supreme Court: how it was, how it is. William Morrow & Co, New York
Resnik J (2006) Democratic responses to the breadth of power of the chief justice. In: Crampton RC, Carrington PD (eds) Reforming the court: term limits for Supreme Court justices. Carolina University Press, Durham, pp 181–200
San Francisco Chronicle (2016) 4 lawmakers blocked from taking office. San Francisco Chronicle, 1 January 2016
Segall EJ (2014) Let's lift the Supreme Court's veil of secrecy. Los Angeles Times, 7 October 2014
Sepp DJ (2006) Our law, their law, history, and the citation of foreign law. Boston Univ Law Rev 86:1417–1446
Stras DR (2007) The Supreme Court's gatekeepers: the role of law clerks in the certiorari process. Texas Law Rev 85:947–997
Study Group on the Case Load of the Supreme Court (1972) Report of the study group on the case load of the Supreme Court. Federal Judicial Center, Washington DC. https://www.fjc.gov/sites/default/files/materials/44/Report_Study_Group_Caseload_Supreme_Court.pdf. Accessed 11 February 2021
The Economist (2016a) The coming confrontation, 9 January 2016
The Economist (2016b) Slowing down, 14 May 2016
Torres P, Neuman W (2015) 13 new justices in Venezuela. New York Times, 24 December 2015
Uzelac A (2014) Supreme courts in the 21st century: should organization follow the function? Paper presented at the conference on the functions of the Supreme Court – issues of process and

administration of justice, Warsaw University, Warsaw 11–14 June 2014. http://colloquium2014.uw.edu.pl/wpcontent/uploads/sites/21/¬2014/01/UZELAC_Supreme-Courts-in-the-21st-Century.pdf. Accessed 21 June 2019
Van Rhee CH (2005) Introduction. In: Van Rhee CH (ed) European traditions in civil procedure. Intersentia, Antwerp, pp 3–23
Vinson F (1949) Work of the federal courts. Address before the American Bar Association. Sup. Ct 70(13):13–15
Ward A, Weiden D (2006) Sorcerers' apprentices: 100 years of law clerks at the United States Supreme Court. New York University Press, New York
Whalen R (2015) Judicial gobbledygook: the readability of Supreme Court writing. Yale Law J Forum 125:200–211
Wright CA, Kane MK (2011) Federal courts, 7th edn. West Publishing Co, St Paul
Wright CA, Miller AR, Kane MK (2012) Federal practice and procedure, vol II. West Publishing, St Paul

Case Selection and Writ of Certiorari in Argentina: 'Transcendence' as a Case-Selection Parameter at the Federal Supreme Court

Leandro J. Giannini

Abstract This contribution explores Argentina's Federal Supreme Court case-selection regime known as the 'Argentine writ of certiorari.' Following an introduction describing the different instruments to confront the qualitative-quantitative crisis of the higher courts, the contribution analyzes the concept of 'transcendence' that constitutes the main parameter which governs the filtering mechanism exercised by the Supreme Court. In the absence of an adequate systematization by the Supreme Court, the author proposes a definition of transcendence based on institutional relevance and general impact. He concludes with an analysis of the possible criteria for a proper exercise of discretion in the selection of what he terms irrelevant cases.

1 Introduction

As is well known, one of the most controversial chapters of extraordinary or last resort appeals is the incorporation of selection methods which to a greater or lesser extent confer discretionary powers on Supreme Courts to admit or deny matters brought to them for judgment. Argentina is no exception to this phenomenon.

In Argentina, case-selection mechanisms were often created, modeled, and administered by the Supreme Court (*Corte Suprema de Justicia de la Nación* (*CSN*)) through a profuse case law that was difficult to systematize and was not always furnished with the consistency required for a jurisdictional body of this level. This occurred historically via two essential elements of the so-called 'discretionary jurisdiction' of the Supreme Court, that is to say, the doctrines of 'arbitrariness' and 'institutional gravity,' born and developed for decades under the jurisprudential impulse of the highest court.

Despite this long jurisprudential tradition of 'easing' the limits of its own jurisdiction, up until 1990 the Argentine Supreme Court had not been provided by

L. J. Giannini (✉)
National University of La Plata, Faculty of Legal and Social Sciences, La Plata, Argentina
e-mail: lgiannini@jursoc.unlp.edu.ar

P. Bravo-Hurtado, C. H. van Rhee (eds.), *Supreme Courts Under Pressure*, Ius Gentium: Comparative Perspectives on Law and Justice 83,
https://doi.org/10.1007/978-3-030-63731-6_10

the Parliament with explicit powers to *determine which cases to decide*. The trend of legislative rigidity and jurisprudential flexibility was definitely reversed in 1990 with the approval of Act No. 23.774, which amended Articles 280 and 285 of the Code of Civil Procedure (CCP) (*Código Procesal Civil y Comercial de la Nación*), and which gave the court located at the apex of the Argentine judicial system the possibility of rejecting, according to its own 'sound discretion' (*sana discreción*), extraordinary appeals that carry insufficient, insubstantial, or irrelevant federal issues. That was the letter of citizenship in Argentina of what has been called the 'Argentine certiorari'[1] or—with a more ironic tone—the 'certiorari criollo,'[2] given the self-proclaimed (and seriously debatable) filiation of the aforementioned amendments to the Code of Civil Procedure with the traditional U.S. 'writ of certiorari.' Using this device, a relevant percentage of cases were denied access to the Argentinian Supreme Court.[3]

More recently, the legislature expressly incorporated in positive law another one of the renowned exponents of the aforementioned 'discretionary jurisdiction' of the Supreme Court, the so-called *per saltum* or leapfrog appeal (Art. 257 *bis* and *ter* CCP, cf. Act No. 26.790 (2012)). This device, born in Argentina in a troubled precedent (the *Dromi* case)[4] and now explicitly enacted into law by Parliament, allows the Supreme Court to review the decisions of federal courts in cases that do not fulfill the requirement of coming from a court of last resort, provided that they involve matters of 'notorious institutional gravity' and that the direct advocation of the Supreme Court is the only effective remedy for the protection of the pertinent federal law. This is an additional advance on the part of the legislator into a subject (the extent of the jurisdiction of the Supreme Court) that is always plagued by indetermination, grey areas, and endless discussions about the way in which the highest court exercises its positive (institutional gravity, *per saltum*) or negative (Article 280 CCP) power of selection, in the thousands of cases that are brought to it each year for its consideration.

I propose in this contribution to explore the Supreme Court's principal selection tool, namely the one provided in Article 280 of the Code of Civil Procedure: the discretionary power to dismiss appeals that present irrelevant issues. We will leave

---

[1] Sagüés (1990), p. 717; Palacio (1995), p. 1056.

[2] Multiple authors have used this terminology to describe the institute referred to in Article 280 CCP, among others Sabelli (2003), p. 1343; Vanossi (2000). Opposed to the use of the term 'Argentine certiorari' or 'certiorari criollo': Lugones (1992), pp. 399–400; Berizonce (2011), pp. 123–124.

[3] Recent research into the Supreme Court's workload shows that in 2016, 81% of appeals were not admitted by application of certiorari, which amounts to 72% of all final decisions given that year by the Supreme Court (Giannini 2018, p. 1240). New data reveals that certiorari maintained its prominence in 2018, being by far the most frequent reason for inadmissibility of extraordinary appeals (a reduction can be noted from 81% in 2016 to 68.5% in 2018). In 2018, 59% of appeals were dismissed by application of certiorari (Article 280 CCP). In short, taking into account the year 2018, it is possible to state that out of ten extraordinary appeals that reached the Supreme Court, 8,5 were declared inadmissible (six of them by application of Article 280 CCP), whereas only one in ten were succesful (see Giannini 2020).

[4] *CSN*, Fallos: 313:863, *Dromi* [1990].

aside the identical power recognized in that article to dismiss 'insufficient' or 'insubstantial' matters. This choice is fundamentally explained by the fact that, as we will see, the category of 'relevance' or 'transcendence' is the most important innovation of the 1990 Act No. 23.774 and configures the deepest reform relating to the extent of the jurisdiction of the Supreme Court in the twentieth century.

2 Filters and the Crisis of the Supreme Courts

2.1 'Quantitative' Crisis

At almost every latitude there is no novelty in asserting concern about the case overload of the highest courts. The most obvious reason for this concern derives from the very position of these courts in the judicial structure. Being institutionally positioned at the apex of the justice system, the Supreme Courts could potentially have to review the entire judicial production of a State. Deliberately taking the example to the extreme, if the jurisdiction of the superior courts would not find in the legislation (*lato sensu*) proper limits, these bodies would be in the position of reviewing each and every decision, resolution, or judgment of each and every lower court, for any injustice alleged by the parties, in any case processed before the respective jurisdiction.

Such an unlimited jurisdiction would be unacceptable, useless, and materially impossible to assume. Traditionally, all kinds of limits have been designed to try to avoid the overexposure of the highest courts to an unbearable burden of work. These attempts were initially based on criteria that were meant to be safe and reasonably predictable. In this sense, there are limits widely found in comparative law, such as those relating to the *type of decision subject to extraordinary appeals* (e.g. the limit based on the concept of 'final judgment' emanating from the 'court of last resort,' or similar formulas), *the elements of the judgment that can be reviewed* (e.g. the always controversial limitation of the appellate jurisdiction of Supreme Courts only to review 'points of law' and the consequent lack of jurisdiction to review questions of fact, such as the evaluation of evidence), *the amount of the damage* produced by the error in the judgment (as happens with the different systems of *summa gravaminis* intended to restrict access to the highest courts), or other punitive-oriented mechanisms aimed at deterring the promotion of unfounded extraordinary appeals (such as the requirement to deposit a sum of money that will be returned to the appellant only if the decision is reversed).

However, all these restrictions have been overcome in real life, and often by the very Supreme Courts whose case overload was to be prevented by these traditional restrictions. In fact, most of these restrictions are subject to exceptions that, more than confirming the rules, threaten to destroy them. In Argentina, examples are: (*a*) the practice of 'matching' decisions to the final judgment rule (e.g. when an interlocutory decision causes an injury that is 'very difficult' or 'impossible' to repair in the future); (*b*) the doctrine known as 'Strada-Di Mascio'; it greatly reduces the effectiveness of the *summa gravaminis* in numerous local jurisdictions by requiring them to review every case in which a federal question is involved;[5] (*c*) the powerful doctrine of 'arbitrariness'; it affects the distinction between questions of fact and questions of law; and (*d*) 'institutional gravity'; it grants access to the Supreme Courts for appeals that suffer from all kinds of imperfections or that are inadmissible. And so on.

This is not the place to detail the ways in which this phenomenon has taken place in the past or in the recent history of the Federal Supreme Court in Argentina nor in the local highest courts such as, for example, the Supreme Court of Buenos Aires. It is enough to say that, through these jurisprudential constructions, supposedly rigid barriers designed by the legislature, among other reasons, to prevent the collapse of the superior courts, are shown, in the best of cases, to be perforated dams: they stop much of the litigious stream, but a flow which the 'downstream' population cannot tolerate passes through the holes. Although this approach allows a Supreme Court to speak virtually in any case that sparks its interest, it also can be transformed into a kind of self-immolation. In other words, in return for not closing its eyes to notorious injustices or for preserving a starring role in any discussion that it feels is of institutional interest, a Supreme Court ends up reaffirming the basis of its own collapse.

And so we return constantly to the initial dilemma: (a) the place reserved to the Supreme Courts in the judicial structure exposes them to the risk of having to carry out an impracticable legality control; and (b) the traditional limits are insufficient to prevent this quantitative crisis.

As a consequence, the environment at the top of the judicature remains the same: it is marked by an overexposure of the superior courts to the need to decide more cases than those that they can reasonably face with their material and human resources.

2.2 'Qualitative' Crisis

Apart from (although related to) the sustained quantitative crisis, there is a phenomenon that is more difficult to verify, define, and categorize, but that can also be observed at different latitudes. We refer to what might be called the 'qualitative' crisis of the Supreme Courts, derived from the profound dilemmas that occur within these courts, when it comes to defining and respecting the institutional role that they are called upon to play in a particular society. In Argentina, for example, the same institutional roles that the superior courts have assumed show a strong heterogeneity and risk of inconsistency, on which I will expand later. Is it possible for the highest judicial body to be at one and the same time the constitutional court of last resort of a certain jurisdiction and the institution commissioned to develop a 'unifying role' to

[5] *CSN*, Fallos: 308:490 *Strada* (1986); 311:2478 *Di Mascio* (1988).

prevent inconsistencies in the case law of inferior courts (on civil, criminal, labor, administrative, or federal law, as the case may be)? Can this body also be the final inspector of egregiousness to prevent flagrant errors or arbitrariness and, even more, the institution responsible for representing the judiciary in its dialogue with the other departments of the State? Can we add to these responsibilities the administration and improvement of the judiciary? Is it possible for such a body, such a court, not to have a 'personality crisis' by attempting to play so many roles at the same time?

Sometimes it is thought that the 'qualitative' crisis is a mere derivative of the 'quantitative' crisis. One renowned Spanish professor considers that the distinction previously made between the 'qualitative' crisis and 'quantitative' crisis is, indeed, a euphemism that conceals an indisputable fact: that the first one is a product of the second one.[6] In other words, that the debate on the institutional role of the Supreme Courts lives and dies in the discussion about their case overload. Without this last phenomenon, it is proposed, no one would speak about the first phenomenon. I do not fully share this point of view.

It is true that when a particular legal system decides to reduce the quantitative restrictions imposed on its superior court there is demonstrably a clear risk of inconsistency in its precedents, with the consequent effects on one of the main missions of any Supreme Court, which is guidance on the interpretation and development of the law and the management of precedents in a particular jurisdiction.

Although I will refer to this issue in greater detail in the following section, what has just been said is enough to express a substantial agreement with those who consider that there is a close relationship between the 'quantitative' and 'qualitative' crises of the courts located at the apex of the judiciary. However, this coincidence is not absolute, since this second manifestation of the dilemmas faced by the highest courts (the qualitative crisis) does not appear only in courts that collapse. Even in courts with a total of no more than 100 rulings per year (the U.S. Supreme Court, for example) it is possible to find deep discrepancies and public debates on the role that they play (or should play) in their respective jurisdictions, and in the way in which they exercise that role. Those debates, which often take the form of sharp criticism of the case-selection criteria, of the decision-making process (or the 'no decision' techniques), of the ideological influence of its composition, of the interpretation of the law, and so on, allow us to affirm the existence of a qualitative crisis that is not necessarily caused by the case overload of the highest courts.

In short, it is true that, in general, the overproduction of decisions derived from the case overload of Supreme Courts causes serious inconveniences for these courts to adequately play their institutional roles. In this sense there is a *close* relationship

---

[6]Nieva Fenoll (2011), pp. 69–90, esp. pp. 69–70, who states: 'All the past controversies about *Cassation* seem to have been cornered in a single discussion: how to remove the overload of appeals? Usually this issue is disguised somewhat through another seemingly more technical one: what is the genuine function of cassation? But what actually it is trying to address even in this euphemistic way, is the overload of cases. In fact, I believe nobody would call into question currently the significance of cassation if it were not for the existence, precisely, of the problem of the excessive workload of the Supreme Courts.'

between the quantitative and qualitative crises. However, we do not believe that there is a *necessary* relationship between the two, by which the second (qualitative crisis) is just an elegant creation to complicate the analysis of the first (quantitative crisis). Qualitative crises (the dilemmas or conflicts concerning the definition and exercise of the institutional role of the Supreme Courts) can also occur in a court with a numerically manageable agenda and, therefore, is a phenomenon that can be (and deserves to be) treated with relative independence from the quantitative crisis.

2.3 Mechanisms to Address the Crisis

This reality has been attacked from various angles both in Argentina and in comparative law. A very general—and deliberately simplified—systematization of the paths followed to alleviate the aforementioned 'quantitative' crisis of Supreme Courts (the overexposure of such courts to a volume of cases that goes beyond their material ability to respond to) distinguishes two categories of instruments: 'overproduction' mechanisms and case-selection mechanisms.

'Overproduction' Mechanisms Regarding the first, Supreme Courts face collapse by resolving more and more cases in their efforts to keep 'up to date.' Examples can include: the decision to increase the number of judges and divide the court into chambers, the allocation of decision-making powers to individual judges within the court, a decrease in the 'burden' of giving reasons, and the enlargement of delegation in the decision-making process (i.e. entrusting to different types of advisers (e.g. clerks) different aspects of the decision-making process—typically, the analysis of the record, legal research, and opinion-drafting). Experience has shown that trying to remedy in this way the collapse of the Supreme Courts, apart from being something similar to cutting off the heads of a hydra,[7] usually ends up in affecting the strength and consistency of Supreme Court precedents and, thus, weakens their main institutional role.

In a comparative perspective, there can easily be found examples of Supreme Courts with more than 100 judges (divided into chambers and sections) that deliver more than 20,000 judgments per year (e.g. the French *Cour de cassation*); or courts such as the Brazilian *Supremo Tribunal Federal* with 11 judges—each judge having powers to decide cases individually (a power that is widely exercised in practice)[8]—with an output of more than 100,000 judgments per year. This reality increases dramatically the risk of inconsistencies and all but eliminates the ability to understand and manage the court's precedents. Thus, the 'omnipresent' court puts at risk its own authority and deviates from its most important role of transforming its case

[7] I borrow the metaphor coined by Stevens (2007), p. xxvii.

[8] From 2011 to 2014, an average of 86% of the decisions of the Federal Supreme Court were taken individually by one of its judges, leaving 14% as collegiate court decisions (see full statistics in Giannini 2016).

law into—using Chiarloni's and Taruffo's metaphor—a sort of supermarket where everyone can find what he is looking for . . . and the opposite too.[9]

Case-Selection Mechanisms Regarding the second category of instruments, multiple case-selection mechanisms are gaining momentum in different legal traditions. Through them, what is sought is to deal with the aforementioned crises through a reverse strategy: reduce the agenda of the superior courts in order to try to focus their material and human resources on deciding only the issues that enable them to satisfy or improve their institutional role.

Filters on appeals, such as the 'certiorari Argentino' (Article 280 CCP at the Federal Supreme Court; Article 31 *bis*, Act 5827 at the Supreme Court of the Province of Buenos Aires), are examples of this kind of strategy. It is a solution that, despite not being innovative, is progressively gaining importance in the courts of different legal traditions, as is the case in the U.S. Supreme Court with its traditional writ of certiorari; in the Supreme Court of the United Kingdom by the 'permission to appeal'; in the Spanish *Tribunal Supremo* and *Tribunal Constitucional* with their case-selection mechanisms, respectively based on 'cassational interest' (*interés casacional*) and 'special constitutional transcendence'; with the 'fundamental significance' in the German Federal Supreme Court (*Bundesgerichtshof*) or the requirement that the matter be 'constitutionally significant' as a condition for the original jurisdiction of the Federal Constitutional Court (*Bundesverfassungsgericht*); and with the 'general impact' (*repercussão geral*) as an admissibility requirement to stand before the *Supremo Tribunal Federal* of Brazil.

In addition to the ordinary filters, other instruments can be included in the category of mechanisms of agenda-rationalization of the higher courts. For example, we can include the resolution mechanisms of repetitive cases, such as the one prevailing in Brazil, which seeks to prevent the entry of a multiplicity of cases that carry similar issues of law, holding them at lower levels and enabling just one or a few paradigmatic cases to reach the Supreme Court. The principle of law adopted in these 'test cases' should subsequently be applied by the judge *a-quo*, to resolve every other case whose proceedings were suspended pending the ruling of the first case.[10]

Another example of case-reduction techniques is the restrictive interpretation that Supreme Courts develop on the extent of their own jurisdiction. In Argentina, for example, as well as the consecration of the 'certiorari' in 1990 as a tool for the qualitative selection of cases, the Federal Supreme Court approached from different

[9]Sergio Chiarloni (2008), p. 61, 'Las tareas fundamentales de la corte suprema de casación, la heterogeneidad de los fines surgida de la garantía constitucional del derecho al recurso y las recientes reformas' (trans.: Juan José Monroy Palacios). Chiarloni (2002), pp. 11–16, esp. p. 6 metaphorically stressing that the jurisprudence of the Italian *Corte di Cassazione* resembles a 'supermarket in which clients—litigants—are able to easily find the product they are looking for,' and that those 'defeated in the judgement on the merits can also find favorable precedents'; Taruffo (2007), p. 90; Taruffo (2006a), p. 757.

[10]On another occasion I analyzed more thoroughly different instruments adopted in comparative law to selectively reduce the agenda of the superior courts: Giannini (2016). I refer to this work here.

other angles the subject of case overload. Thus, in addition to propagating the use of the mentioned filters to get rid of irrelevant issues, the court cut back, through its own interpretations, most of its 'mandatory' jurisdiction. To quote from some of the paradigmatic cases relating to this restrictive trend, supported for reasons of 'institutional significance' which, in the Supreme Court's opinion, forced it to reexamine access to the court and rationalize its agenda, we can mention: (*a*) the reduction of original jurisdiction in cases in which a state is a party, attending the restrictive interpretation of Articles 116 and 117 of the Argentine Federal Constitution (*Constitución Nacional Argentina*) and Article 24, inc. No. 1 of Act 1285/58;[11] and also (*b*) the recent invalidation (unconstitutionality declared by the Supreme Court) of the ordinary mandatory appeal established in cases in which the federal government is a party (Article 24, inc. 6), ap. a), Dec. Ley 1285/58 (*CSN*, *Anadon*, 2015).[12] Such jurisdictional strategies (restrictive interpretation of the conditions to access the Supreme Court or invalidation of rules that allow a too extensive mandatory jurisdiction) can also be considered examples of case-selection mechanisms different from access filters themselves.

3 The Requirement of 'Transcendence' in the Extraordinary Appeal at the Federal Supreme Court

3.1 Introduction

As was anticipated, the debated (and often fought against) category of 'irrelevance' (*intrascendencia*), introduced by Act 23.774 (1990), constituted the only real innovation as regards the appellate jurisdiction of the Supreme Court. The remaining parameters ('insubstantiality' and 'insufficiency' of the issues presented in the extraordinary appeal) had, already in 1990, a long tradition. In other words, the Supreme Court turned repeatedly to its case law, even in the absence of an explicit

[11] *CSN*, Fallos: 329:759, *Barreto* (2006).

[12] *CSN*, Fallos: 338:724, *Anadon* (2015). In this precedent, the Supreme Court departed expressly from its historical jurisprudence which considered legitimate this formal path to its courtrooms. Attending a 'dynamic' interpretation, it went on to consider that the subsistence of this mandatory appeal (only subjected to the classical quantitative admissibility requirement *summa gravaminis*) constitutes an unreasonable exercise of the powers of Parliament to legislate on the jurisdiction of the Supreme Court (Article 117, *Constitución Nacional Argentina*). The concepts used to question the reasonableness of *summa gravaminis* are quite eloquent: 'The Supreme Court must decide all matters in which some constitutional principle may be involved, issues that cannot be measured by the amount of money at stake, because a case in which a large amount of money is at stake can be resolved based on local or common legislation, and a problem of a few cents can affect the property clause as a whole and even the whole constitutional system. Thus, quantitative criteria can never be taken into account, as it should be the qualitative criteria alone.'

legal text, to dismiss appeals of these kinds, through relatively stereotyped formulas designed to relieve the agenda. Thus, regarding these categories, the only significant change consisted in providing legal support to this practice.

In contrast, the introduction of the 'transcendence' parameter significantly changed the landscape in this area, since: (*a*) in contrast to what happens with 'unsubstantial' or 'insufficient' issues, 'relevance' was not included in the previous practice of the Supreme Court as a widespread motive to reject; (*b*) the notion of 'transcendence' is capable of defining by itself the outcome of the case. With respect to the latter, it is enough to stress that the filter based on the relevance of the matter involved allows invalidating flagrant judicial errors that could have been corrected in the traditional system of extraordinary appeals, but it will not be so if the case does not stir the interest of the court as the 'ultimate and most authentic interpreter of the Constitution,' using its own words.

In this sense, the 'Argentine certiorari' based on the concept of transcendence is a 'proper' filter, unlike the one based on the notions of 'insubstantiality' and 'insufficiency,' which can be qualified as 'improper.' The latter ('improper' filters), unlike the former, constitute the mere streamlining of the decision-making process, since they only allow the court to decide in a simpler manner (with fewer formalities, in any instance of the proceeding, and fading to the point of almost getting rid of reasons) the same thing that would have been decided if access to the court had been granted. 'Proper' filters, on the other hand, are selection tools in strict terms, and not mere instruments to decide the same thing, but more nimbly.

3.2 The Partial Discretion of Article 280 of the Code of Civil Procedure

Article 280 of the Code of Civil Procedure expressly provides for the discretionary nature of the authority to reject appeals that carry insufficient, unsubstantial, or irrelevant federal issues. So it says in the article alluded to, establishing that the Supreme Court, 'according to its sound discretion,' can apply this instrument to deny extraordinary appeals under such conditions.

The expression used in Article 280 persuades us that the reform only introduced a *partial discretionary power* into the original federal court jurisdiction. Indeed, the Supreme Court cannot refuse by 'certiorari' *relevant* cases with self-proclaimed grounds of opportunity or convenience. Instead, it is only authorized to use such tools for the purpose of admitting or discarding *irrelevant* cases under the aforementioned article.

Far from being a grammatical debate, the previous matter concerns a definition that I consider important to clarify the scope of the discretion that the mentioned legal provision has granted to the Argentine Supreme Court. When, in Argentina, the Supreme Court makes use of Article 280 of the Code of Civil Procedure as a qualitative intake filter, the first question that it must answer is whether the issues raised on appeal are 'transcendental.' If so, the appeal *should* be admitted. It is, in this first phase, a problem of the interpretation of an indeterminate legal concept introduced by the legislator. That test demands examining: (*a*) the proper sense of the standard established by the legislator; and (*b*) its application to the specific case.

In the event of a negative answer to this question (that is, Were the issues raised 'irrelevant' or not?) the Supreme Court *may* still admit the extraordinary appeal, according to its 'sound discretion,' as the provision indicates. In this field, Article 280 does not impose any parameters different from the reasonableness that qualifies the exercise of such authority ('sound' discretion). Therefore, the legislator vested the court with a broad freedom to determine what criteria are to be used to place on its agenda an 'irrelevant' matter. For example, the Supreme Court could use different alternatives such as choosing the 'more relevant issues within the irrelevant' ones, or it could only pick those irrelevant appeals that have a real prospect of success. It could take into account the severity, intensity, or economic importance of the reported injury, or the need to address some irrelevant 'issue' brought in an important 'case,' etc.

Some of these guidelines would, in my view, be inconvenient, as we shall see, but should not for that reason banned from the approaches that the legal provision allows the court to follow. Different from the traditional distinction that some authors[13] make between the exercise of discretionary powers and the interpretation of indeterminate legal concepts, I understand that Article 280 of the Code of Civil Procedure includes both types of activity. In part, it recognizes a proper discretionary selection power, allowing the court to 'decide which cases to decide' according to primarily self-proclaimed criteria. But it also imposes a typical hermeneutic analysis, which consists in finding the right sense of an open-textured expression (the notion of 'transcendence') and applying it as the first admission test.

In other words, Article 280 of the Code of Civil Procedure demands that the extraordinary appeal presents relevant issues as an admissibility requirement, but, at the same time, it authorizes the court to supplement the absence of this attribute by using its 'sound discretion.' If the point of law is relevant, the appeal *must* be admitted; otherwise, it could be admitted or not, according to the reasonable discretion granted to the court.

If 'relevance' were a mandatory requirement for the admissibility of the analyzed remedy, the work of the court would consist of: (*a*) defining effective parameters for judging the relevance of a case generally worthy of its attention; (*b*) examining

[13]See, among others, García de Entrerría (1983), pp. 33–35; García de Entrerría and Fernández (1993), pp. 440–462. See also, Sainz Moreno (1976), pp. 347–348; Gordillo (2017), pp. 9–18; Linares (1958), p. 18; Bianchi (1988); Grecco (1980); Cassagne (2008). Also in modern Brazilian doctrine, endorsed by Teresa Arruda Alvim Wambier, stands the idea that the interpretation of an indeterminate legal concept should not be confused with the exercise of discretionary powers (Arruda Alvim Wambier 2001, pp. 351–357; Arruda Alvim Wambier 2008, pp. 151–161); see also: José Miguel García Medina et al. (2008). To mention some authors who concur with Arruda Alvim Wambier's opinion: Santos Fernandes Góes (2008), pp. 87–93; De Castro Lopes (2008), pp. 94–98; De Oliveira Guimarães (2008), pp. 99–106; Cramer (2008), pp. 107–114.

whether the issues presented in each case comply with that condition; (*c*) then granting the appeal if the response was positive, dismissing the appeal if it was negative.

Something different happens with Article 280 of the Code of Civil Procedure. As was anticipated, this rule authorizes the court to dismiss, using its 'sound discretion,' remedies that bring irrelevant issues. With a similar pattern of reasoning, and according to the current provision, the steps that the court should follow when deciding about the use of 'certiorari' in a given case can be synthesized in this way. To cope with this task, the court should: (*a*) define effective parameters for judging the relevance of a case generally worthy of its attention; (*b*) examine whether the issues presented in each case comply with that condition; (*c*) if the response is positive, the appeal should be granted, while if it is negative, the court would have the discretion to admit, or not admit, the matter.

As may be noticed, the main difference between a system that establishes 'transcendence' as a mandatory requirement and the one provided for in Article 280 of the Code of Civil Procedure, lies in the last phase of the case-selection decision. In the first model (e.g. the Brazilian filter based on the *repercussão geral* prerequisite), there is no proper discretion but interpretation of a flexible legal concept, while in the second there is a wider discretion, but only in the second phase of the decision-making process (the admission or not of irrelevant questions).

Even acknowledging that the distinction between the interpretation of indeterminate legal concepts and discretionary powers of the judiciary is largely a terminological discussion, the solution adopted by Article 280 of the Code of Civil Procedure did not introduce 'importance' as a mandatory qualitative condition to examine the admissibility of an extraordinary appeal. It did not establish a purely discretionary admission regime either, since the 'sound discretion' of the court can only be used to admit irrelevant appeals using, wisely, self-proclaimed criteria, but not to deny relevant matters of law adequately brought to the court's knowledge.

3.3 The Requirement of 'Transcendence' and the Definition of Irrelevant Issues

In the previous section I have sought to build the foundation to guide us in this last part of my contribution in which I extend the analysis, trying to identify suitable parameters to study the exercise of a Supreme Court's case-selection powers. The importance of this line of research is greater in countries that—like Argentina—have no regulation to allow the operators who act before (and within) the Supreme Court to determine with some accuracy the guidelines used to decide which cases to decide. Thus, in this kind of environment it is extremely difficult to approximately predict (or even decide without the risk of inconsistency or unfairness) which issues will trespass on the highest court's territory.

This complexity, coupled with the lack of reasons in decisions admitting appeals and the lack of commitment to improving transparency in the selection process, has been the primary source of criticism suffered by this kind of filter, due to the distrust towards the equity and coherence of the 'picking-up' exercise. That disrepute explains the radical skepticism of many authors who consider that the only criterion followed in this field is the 'taste' or 'palate' of the operators involved in the selection process. In Argentina, this absence of reasons and lack of commitment to improving transparency leads me to openly proclaim the unconstitutionality of Article 280 of the Code of Civil Procedure,[14] since it encourages arbitrariness in case selection. However, as was foreseeable, the Supreme Court has repeatedly overruled this challenge to the validity of its main filtering mechanism.[15]

We will not delve deeper into the interesting constitutional and conventional debate on the 'Argentine certiorari,' for that is a subject addressed elsewhere.[16] However, once this first problem is overcome, it is necessary to build a theory that provides tools to improve our experience in this area. What looks attractive is to put aside the initial skepticism and propose a model that allows a better understanding and operation of this case-selection device. Even for those who question filtering devices, developing acceptable categories in this area helps to build up a sharper critique of the exercise of that power.

3.3.1 Introduction: 'Transcendence' and the Institutional Role of the Supreme Court

One of the important general aspects in the definition of what is considered 'relevant' for case selection is the departure from a teleological approach to filtering mechanisms. This option allows associating the exercise of selection attributions by the Supreme Courts with their most eminent institutional missions. In this way, filters like the 'Argentine certiorari' are conceived as devices aimed towards an end, which is not primarily the quantitative decongestion of the Supreme Courts, but the improvement of their institutional role, by allowing them to concentrate on their core missions. However, we must avoid a common mistake that leads to an over-simplification of the topic.

[14]Among the authors who proclaim the unconstitutionality of this provision see Vitale (2003), p. 1244; Sabelli (2003), p. 1343; Ekmedjian (1999), p. 551; Ekmedjian (1997), pp. 57–58; Oclese (1997), p. 981; Padilla (1992), p. 358; Gil Domínguez (2003), p. 1325; Trionfetti (2001), pp. 313–324.

[15]*CSN*, Fallos: 322:3217, *Asociación de Prestaciones Sociales para Empresarios c/ Set Sociedad Anónima* [1999]. See also: *CSN* Fallos: 323:86 [2000] and 325:2431 [2002]. Nowadays, paradoxically, the validity of Article 280 CCP is rejected by the application of the same filter, as it constitutes an 'insubstantial' federal question (*CSN*, Fallos: 330:694, *Hase* [2007], Fallos: 331:303, *Ventura* [2008]).

[16]See Giannini (2016), Chapter 2, para III.

When we associate the purpose of filters (such as the Argentine Article 280 CCP) with the institutional role of the Supreme Court, it is not to suggest that to define the 'significance' of a case it is enough to verify whether a decision on the merits upon it would allow the highest body to meet some part of its mission. That kind of standard would not be too complex to implement but would end up becoming ineffective as a selection device, since—as we shall see—the heterogeneity of the functions of the court could result in all matters passing the aforementioned filter. That is not a minor clarification, as will be seen in the following sections. It is not the same to say that filters are instruments that allow Supreme Courts to rationalize their agendas and focus on their most eminent roles as to hold it is the 'transcendence' or 'significance' of each case that leads those courts to carry out one of their varied missions. As I will try to prove later, the first is true, while the second is not, particularly in systems where these courts have assumed multiple and heterogeneous institutional roles.

Indeed, the task of defining transcendence or significance would lose part of its difficulty if, in assessing this condition of admissibility, it was enough to verify the potential of a specific case to allow the court to carry out one of its traditional missions. The problem is that the roles imposed upon or assumed by these highest judicial bodies are sometimes so heterogeneous that the aforementioned scrutiny (i.e. 'deciding whether this case would allow the Supreme Court to exercise one of its institutional missions') could lead to opposite answers. In Argentina, this difficulty has caused perplexity in astute authors who, being unable to find consistent criteria in the Supreme Court agenda, have come to the conclusion that it lacks a precise course.[17] This example will be useful to illustrate the previous reflection.

Just as in the case of the U.S. Supreme Court, there are not many controversies surrounding the purposes for which the Argentine highest federal body has been crafted. That is so, at least from a static perspective—in other words, regardless of the differences between the way in which these roles are or should be articulated in real life (an issue that will be left aside for the moment, to return to later). There is sufficient consensus on the roles of the Supreme Court, which are: (*a*) the final safeguarding and interpretation of the Federal Constitution; (*b*) a sort of 'cassation' role of federal law (final supervision of the interpretation and application of federal law, which should lend consistency to the court's decisions); (*c*) the exercise of a broad and diverse 'axiological' mission (mainly exerted through the doctrine of 'arbitrariness'); and (*d*) its performance as 'head' of the judiciary, which combines an heterogeneous mix of institutional, administrative, and jurisdictional tasks oriented towards a dialogue between the judiciary and the other branches of government, the preservation of judicial independence, and the improvement of judicial services.

Regarding the aforementioned 'axiological role,' it is fair to say that it does not imply that the court will remedy any and all injustices, but only those which, through their gravity and egregiousness, configure an unacceptable departure from the due process constitutional clause. However, the breadth and vagueness of the formulas

[17] See Oteiza (1998), pp. 71–85.

used by the court to define the scope of the doctrine of 'arbitrariness' transformed it into a versatile and ungraspable device on which any litigant (internalized in the extraordinary appeal technique) can rely to try to open the gates of the Supreme Court.

3.3.2 Heterogeneity of the Supreme Court's Roles. Variability of Parameters. Importance

Earlier (Sect. 2.3 above) I synthetically explained the fundamental roles of the Argentine Federal Supreme Court as an example of the ambiguity at the apex of the judicial system by using Taruffo's amusing metaphor.[18] If we examine these roles, two trends can be distinguished: (*a*) on the one hand, there are roles that have an overall impact, that is to say, an impact on a relevant group of people directly or indirectly interested in the resolution of the case, an influence that, in severe cases, may even affect the very foundations of the republican system; (*b*) on the other hand, there is the role of protection of individual guarantees potentially violated, an attribution that is mainly (but not exclusively) exerted through the 'arbitrariness doctrine.'

The confrontation between the two guidelines is not novel and assumes different forms according to the particular Supreme Court under discussion. In regard to filtering mechanisms, this diversity explains the difficulties that face a model which seeks to examine the 'significance' or 'importance' of a case by simply 'measuring' its ability to cover any of these purposes.

For example, when an appellant alleges the existence of serious arbitrariness in the previous judgment (e.g. the omission of core arguments, which will be discussed below, or of fundamental questions that could have altered the fate of the case, an unacceptable evaluation of evidence, a flagrant lack of motivation, etc.) it can be argued that the case places the court in full exercise of its axiological role of safeguarding the due process protection clause of the constitution. However, a judgment on the merits in this kind of case can hardly be considered interesting for anybody apart from the appellant.

Thus, a teleological approach to filters that is only based on the idea of coupling the case to the court's institutional roles ends up transforming the so-called 'filter' into a tautological mechanism: as every appeal based on the existence of a federal matter (including the hypothesis in which the judgment is attacked by 'arbitrariness') could compromise the exercise of some of the roles of the highest body, none of them could be considered 'irrelevant.' In that manner, filters such as the 'Argentine certiorari' would lose all possible effectiveness.

Now, the tension of these institutional missions in determining the parameters for case selection does not seem to be solvable by simply 'deleting' one of such tasks (in Argentina, for example, overturning the 'arbitrariness doctrine'). After more than

[18]Taruffo (2006b).

25 years of 'certiorari,' the Supreme Court insists on including within its core missions the protection of due process and fundamental guarantees. In other words: the 'arbitrariness doctrine' is still alive in its case law.

If there are no shortcuts, some further analysis must be developed to identify how to apply the 'transcendence' standard, in accordance with the institutional role that the court is called upon to play in each case. For this purpose, I will present three central aspects of the problem. As will be explained below, there are two conditions that must necessarily coexist in assessing the significance of the issues raised in an appeal. The first is the correspondence between the matter involved and the institutional missions of the highest judicial body, so that a case can fulfill this requirement only if a ruling on the merits places the court in the exercise of one of its fundamental roles. But, as has been pointed out, that condition is not sufficient, since if that were the only parameter, the 'filter' examined would be a tautological and ineffective instrument. That is why a second condition *sine qua non* should be added: the general impact of the topic discussed, understood as the ability to increase its impact, directly or indirectly, in a considerable part of the community.

The aforementioned examination would leave an important number of cases outside the appellate jurisdiction of the Supreme Court despite the presence of a constitutional violation, since the constitutional remedy would only be of interest to the parties (*ius litigatoris*). However, as we have seen, Article 280 of the Code of Civil Procedure empowers the Supreme Court to admit irrelevant issues, according to its sound discretion. Therefore, it is possible that even a question with no general impact could, on its merits, be ruled on. Now, to avoid a selection based on the subjective instincts of 'taste' or 'palate,' the court should establish a series of appropriate parameters to guide itself and the community.

Let us look at the three fundamental aspects of a transcendence-based case-selection procedure.

3.3.3 First Requirement to Define 'Transcendence' or 'Significance': Suitability of the Case to Allow the Supreme Court to Accomplish One of Its Institutional Roles (Institutional Relevance)

What has previously been said is almost enough to identify a first element for the qualification of cases as 'significant,' 'important,' or 'transcendent' (in terms of Article 280 CCP): their tendency to place the highest court in the exercise of its fundamental missions. We call this element 'institutional relevance.'

These matters have already been presented before (final safeguarding and interpretation of the Federal Constitution, federal 'cassation,' axiological safeguarding from arbitrariness, institutional leadership of the judiciary), so I will not go into them here. It is enough to simply point out that a case could not meet this requirement despite its 'coast to coast' impact (e.g. a nationwide class action) if the matter involved is alien to the institutional missions of a Supreme Court (e.g. if the case raises a non-federal question of law, as happens in Argentina—as a principle—with civil, commercial, criminal, and labor law).

Therefore, the first (and most obvious) effect of the implementation of this initial line of selection consists in leaving outside the confines of the appellate jurisdiction of the court cases that do not raise issues proper to its institutional tasks. In such an event, the court may rule out, without providing reasons, the appeal as 'irrelevant.'

3.3.4 Second Requirement to Define 'Transcendence' or 'Significance': General Impact of Discussed Issues. Distinction Between Transcendence and 'Institutional Gravity,' Transcendental 'Cases' and Transcendental 'Issues'

It has already been explained why the 'institutional pertinence' set forth in the preceding section, although necessary, is not sufficient to assess properly the transcendence or significance of an issue. That is how it is possible to arrive at a second condition needed to determine the relevance of the questions presented before the highest court: their *general impact*. This second requirement is present when the issues at stake are *directly or indirectly relevant for a part of the community*.

There is no need to emphasize that the definition contains considerably vague elements. Indeed, it is extremely difficult to think of a complete list of situations in which, unfailingly, the rule emanating from precedent would have this kind of impact. It is, however, possible to specify certain guidelines for such a test.

This second definition is based on two central elements: (*a*) the *direct or indirect scope* of the precedent that is to be established by deciding the case; (*b*) the size of the part of the community that will be affected by it.

Let us take a brief look at each of these elements.

The Direct or Indirect Scope of the Precedent

By referring to the 'direct' or 'indirect' scope of the rule to be established, we seek to include two different situations.

The first ('direct' scope) is probably the simplest one, since it is based on the subjective authority of *res iudicata*. When the judgment to be imposed has the authority of *res iudicata* for a relevant group of people (we will focus on this last point) for whom the precedent would be enforceable or it defines a standard of conduct, then the case meets this requirement. A nationwide class action is a possible example.

The second ('indirect general scope') is not linked to the subjective effect of the judgment or its authority of *res iudicata*, but to the scope of the legal doctrine emanating from the precedent. As is well known, the judge-made law emanating from the superior courts has a particular 'contagious' effect (if not a legally binding one) that transforms the standard of individual conduct contained in the decision into a usable abstract rule to decide similar cases. Whatever the opinion adopted regarding the binding effect of Supreme Court precedents, the truth is that when these precedents are set, at least as relevant parameters to decide a significant number of similar cases, an indirect impact will be present.

The two underlined aspects of the overall impact (direct and indirect) differ as to their nature, since the first refers to the effectiveness and authority of the ruling, while the second refers to the scope of its legal doctrine. It should also be pointed out that the general impact, either direct or indirect, must have a sufficient degree of concreteness in order to avoid the frequent confusion between this requirement and the journalistic dissemination of a case. The truth is that many of the cases that enter into the public domain via the mass media do so precisely because they focus on issues that concern society as a whole. But this is not necessarily so, given the obvious circumstance that the interests of the press may originate in reasons quite different from the interests of the community. The most basic example of this distinction concerns the public dissemination of aspects of people's private lives. Although these aspects may arouse the curiosity of many consumers of this kind of information, and can generate even deep public media controversies, they usually do not concern profound values of the community so as to pass the gates of the Supreme Court.

In general, the difference between transcendence and media coverage is quite clear and should not lead to greater confusion even if the warning is sometimes heard that the court fails to distinguish them properly.[19]

Another example, less extreme and more often giving rise to misunderstanding, stems from undue confusion between the general impact *of a case* and *of the issues raised* in the case. In 'Argentine certiorari,' Article 280 of the Code of Civil Procedure does not refer to the significance of *cases* brought before the Supreme Court, but to the importance of the *questions* presented in the extraordinary appeal. It is easy to provide examples of this difference with cases that genuinely possess an authentic overall impact, but will not reach the highest court if the parties want to review at that instance accessory or circumstantial aspects (e.g. costs, lawyers' fees, etc.).

The Size of the Group of Person Affected

As previously mentioned, the second element that should be taken into account to judge the general impact of an issue is the number of persons affected. The problem

[19]In Argentina, the *Veira* case (the case of a well-known athlete charged with child abuse that received nationwide media coverage) can be cited as an example of this kind of deviation, as may be appreciated by the dissenting opinions adopted within the Supreme Court on the subject (the minority correctly stressed the confusion that arose due to the appellant's allegation that the case presented 'institutional gravity'; *CSN* Fallos: 315:2056 [1992]). In the right line of reasoning, the Supreme Court has made clear, at least as a rule to follow, that such qualities are not fungible: 'We must reject the institutional gravity invoked based on the journalistic impact of the matter, if principles of social order are not affected and what was decided does not go beyond the personal interests of the appellant' (*CSN*, Fallos: 325:2534, *Risso* [2002]).

to solve at this point is the size of the social group that should be interested (either directly or indirectly, as we saw) in the topic addressed in the dispute.

Again, it is a standard that lacks infallible arithmetic rules, for two fundamental reasons. First of all, because even though the group affected by or benefiting from the decision can be defined sufficiently in general terms, concrete members often remain anonymous. Secondly, because even if personal identification were possible (that is to say, if the people involved in the matter could be defined), the 'relevance' of the proportion of the community concerned would still be unknown. Here we enter into one of the aspects of the notion of 'transcendence' in which the problems of the open texture of language become evident.

Thus, in each case one might inquire about the proportion of society involved in the debated subject. Examples multiply, and so too the questions, such as: Will the trial on the constitutionality of a regulation pertaining exclusively to a group of people (e.g. teachers at private schools, the members of the security forces or the armed forces, cancer patients, etc.) affect a 'relevant' part of the community? And: What would we have to say about a constitutional question or interpretation of federal provisions raised in an environmental case that only affects the inhabitants of a small community, a local state, or a region?

It should be noted that it is not common to find legal dilemmas impacting directly or indirectly on each and every member of the community. If that were the case (e.g. an appeal that involves the validity of the declaration of martial law throughout the whole national territory or of acts of force that violate the institutional order and the democratic system, or an appeal against measures that involve the survival of fundamental natural resources, freedom of speech at the national level, etc.), then there would be no doubt with respect to compliance with the analyzed standard ('general impact'). However, there is no reason to affirm that this requirement would only be present in 'universal' cases. That is why we have been referring to the 'relevance' of the 'group of people' and not to the 'community as a whole.' In fact, the distinction between both standards ('relevant group' and 'entire community') should serve as a guideline to distinguish the presence of the 'transcendence' requirement from the application of the historical doctrine of 'institutional gravity,' which allows the court to make an exception to almost every traditional admission requirement (the final judgment rule, court of final resort—*per saltum*—etc.). For the first, the relevant group standard is enough, for the second, the impact should be global.

3.3.5 Irrelevant Issues, Discretion and Verisimilitude. 'Argentine Certiorari' and the Doctrine of 'Arbitrariness'

We have previously distinguished two defining aspects of the requirement of 'transcendence' in the terms of Article 280 of the Code of Civil Procedure. In a nutshell, that requirement is present whenever: (*a*) addressing the discussed issues belongs to the institutional responsibilities of the court (institutional pertinence); and (*b*) the questions presented in the extraordinary appeal have general impact (direct or indirect influence on a significant part of the community).

As can be seen without much difficulty, the second of the aforementioned requirements would not allow the court to decide on matters that, even if belonging to its traditional institutional missions, concern only the parties involved (*ius litigatoris*). As explained, this often happens when the Supreme Court performs the role of preserving individual guarantees, a function through which the court ensures respect for some unquestioned constitutional principle (for instance, the traditional elements of due process that are violated in a single case), not reaching to establish a relevant line of interpretation as regards that principle; for example, when the court reverses arbitrary rulings for lack of grounds. In such situations, the court does not ascertain relevant criteria for the future. On the contrary, those kinds of matters are—in general—a repetitive application of traditional legal rules and principles, limiting the activity of the court to an examination of their violation in a single case.

This activity, therefore, is dominated by the safeguarding of the subjective interests of the parties. As a result of that prevalence, the issues addressed have no general impact and, therefore, no importance for a Supreme Court. Consequently, the case may be ignored when applying Article 280 of the Code of Civil Procedure.

Now, limiting the conversation to this conclusion would mean an incomplete study of the problems associated with the aforementioned selection instrument. Indeed, as noted, the quoted provision allows the Supreme Court, according to its sound discretion, to pass over the irrelevance of the question and examine the case. As explained, it is in this field that the proper discretion of the court appears, permitting the high body to auto-determine, with no primary legal guidelines, the parameters for that 'positive' selection of irrelevant appeals.

Despite the strength of the Supreme Court's discretion in this final chapter of the case-selection process, it is possible to identify some sort of parameter to guide the operators. In this regard, it has been pointed out that this form of discretion ('sound') does not allow the Supreme Court to 'do what it wants,' but to set its own agenda based on reasonable (although self-defined) criteria. In other words, Article 280 of the Code of Civil Procedure omits all legal parameters, allowing generously the highest judicial body to determine which guidelines will be used in this selection process. Therefore, once having defined these patterns with wide discretion (either internally or through some form of regulation such as the U.S. Supreme Court's Rule 10, or even setting some criteria in a precedent that could be referential for those who try to pass through the court's gates), it would be inconsonant to arbitrarily depart from them.

Then, the question is: Which parameter would allow the Supreme Court to address issues that lack general impact, respecting the principles of consistency and equal treatment, on the one hand, and efficiency in the use of its resources, on the other? In this phase it is no longer possible to find answers within the standard of transcendence. It would, for example, not be adequate to distinguish absolute banal questions from those affairs that 'aren't so irrelevant,' to allow only the latter to pass through the filter. Once the case has been considered irrelevant, another more efficient selection criterion should be adopted.

Two parameters primarily prevail in this instance of the test (that is: once the irrelevance of the issues is recognized, to launch a search for guidelines to establish which cases may be admitted). The first is the *verisimilitude* of the appeal, similar to a 'real prospect of success' test. In this line of thought, for example, when multiple extraordinary appeals allege serious abuses of due process (usually by means of the doctrine of 'arbitrariness'), the Supreme Court could justify its decision to consider some cases and not to consider others, based on this prima facie examination. The second is the possibility of treating *irrelevant questions* raised in *relevant cases* when elucidating the first is essential to resolving the second (*necessity* standard). This is an additional, perfectly compatible and complementary element of the first parameter (*verisimilitude*) although based on a completely different test. In this case, it is not necessary to examine the prospects of success of the appeal (i.e. the flagrant nature of the alleged arbitrariness), but one needs to reexamine an 'irrelevant' issue of the appealed judgment in order to be able to rule on a relevant issue (e.g. the unconstitutionality of a regulation specifying alleged discriminatory conditions for accessing health care services or social security).[20]

Those parameters are examples of criteria that are useful in preventing extreme solutions to the Supreme Court crisis. On the one hand, they resist the constitutional challenge of the traditional equal protection clause, giving reasonable (although flexible) guidelines different from a mere whim or the caprice of the gatekeepers. On the other hand, they prevent 'all or nothing' responses to the *ius litigatoris* dilemma. Anyone could prevent randomness in case selection by proclaiming that no *ius litigatoris* case shall pass. That could be the point in some legal systems, but, for example, in Argentina this would destroy every practical application of the traditional 'arbitrariness doctrine.' Others could say that, to be fair, every case that raises a proper constitutional question of 'arbitrariness' should be heard. In this situation, as was shown above, the filter would end up being an absurd and ineffective device.

For that reason, among the various parameters by which the Supreme Court could systematize the exercise of its power to select questions with no general impact, standards such as *verisimilitude* (real prospect of success) and 'necessity' (need to resolve an irrelevant issue to address relevant topics) appear as criteria which allow reducing the case overload without ignoring the principle of a fair treatment.

[20]An example of this parameter could be found in the *Yapur* case (*CSN*, Fallos: 332:1616, *Yapur* [2009]).

4 Conclusion

The Federal Supreme Court of Argentina (composed of five judges, hearing approximately 14,000 cases a year) is a court of last resort with jurisdiction to review final judgments in civil, criminal, labor and administrative cases when they raise questions of federal law (national interest legislation) including constitutional matters. There is no other specialized constitutional Supreme Court in Argentina.

The Argentine Supreme Court fundamentally conserves the original U.S.-style Supreme Court design and competence, but—in practice—it develops a broader role in the correction of errors, with a significant use of the so-called 'arbitrariness doctrine' to review gross deviations in factual determinations and non-federal legal interpretations.

Since 1990, with the enactment of the so-called 'Argentine certiorari,' the Federal Supreme Court has completed the development towards a full discretionary jurisdiction that allows the court to decide almost every case that it finds to be 'institutionally significant' or dismiss with no justification any appeal considered irrelevant ('intranscendent').

No parameters are settled by legislation or by Supreme Court rules or precedents that allow litigants to know precisely what a 'relevant' or 'transcendent' issue is. The problem deepens as the court does not give reasons when it decides to dismiss an irrelevant appeal.

To address the problem of determining when a case is likely to pass through the certiorari barrier, it is useful to follow a two-stage analysis. First, it must be determined whether the issues involved in the appeal are relevant, which requires verification of the presence of two main conditions: (*a*) that addressing those issues belongs to the institutional responsibilities of the court (institutional pertinence); and (*b*) that the questions have general impact (direct or indirect influence on a significant part of the community). Second, if the first test is negative, typically when an arbitrary decision is challenged, the appellant has to bring forward compelling reasons to verify the presence of factors such as the 'real prospect of success' of the appeal or 'necessity' to treat an irrelevant matter.

References

Arruda Alvim Wambier T (2001) Controle das decisões judiciais por meio de recursos de estrito direito e de ação rescisória: recurso especial, recurso extraordinário e ação rescisória: O que é uma decisão contrária a lei? Revista dos Tribunais, São Paulo

Arruda Alvim Wambier T (2008) Recurso especial, recurso extraordinário e ação rescisória, 2nd edn. Revista dos Tribunais, São Paulo

Berizonce RO (2011) Las funciones de la Corte Suprema: en el tránsito hacia un nuevo modelo. In: VVAA, Oteiza E (ed) Cortes Supremas. Funciones y recursos extraordinarios. Rubinzal Culzoni, Santa Fe, pp 107–138

Bianchi AB (1988) El *writ of certiorari* en nuestra Corte Suprema (la cuestión federal suficiente como concepto jurídico indeterminado). Revista El Derecho 125:857–864

Cassagne JC (2008) La discrecionalidad administrativa. Foro Jurídico 09:82–91
Chiarloni S (2002) Ruolo della giurisprudenza e attività creative di nuovo diritto. Rivista Trimestrale de Diritto e Procedura Civile 56(1):11–16
Chiarloni S (2008) Las tareas fundamentales de la corte suprema de casación, la heterogeneidad de los fines surgida de la garantía constitucional del derecho al recurso y las recientes reformas (trans: Monroy Palacios JJ). In: VVAA, Ortells Ramos M (ed) Los recursos ante los Tribunales Supremos en Europa. Appeals to Supreme Courts in Europe. Difusión, Madrid, pp 55–76
Cramer R (2008) Conceitos jurídicos indeterminados e discricionariedade judicial no processo civil. In: García Medina JM et al (eds) Os Poderes do juiz e o controle das decisões judiciais. Estudos em homenagem à Professora Teresa Arruda Alvim Wambier. Revista dos Tribunais, São Paulo, pp 107–114
De Castro Lopes ME (2008) Anotações sobre a discricionariedade judicial. In: García Medina JM et al (eds) Os Poderes do juiz e o controle das decisões judiciais. Estudos em homenagem à Professora Teresa Arruda Alvim Wambier. Revista dos Tribunais, São Paulo, pp 94–98
De Oliveira Guimarães R (2008) A (im)possibilidade de discricionariedade judicial na inscrição do Magistrado no sistema Bacen-Jud. In: García Medina JM et al (eds) Os Poderes do juiz e o controle das decisões judiciais. Estudos em homenagem à Professora Teresa Arruda Alvim Wambier. Revista dos Tribunais, São Paulo, pp 99–106
Ekmedjian MA (1997) Manual de la Constitución Argentina, 3rd edn. Depalma, Buenos Aires
Ekmedjian MA (1999) Tratado de Derecho Constitucional, vol V. Depalma, Buenos Aires
García de Entrerría E (1983) La lucha contra las inmunidades del poder, 3rd edn. Civitas, Madrid (reimpr.: 1995)
García de Entrerría E, Fernández TR (1993) Curso de derecho administrativo, 6th edn. Civitas, Madrid
García Medina JM et al (2008) Os Poderes do juiz e o controle das decisões judiciais. Estudos em homenagem à Professora Teresa Arruda Alvim Wambier. Revista dos Tribunais, São Paulo
Giannini L (2016) El certiorari. La jurisdicción discrecional de las cortes supremas. Editora Platense, La Plata
Giannini L (2018) La producción jurisdiccional de la Corte Suprema de Justicia de la Nación en su actual integración. Revista Anales de la Facultad de Ciencias Jurídicas y Sociales de la Universidad Nacional de La Plata 48:1208–1259
Giannini L (2020) Análisis de la producción jurisdiccional de la Corte Suprema (2018), Revista Anales de la Facultad de Ciencias Jurídicas y Sociales de la Universidad Nacional de La Plata 50:791–832
Gil Domínguez A (2003) ¿Es la República Argentina un Estado violador de los derechos humanos en virtud del art. 280 del CPCN?, Revista Jurisprudencia Argentina 1:1325–1328
Gordillo A (2017) Tratado de Derecho Administrativo, vol I, 8th edn. Fundación de Derecho Administrativo, Buenos Aires
Grecco CM (1980) La doctrina de los conceptos jurídicos indeterminados y la fiscalización judicial de la actividad administrativa. Revista La Ley D:1306–1309
Linares JF (1958) Poder discrecional administrativo. Abeledo Perrot, Buenos Aires
Lugones N (1992) Recurso extraordinario, 2nd edn. LexisNexis, Buenos Aires (1st edn, Depalma, 1992)
Nieva Fenoll J (2011) El modelo anglosajón en las cortes supremas: ¿Solución o elusión del problema de la casación? In: VVAA, Oteiza E (ed) Cortes Supremas. Funciones y recursos extraordinarios. Rubinzal Culzoni, Santa Fe, pp 69–90
Oclese JM (1997) La institución del certiorari repugna al concepto nacional del derecho de defensa, Revista Jurisprudencia Argentina, Buenos Aires 4:981–1097
Oteiza E (1998) El *certiorari* o el uso de la discrecionalidad por la Corte Suprema de Justicia de la Nación sin rumbo preciso. Revista Jurídica de la Universidad de Palermo 3(1):71–85
Padilla MM (1992) El art. 280 del Código Procesal Civil y Comercial de la Nación y el derecho al acceso a la justicia, Revista La Ley E:358

Palacio LE (1995) Experiencia del denominado 'certiorari argentino'. Revista La Ley E (sección doctrina):1056

Sabelli HE (2003) El rechazo 'sin motivación' del recurso extraordinario cuando la cuestión federal es intrascendente, ¿es constitucional? (sobre el *certiorari* criollo). Revista Jurisprudencia Argentina I:1343–1362

Sagüés N (1990) El 'writ of certiorari' argentino (las reformas de la ley 23.774, respecto al recurso extraordinario). Revista La Ley C (sección doctrina):717

Sainz Moreno F (1976) Conceptos jurídicos, interpretación y discrecionalidad administrativa. Civitas, Madrid

Santos Fernandes Góes G (2008) Existe discricionariedade judicial? Discricionariedade x termos jurídicos indeterminados e cláusulas gerais. In: García Medina JM et al (eds) Os Poderes do juiz e o controle das decisões judiciais. Estudos em homenagem à Professora Teresa Arruda Alvim Wambier. Revista dos Tribunais, São Paulo, pp 87–93

Stevens RG (2007) Introduction. In: Landis JM, Frankfurter F (eds) The business of the Supreme Court. A study in the federal judicial system. Transaction Publishers, New Brunswick

Taruffo M (2006a) Una reforma della cassazione civile? Rivista trimestrale di diritto e procedura civile. Rivista trimestrale di diritto e procedura civile 60(3):755–786

Taruffo M (2006b) El vértice ambiguo. Ensayos sobre la Casación civil (trans: Monroy Palacios JJ, Monroy Gálvez JJ), 1st edn. Palestra, Lima

Taruffo M (2007) Precedente y jurisprudencia (trans: Martínez Vallecilla C, Gandini F). Precedente. Anuario Jurídico:85–99

Trionfetti V (2001) Reflexiones acerca del art. 280 del CPCCN: Un aporte constructivo a la ley 402. Revista Argentina de Derecho Constitucional II(3):313–324

Vanossi JR (2000) La extensión jurisprudencial del control de constitucionalidad por obra de la Corte de la Argentina (Balance de una década de 'certiorari' criollo). Anales de la Academia Nacional de Derecho y Ciencias Sociales de Buenos Aires 2:228–260

Vitale GL (2003) La indefinición de la Corte Suprema de Justicia de la Nación en un caso de suspensión del proceso a prueba (el ilegítimo 'certiorari' al revés). Revista Jurisprudencia Argentina 2003(2):1244–1248

The manufacturer's authorised representative in the EU is Springer Nature Customer Service Centre GmbH, Europaplatz 3, 69115 Heidelberg, Germany. If you have any concerns regarding our products, please contact ProductSafety@springernature.com

Printed and bound by CPI Group (UK) Ltd, Croydon, CR0 4YY
07/10/2026
02229094-0001